PRODUCT
LEADERSHIP

Also by Robert G. Cooper
*Winning at New Products: Accelerating the Process
from Idea to Launch,* 3rd ed., Perseus, 2001

Portfolio Management for New Products, 2nd ed.
(co-author with Edgett & Kleinschmidt), Perseus, 2002

PRODUCT LEADERSHIP

Pathways to Profitable Innovation

Second Edition

ROBERT G. COOPER

BASIC
BOOKS

A Member of the Perseus Books Group
New York

Designed by Bookcomp, Inc.

Library of Congress Cataloging-in-Publication Data
Cooper, Robert G. (Robert Gravlin), 1943–
    Product leadership : pathways to profitable innovation / Robert G. Cooper.
       p.   cm.
    Includes bibliographical references and index.
    ISBN 0-465-01433-X (alk. paper)
1. New products—Management.   2. New products—Marketing.   3. Product
Management.   I. Title.
    HF5415.153.C643 2005
    658.5'76—dc22
                                                                    2004017395

05 06 07 / 10 9 8 7 6 5 4 3

To the three ladies in my life . . . my wife, Linda,
who provided some great presentation insights and ideas
for the book; and to my two daughters, Barbara and Heather,
who no longer live at home, but still provided
encouragement and moral support

Contents

Preface

This is the second edition of this book on product innovation aimed strictly at senior executives. The first edition (1998) must have had some impact, because nearly all leading firms in North America and many in Europe, Japan, Australia, and even China have implemented my *Stage-Gate®* process,* which was a key message in that edition. And the need for such a book remains: More so than in the 1990s, the demand for innovation is heard loud and clear in corporate boardrooms across the world. No executive today is unaware of the strategic need for winning new products. As one senior person put it, "Ten years ago, all you had to do was demonstrate positive profits. That's not enough anymore. Now Wall Street seems to expect great product innovations along with profits." And so the pressure is on virtually every leadership team to deliver great new products. The new corporate motto is "innovate or die."

This book is aimed at senior executives, leadership teams, and senior managers who want to win the product innovation war. And who doesn't? Over the last two decades, I've been privileged to give presentations to a great number of CEOs and leadership teams of businesses in North America, Europe, China, Japan, and Australia–New Zealand. What never ceases to amaze me is how mystified senior people are by product innovation. Their intentions are good, but they don't seem to quite know what to do in order to help their businesses to get a steady stream of winning new products—and big winners—to market.

The trouble is, winning the product innovation war is not so easy. Where does one start? Leading product innovation efforts is a new challenge for many leadership teams. Many senior people appear somewhat at a loss. Perhaps the problem is that, until recently, product development was "an R&D thing"—effectively taken care of by the technical community in the company. No longer. Now product development is a business-wide activity, and one where the leadership team of the business must be front and center, clearly in charge—indeed, *leading* the charge!

---

*The term *Stage-Gate®* was coined by the author in the 1980s, and is a trademark of the Product Development Institute, Inc. (PDI): www.prod-dev.com.

Much has happened since 1998 and the book's first edition, and it is time for an update and some new messages and calls to action. I've seen a lot of downsizing and hollowing out of corporations, as executives strive to meet shareholder profit expectations by cutting costs. Unfortunately, this has put some businesses' product innovation efforts in jeopardy. And for many companies, the mix of product development effort has changed: With tighter budgets, they have taken on less challenging new product projects. And so for many, the blockbuster projects and "game-changers" of yesterday—the products that made the company—are missing. So I emphasize developing a product innovation strategy in this new edition, with an emphasis on setting product innovation goals, targeting the right arenas, and dealing with the resource issues—how much should you spend on R&D? Technology developments and disruptive technologies (or radical innovations) yield both opportunities and threats in the product innovation war, and so are key areas for which I propose approaches.

I introduce the *Innovation Diamond* for the first time in this book, although I certainly have shared the concept with executive teams in numerous in-company meetings. The *Innovation Diamond* with its *four points of performance* is based on recent benchmarking studies into new product practices and performance—why winners win. And the diamond is a novel and practical way of visualizing the major forces that drive a business's product innovation efforts to success. I hope this diamond helps you and your leadership team guide your business to victory, because this diamond has power! For example, Procter & Gamble has based its *Initiatives Diamond*, which guides its many global business units' product development efforts, on the predecessor of my latest *Innovation Diamond*.

Portfolio management has come into its own in the field of product innovation in the last five years. With limited resources, senior management must be more vigilant than ever about where it spends these resources. And so strategic portfolio management, strategic buckets, and strategic product roadmaps are key topics I highlight. Because better ways to select projects—how to make the right investment decisions—remains a mystery for many management teams, I provide new insights into effective methods you can employ here.

Back to basics is a recurring underlying theme in this book. Many executives seek *the silver bullet*—that one "aha" or management principle that will dramatically alter their fortunes in product innovation. Alas, it does not exist . . . at least according to all the recent studies into what distinguishes the top-performing businesses. As ever, winners win because they get the basics right. In the case of the product innovation war, it's how well your teams conceive big ideas, and then move these concepts from inception through to launch and beyond. So I spend much time in this book on the basics of your innovation process or idea-to-launch framework—your *Stage-Gate®* process—and how to get it right. I fear that many firms have implemented such a process since the first edition, but lots of businesses missed some key points along the way and got it wrong. I attempt to straighten things out in this edition!

Finally, the topics of climate and culture, and managing the "people side" in the innovation war, are drivers that separate winners from losers in the innovation war. So I devote an entire chapter to these *people topics*, and most important, to your role as the leaders.

A number of people helped me in the writing of this book. My two closest colleagues are Dr. Elko Kleinschmidt, professor at McMaster University's Michael G. DeGroote School of Business, and Dr. Scott Edgett, CEO of the Product Development Institute and a former professor at McMaster. Over the years we have done much research together, and we have co-authored numerous articles. This book draws heavily on this research and resulting articles. Sources for this book include a recently co-authored book with Elko and Scott: *Portfolio Management for New Products* (Perseus, 2002), and our most recent benchmarking study with the American Productivity & Quality Center (APQC). Both of these colleagues are world-class scholars in the field of product innovation management, and they have both been invaluable in the preparation of this book. I thank both of them.

Ms. Barb Pitts, chief operating officer of the consulting and innovation services firm, Stage-Gate Inc., is a close associate and is the source of many ideas and insights into management practices in the field of product innovation. She is a real professional, and "the best" in terms of implementing much of what you read in this book (www.stage-gate.com). And of course, a special thanks to all the special people at Stage-Gate Inc., who preach and live these innovation principles daily as they work to help their clients win the product innovation war.

Two other close colleagues are in Europe and provide both insights on and implementation sites for the concepts you'll see in this book. They are Mr. Jens Arleth, managing director of Innovation Management U3, a leading new products consulting firm located in Copenhagen. Jens has been instrumental in introducing *Stage-Gate®*, portfolio management, and other concepts highlighted in this book into Scandinavia over the last 20 years. Today, most Scandinavian product-developers use some form of *Stage-Gate®*, due largely to Jens's efforts. My second European colleague is Dr. Angelika Dreher, senior partner in the Austrian consulting firm, Five I's Innovation Consulting gmbh. Like Mr. Arleth, Angelika has been a leading force in successfully introducing *Stage-Gate®* and our portfolio management concepts to German-speaking countries, and has had great success with leading German, Austrian, and Swiss firms in implementing the principles outlined in the book.

While many of our studies into innovation management and practices are the sources for the facts and foundation for my prescriptions on innovation management, our most recent benchmarking study—perhaps the most comprehensive best practices study ever done in the field of product innovation—provides a strong basis for this book. This study was undertaken with the APQC, the premier benchmarking institute in the United States. Thus, I thank Mr. Ron Webb, director of the APQC, for his support and for making the study possible; and also Ms. Marisa Brown and Mr. Steve Wright of the APQC for the hard work they put into making this study the huge success it was. A co-sponsor of the APQC study was the Institute for the Study of Business Markets (ISBM), Pennsylvania State University. I thank Mr. Ralph Oliva, managing director of the ISBM, always a strong supporter of our work, for suggesting the study, helping to get it underway, and gaining the cooperation and help from his ISBM member firms.

A number of companies provided case histories and examples for the book. And I truly appreciate the efforts they made:

- From Procter & Gamble: Mr. Mike Mills, manager, corporate new initiative delivery, who has brought me into the company a number of times, and remains a steadfast supporter of the principles outlined in this book. I thank him for his help in securing case studies within the company. For the efforts in preparing the cosmetics case history in Chapter 2, I thank the following people: Mr. Marc Pritchard, president, global cosmetics; Mr. Dan Edelstein, director, global cosmetics product supply; Mr. Mike Beeby, associate director, personal beauty care program manager; and Mr. Bill Massey, group manager, cosmetics initiative leadership.
- From Mega Bloks, Inc.: Mr. Daniel Bourgeois, VP research and development, who has employed the concepts in this book to help build Mega Bloks into a successful and profitable company focused on product innovation (Dan also supplied the material for the Mega Bloks case history); and Ms. Catherine Cerezuela, technology and method supervisor, who runs the Mega Process, and who helped in the development of the Mega Bloks case history.
- From EXFO Engineering: Mr. Stephen Bull, VP of R&D, EXFO Electro-Optical Engineering, Inc., for his strong contributions to the APQC study, and also for providing a case history that is frequently cited in this book.

- From ExxonMobil Chemical Company: Dr. Carol P. Fitzpatrick, manager, technology innovation processes, who also contributed to the APQC study, and provided a case study also frequently cited in this book.

A number of people also helped me gather data for the book. I thank Mr. Tyrone Shephard, my research assistant and an MBA student at McMaster University, for gathering much of the data in Chapter 1; Mr. Mike Wolff, editor of *Research-Technology Management*, for his help in tracking down background information and data (and also for his continuing support of our research as editor of the major practitioners' journal in this field). I also acknowledge Dr. Al Bean, executive director, Center for Innovation Management Studies, North Carolina State University, and Mr. Roger L. Whitely, independent consultant, who have conducted a number of Industrial Research Institute surveys on R&D spending, for providing data and insights into data sources for Chapter 1.

I would also like to thank the editorial staff of Bookcomp, Inc., who did a superb job copy-editing the book, and helped to make the text flow so smoothly.

And most of all, I thank you, the readers, for buying this book and showing support for the principles—that our research and prescriptions really have found an ear. But mostly, I thank you for coming to seminars and events with a comment like, "Hey, I read your book . . . and this stuff really works!" So I'll see you at the next product innovation conference or seminar . . . and bring your book!

1

Winning Is Everything

In war, there is no prize for the runner-up.
—Omar Bradley, U.S. General

Product Innovation Warfare

The *USA Today* headline reads: "New, Smaller, Flashier iPod Sells Out Fast."[1] The story continues: "Apple has a smash hit on its hands with the new iPod mini digital music player. The little cousin of the full-size iPod is virtually sold out after less than two weeks in stores, with nearly 10,000 snapped up." Does this make you wonder how Apple did it once again? The story continues to note that the key to success was iPod's small size (about the size of a small mobile phone) and cool appearance, which appeals to young people. Chalk up another big victory for Apple Computer in the ongoing innovation war!

Companies everywhere like Apple are engaged in a product innovation war. The battlefields are the marketplaces around the world for everything from consumer electronics to new engineering resins, from potato chips to computer chips, from a new coffee experience to new financial services.

The combatants are the many companies who vie for a better position, a better share, or new territory on each battlefield or in each marketplace. They include the large and well-known combatants—the IBMs, Procter & Gambles, Apples, GEs, GMs, Pfizers, and 3Ms, as well as a number of foreign players—Sony, JVC, Nestle, DaimlerChrysler, ABB, and Siemens. More recent entrants have gained prominence in the last few decades because of big new product victories: Microsoft with computer software, GlaxoSmithKline with pharmaceuticals, Hewlett Packard with laser printers, Nokia with cell phones, and Intel with computer chips.

The costs of this warfare are enormous. By 2002, the total cost of R&D in the 1000 largest companies in the world had equaled *one billion dollars per working day!*[2] That's right: These 1000 firms spent $273 billion on R&D in

1

2002—one-quarter of a trillion dollars.* As far as the modern economies go as a whole, the 29 OECD countries spent $579 billion on R&D in 2001.[3] These are *huge amounts of money*, far higher than the cost of any recent military war, which is why some pundits have labeled this phenomenon "the product innovation war."[4] And as a proportion of economic activity within a country, significant percentages of national economies are devoted to new products warfare: For example, the United States spends 2.82% of its gross domestic product (GDP) on R&D. Other, not so obvious, costs are the many victims of this war—the companies that simply disappear or are gobbled up by the victors.

The weapons of this war are the thousands of new products developed every year in the hope of successfully invading chosen marketplaces. But many new product attempts fail. So, increasingly the quest is for weapon superiority—seeking product differentiation in order to secure a sustainable competitive advantage; and speed and mobility, rapidly moving innovations to market. Positioning plays a key role, too, as combatants deploy their troops to secure an advantageous position on the battlefield. They use tactics such as frontal assaults, outflankings, and even attempts to reposition the enemy.

The combatants have their shock troops that lead the way into battle: the sales teams, advertising people, and promotional experts. The cost of these shock troops is enormous (it costs Procter & Gamble hundreds of millions of dollars to launch a new brand in the United States). But the battle is often decided by the unsung heroes: the infantry, the many engineers and scientists in R&D labs and engineering departments around the world—less glamorous and less visible, but at the heart of almost every victory.

You Are the Generals

As the senior executives, you are the generals. You generals plan and chart direction, and define a *business* and *product innovation strategy* for your business. You generals speak in terms of strategic thrusts, strategic arenas, and the need for strategic alignment. And you generals also deal with *resources and their deployment:* about how many resources to commit to product innovation, and about where to deploy them—to which battlefields or arenas of strategic focus, and to which major initiatives. Sadly,

---

*From our studies, we estimate that about half of this R&D goes to product development (as opposed to process development and improvements, and other technical activities). And for every dollar spent on new product R&D, about another two dollars are required for marketing, capital, and production expenditures.

many generals have not grasped the art of new product or technology strategy very well. So, as is often the case with ill-defined strategy, the battle is won or lost tactically in the trenches by the shock troops and infantry. As a result, you generals must be concerned about tactics as well—about the details of how the battle will be fought. This means that the generals should ensure that the right processes are in place to make the tactics happen, namely, *an effective idea-to-launch process*. And finally, generals must

Notes for Senior Management

Unlike a military war, the product innovation war is a beneficial one—no deaths, no violence, and no burned-out buildings. The victors gain riches and fame; the losers are vanquished, merged, or disappear; and society and humankind benefit from the new products and services that previous generations did not have.

Make no mistake, however: Product innovation is still very much a war. And victory in this war ultimately decides the fate of your business. So here are some key questions for you and your business's leadership team to ponder:

▶ Does your business's leadership team recognize that you are indeed at war, and that guiding your business through this war merits your undivided time and attention?
▶ Are you leading your business the way that professional generals would run their warfare operations? For example. . .
  • Have you mapped out your strategy for this war—a product innovation and technology strategy for your business?
  • Have you defined the battlefields or arenas where you will focus your attack?
  • Have you thought about your tactics—the methods and procedures that your troops will rely on to move new products from idea through to launch?
  • What have you done to lead your troops—to create a positive environment and the right climate needed to win this innovation war?

If you have not thought about these questions, then you're not quite equipped for this war. So read on, and prepare yourself.

deal with the people issues—about how to organize for product development, how to foster effective teams, and how to create a positive, enthusiastic morale—the right climate and culture for innovation—within the ranks.

It's War: Innovate or Die

As the twenty-first century gets underway, the product innovation war looms as the most important and critical war the companies of the world have ever fought. The message to senior people is this: Innovate or die! Winning in this new products war is everything. It is vital to the success, prosperity, and even survival of your organization. Losing the war, or failing to take an active part in it, spells disaster. The annals of business history are replete with examples of companies that simply disappeared because they failed to innovate, didn't keep their product portfolio current and competitive, and were surpassed by more innovative competitors. Look at the plight of the traditional airlines, which have failed to deal with the new and harsh realities of air travel today; yet a whole new breed of innovative airlines appears to be succeeding. Or what happened to all those companies that were born in the heyday of the tech-boom, and are no longer with us? What many of them failed to understand is that not only do you have to have a novel business model; you also need to produce and market innovative products that really work and actually satisfy real customer needs!

New Products: The Key to Your Business's Prosperity

The Mega Bloks Story

If you are a parent or grandparent, chances are you know the name "Mega Bloks." The company has been well-known for over a decade for its first new major product: a large version of construction toy blocks designed for preschool children. Numerous awards have been won by the firm for its innovative children's products, including awards from *Parents Magazine*, *Learning Magazine*, *American Baby*, *FamilyFun*, and the Parents Choice Foundation. Here's the Mega Bloks' story.

The company's rise to stardom began in 1985, when the owner and manager of a small toy manufacturer had a dream about a Lego-style toy, but aimed at younger children: a larger, easier-to-use building block set. And so Mega Bloks was born. In those early days, the company was small and easy to manage: There were only one or two development projects underway; an entrepreneurial "can do" spirit prevailed; and management was close to their customers.

For the next 15 years, Mega Bloks boasted a steady stream of successful new products. The company progressed from merely selling a bag of blocks to major themes, such as fire stations and farms. It also introduced other product lines. For example, the highly successful *Dragon*™ line—a building-block toy based on the "dungeons and dragons" game theme—hit the market in 2002. The toy is built around a castle with surrounding countryside, but with a difference: There are also action figures, each with a name and story line. Kids can identify with action figures, and begin to role-play. Subsequent *Dragon*™ themes moved from "the land" to a "sea" theme in 2003, and to "fire and ice" in 2004. And sales are going through the roof!

Mega Bloks continues to go from strength to strength. Sales grew by 16% in 2003 in spite of a sluggish economy, the 17th year of continuous sales and profits growth. And in 2003, the company won the vendor-of-the-year award from Toys "R" Us and the toy vendor of the year award from Wal-Mart.

The keys to success: What is the secret to Mega Bloks' stunning and continuing success in such a competitive business? The first key is a *vision and strategy,* based on product innovation, according to Dan Bourgeois, VP of R&D. From the beginning, senior management focused on growth through innovation—"new products drive the company." The emphasis is on innovativeness, creativity, and themes, the *Dragon*™ line being an example. The company spends about 4% of revenue on R&D, and 30 to 40% of that goes to *innovative projects* (the rest to extensions, modifications, etc.).

The right culture: Senior management's commitment to new products coupled with the company's entrepreneurial spirit led to the second key to success: a very supportive climate for product innovation. Walk into any office, design space, or lab in the company, and watch the people—they're excited, bubbling with enthusiasm, and having fun. And no idea is a bad one!

The Mega Process: A third and vital key to success has been the company's new project methodology—their idea-to-launch framework (see Exhibit 1.1). By 1999, product development, the engine of Mega Bloks' growth, was in trouble. There were far too many projects underway, no focus, and no priorities; too many people with undefined roles were involved, and accountabilities and communication suffered. The result was many false starts on development projects—"start, then stop, go back, then start

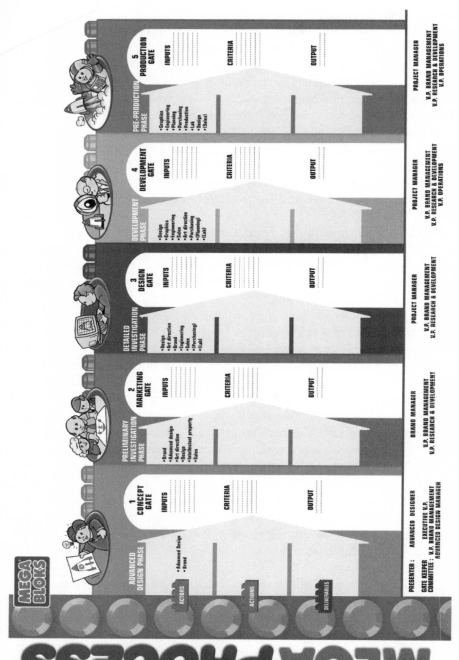

Exhibit 1.1 The Mega Process—An Idea-to-Launch *Stage-Gate®* Framework

again"—a back-and-forth motion that wasted a lot of time, resulting in many products being late to market. As Dan pointed out, "The old way of going fast—with no discipline—was actually causing us to go slow!"

In 1999, Dan and the rest of the executive committee attended one of my seminars on new products, and learned about the *Stage-Gate®* idea-to-launch process. "That changed the business," exclaimed Dan. "The day after the seminar, as the leadership team traveled home, we had a discussion and a key decision was made." It took one year to design and implement the Mega Process in Exhibit 1.1 (Mega Bloks' *Stage-Gate®* method). "The goal was to have a system, but at the same time, to have the entrepreneurial methods, spirit, and way of doing things we had when we were small—we wanted to make a big company act small again."

The immediate result of implementing their Mega Process was dramatic: Mega Bloks was able to *double the number of projects* with about the same resources in the following year. Why? Because of much more discipline, better integration among functions, effective cross-functional teams with better communication, faster Go/Kill decisions, and more emphasis on superb upfront homework and consumer insights (resulting in less "go-forward, go-back" motion). The Mega Process has also become a tool for the entire company. For example, salespeople understand the process, recognize where the project is, and know what they can tell and promise the customer—they even use the process with customers (retailers) to explain how the business is run. Even the finance department is engaged—data reliability and integrity is understood as a function of each stage.

Portfolio management: In 2003 the company embarked on the fourth key to success: more effective allocation of new product resources. With 200 projects underway at any one time, the question of priorities and the right mix and balance of projects looms large. Previously, if the project was rated positively, it was put into the Mega Process based on its own merits; there was little concern about the impact that one project might have on the entire pipeline of projects—on mix, balance, priorities, and resource limits. Now management has adopted a portfolio management system that enables them to run the development pipeline as a *portfolio of projects:* to make better project selection decisions, and to prioritize projects more effectively.

Mega Bloks is one of but countless stories about how companies are born, grow, and prosper on the basis of product innovation. There are several lessons in this and other such tales: One fact that stands out is how management made the transition from a one-product toy company to a large and sustainable business. To do so, senior management wisely put in place the methods, procedures, and frameworks to drive new products to market and to manage the myriad projects underway. But the overriding message I hear from Mega Bloks is senior management's undying belief in the central role that product innovation must play in their growth strategy. The company's heavy spending on R&D from the outset and the large proportion that is spent on innovative products (not just tweaks and extensions) is testament to their commitment.

Why Are New Products So Critical?

Mega Bloks and other case studies might convince you of the central role that product innovation must play in your own business. But before you embark on your journey seeking more successful product innovation, first consider *why there is all this emphasis on new products in today's business world*. Back in the early 1970s, when I began my research into product innovation practices, my literature review revealed that there was *hardly anything* written on the topic. Why, then, are we so preoccupied today with product innovation and getting new products to market?

Simple! New products are the future: They are vital to the success and prosperity of the modern corporation. The period of downsizing that characterized the recent economic slowdown is over: Senior executives and investors are sobering up to the reality that *no corporation ever shrank itself to greatness*. As we move forward in this new millennium, the organic growth game is on, faster than ever. Front and center in this game is the desire for new products—successful, significant, winning new products. Driven by rapidly advancing technologies, globalization of markets, and increasing competition at home and abroad, effective new product development (NPD) is emerging as *the major corporate strategic initiative* of the decades ahead. Those corporations that succeed at new product development will be the future Pfizers, Hewlett-Packards, 3Ms, and Microsofts; those companies that fail to excel at new products will disappear or be gobbled up by the winners.[5]

Innovation is no longer an optional investment, according to a recent Cheskin and Fitch:Worldwide study.[6] Only a small percentage of executives (13%) consider product or brand innovation to be less than "somewhat critical" to their company's overall success (see Exhibit 1.2). And almost half rate innovation as "very critical" to their future business success.

The impact on sales and profits: New products now account for about 32% of company sales, on average, up significantly from the 1980s.[7] (Here a product is defined as "new" if it has been on the market by that company for five years or less.) New products have a similar impact on corporate profits: In the period from 1976 to 1981, new products contributed only 22% of

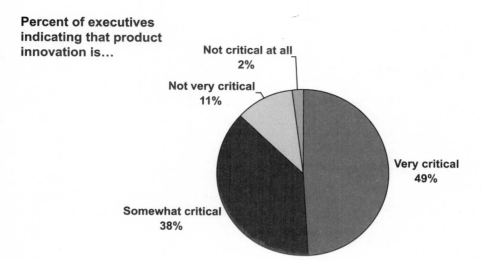

**Percent of executives
indicating that product
innovation is...**

Not critical at all
2%

Not very critical
11%

Very critical
49%

Somewhat critical
38%

Exhibit 1.2   Importance of Product Innovation to Business Success
Source: Results of an executive survey by Cheskin & Fitch: Worldwide: see note 6.

corporate profits; this *had grown to 30%* by the late 1990s. That is, profits from new products account for almost one-third of the bottom line of corporations! On an industry-by-industry basis, while some high-technology industries approach 100% of sales and profits from new products, even mature industries are remarkably close to the mean values here. (Exhibit 1.3 shows the impact of new products on selected industries.[8])

These percentages are only averages, and thus understate the true potential. What CEO wants to be average! A minority of firms do much better than average, according to the Product Development and Management Association's (PDMA) best practices study.[9] These Best firms are compared to the Rest. The Best . . .

 ▶ have 49.2% of sales derived from new products (versus 25.2% for the Rest)
 ▶ see 49.2% of profits derived from new products (versus 22.0% for the Rest)
 ▶ start with 3.5 ideas to achieve one winner (versus 8.4 ideas for the Rest)

The point is that stellar performance is indeed within your grasp in new products warfare: These Best firms model the way.

Exceptional profits: New products are also very profitable, on average. A study of 203 representative new product launches in U.S. businesses

Industry sector	% of Sales by New Products – launched last 5 years
Food products (& related products)	15%
Wood, paper & allied products	14%
Industrial inorganic chemicals	1%
Plastic materials & synthetics	19%
Pharmaceuticals & drugs	28%
Soap, cleaners & toiletries	18.5%
Industrial organic chemicals	16.5%
Agricultural chemicals	19%
Misc. chemical products	15.5%
Fabricated polymer products	18.5%
Industrial machinery & equipment	26%
Food products (& related products)	15%
Instruments & related products	26%

Exhibit 1.3 Impact of New Products by Industry

Source: Data from *Research-Technology Management:* see note 8.

reveals that approximately two-thirds are considered to be commercial successes.[10] And these winning products do exceptionally well:[11]

- Return on investment (ROI) is astounding: The average ROI for successful new products is 96.9%.
- New products pay off very quickly: The average payback period is 2.49 years.
- They achieve an excellent market position, too: The average market share in their defined target markets is 47.3%.

Averages don't tell the entire truth, because, as might be expected, a handful of very big winners skews the results. So consider the median values, which are almost as impressive (Exhibit 1.4):

- Fifty percent of successful new products achieve a 33% ROI or better.
- Half have a payback period of two years or less.
- Half achieve a market share in excess of 35%.

Not all the new ventures studied are winners, however, so these exceptional performance results must be tempered with the cost of failure. And

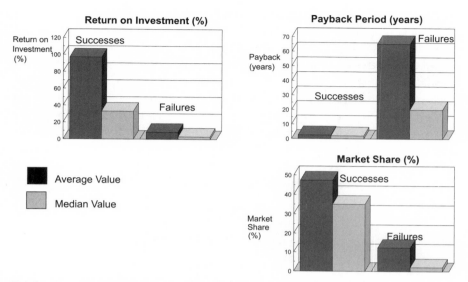

Exhibit 1.4   Profitability of New Products—Successes Versus Failures

in this study, about one-third are unsuccessful launches. But even factoring in these losses, product development must be considered a very profitable undertaking, overall.

Impact on investment value: Another reason why product innovation is so important these days are the financial markets, which seem to dominate corporate behavior. An annual *Fortune* survey rates top U.S. corporations on a number of criteria, including "value as a long-term investment." Using data supplied by *Fortune Magazine*, I studied various predictors of investment value. The results are provocative. *The single strongest predictor of investment value is "degree of innovativeness of the company."* The conclusion is that product innovation is not only important to remain competitive in the business's marketplace, it also seems to be important to financial markets in determining the value of the company as a long-term investment, and hence to the cost of capital to the firm.

Each year, this *Fortune Magazine* survey lists the most admired major corporations in America. In the top 10 typically are firms such as Merck, Microsoft, Johnson & Johnson, Intel, Pfizer, 3M, GE, and Procter & Gamble. Coincidentally, all of the most admired companies are the top one or two firms in their industries in terms of *innovativeness.* Another article in *Fortune Magazine*, entitled "Secrets of America's Most Admired Corporations," reveals that *new ideas* and *new products* are the key: To be genuinely admired, these businesses possess a common quality: "that ingredient is innovation, and all the top companies embrace it passionately."[12]

Huge amounts at stake: The payoffs are high, but so are the costs. The *average company* among the top 1000 R&D companies in the world spends about $273 million annually on R&D, or 4.2% of annual sales.[13] In the United States alone, total R&D expenditures amounted to $253 billion annually in 2002, or about 2.82% of its GDP. In Japan and Germany, R&D spending is similarly high at 3.09 and 2.50% of GDP, respectively.[14]

Certain industries, noted for their growth and profitability in recent decades, spend heavily on R&D. For example, the software industry spends almost 20% of sales on R&D; the computer communication equipment industry averages 12.5% of sales on R&D; pharmaceuticals averages 12%; and chemicals averages almost 6% (see Exhibit 1.5 for an industry breakdown).

The Drivers of Innovation

New products are clearly the key to corporate prosperity. They drive corporate revenues, market shares, bottom lines, and even share prices. But why is product innovation speeding up so much, and why is so much more emphasis being placed on your product innovation track record? One pundit even likens the innovation phenomenon to the *international arms race* between 1950 and 1990.[15] The recent Cheskin and Fitch:Worldwide survey reveals that *greater competitive pressures* and *new technology, invention, and discovery* are what executives see as the two principal drivers of innovation and the heavy emphasis on new products.[16] And there have been other studies that have revealed similar forces.[17] Overall, the main drivers of product innovation today are:

▶ *Increased globalization of markets*: Your business now has access to foreign markets like never before, but at the same time, your domestic market has become someone else's international one. This globalization of markets has created significant opportunities for the product innovator: *access to global markets* and also the prospect of *the world product* targeted at global markets. It has also intensified competition in every domestic market. Both factors have sped up the pace of product innovation.

▶ *Increased competitive pressure*: Gone are the days when a single company could dominate a market without challenge—when IBM owned the computer market, DuPont dominated the nylon business, and Boeing was alone in the jumbo-aircraft market. Not even Microsoft is secure within its competitive fortress today. These intensely competitive markets have created much pressure on businesses to regain or secure competitive advantage. And new products are seen as a vital

Industry	R&D as a Percent of Sales	Industry	R&D as a Percent of Sales
All industry	4.4%	Glass, stone, & clay products	2.2
Aircraft & aerospace	3.4	Instruments	6.8
Automotive (motor vehicles)	4.2	Machinery (non-electrical)	3.2
Chemicals	5.8	Metal products (fabricated)	1.6
Communications equipment	12.1	Metals – primary	0.8
Computers & office equipment.	6.7	Paper	2.0
Computer services	11.8	Petroleum & coal	0.6
Electronic components	10.3	Pharmaceutical	12.3
Electrical equipment	2.1	Phone & telecommunications services	2.0
Food	0.7	Polymers & rubber	2.4
Furniture & wood products	1.7	Textiles	1.8

Exhibit 1.5   R&D Spending by Industry

Source: Industrial Research and Development Facts with the 1998 Industrial R & D Scorecard, Industrial Research Institute, Wasington, DC, 1999.

route to gaining market leadership and sustainable advantage over competitors.

▶ *Technology advances:* Not even a slower economy slows down technology. The world's base of technology and know-how increases at an exponential rate, making possible solutions and products not even dreamed of a decade or so ago. What was science fiction and featured on *Star Trek* in the 1970s—for example, hand-held computers, portable picture phones, and nonintrusive surgery—is suddenly a technological reality today.

▶ *Changing customer needs*: Marketplaces are also in turmoil, with market needs and wants and customer preferences changing regularly. The company that seemed omnipotent only a few years ago suddenly falls from favor with the consumer. Witness IBM's problems of the 1990s, as corporate customers shifted their desires dramatically away from mainframe computers (IBM's traditional strength) and to much smaller computers and LAN servers; or GM's problems, as customers seek technology, features, and performance more typical of German or Japanese luxury cars. In other markets, customers have come to expect new products with significant improvements on a regular basis. Look at the new photo-cell phones—take a picture and email it to a friend! We consumers have become like kids in a candy shop: We see what is possible, and we want it.

▶ *Shortening product life cycles*: If you have the impression that the world is moving much faster, it's not that you're getting older—it really has speeded up! A study done by A. D. Little shows that product life cycles have been cut by *a factor of about four* over the last 50 years (see Exhibit 1.6).[18] Your new product no longer has a life of five to 10 years, but within a few years, sometimes even months, it is superseded by a competitive entry, rendering yours obsolete and necessitating a new product. This has placed much pressure on businesses and their managements: For example, in one leading electronics firm in the United States, as product version number 1 is hitting the market, its replacement, product version 2, is already in the Development phase, and product version 3 is waiting in the wings for a Go-to-Development decision.

A quick review of all five drivers of product innovation reveals that none is likely to disappear in the next decade or two. Technology advances will continue to occur, as will changes in market needs and demands; globalization of markets marches on, spurred by trade agreements and the creation of free trade zones; and competitive pressure will continue to mount, and will also drive life cycles to become even shorter. Product

Notes for Senior Management

Senior management must lead, because new products are your key to business prosperity. Look at the facts . . .

- the high profit impact that new products have (or should have) on your business
- the impact that product innovation has on your business valuation or share prices
- where your future sales and profit will come from

Compare yourself to the industry averages: 32% of sales and 30% of profits coming from new products launched in the last five years! And compare yourself to the averages in your industry (Exhibit 1.3).

Next, recall the vital importance that other executives accord product innovation—that half believe it to be *critically important to the success of their busine*sses (Exhibit 1.2). And think about how profitable new products are when they are successful: the spectacular ROIs, paybacks, and market shares achieved by winning new products (Exhibit 1.4). Very few other investments in your business have the potential for these high returns and rewards.

Next there are the financial markets to consider. Not so long ago a steady and profitable business was what Wall Street valued. That is still true, except that increasingly the investment community is looking for organic growth and evidence of a solid new product track record. The investment community cannot be ignored: It dictates the rules of the game for your business!

Don't forget resource commitments. If your business is typical, chances are you are already spending a lot on product innovation. But are you spending enough? Compare yourself to the norms in Exhibit 1.5.

Finally, as you look into the future, consider the drivers of innovation in your industry and why things are changing ever so quickly: globalization of markets; increased competitive pressure; advancing technology; changing customer needs; and shorter product life cycles. None of these drivers is likely to disappear; indeed, we can expect them to be stronger than ever in the years ahead.

So ready or not, you're in the innovation war today! And either you succeed in this war, or you likely won't last long as a viable business. So take charge of your business's product innovation efforts! The payoffs are too huge and the costs to great to be ignored.

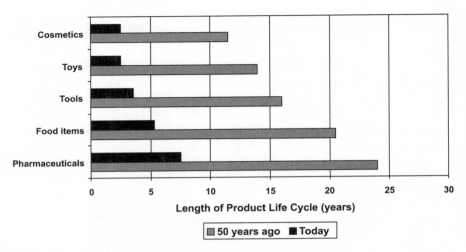

Length of Product Life Cycle (years)

50 years ago ■ Today

Exhibit 1.6 Product Life Cycles Have Decreased Dramatically
Source: A. D. Little, as cited in von Braun. See note 4.

innovation will be even more critical to corporate prosperity in the years ahead than it has been in the recent past.

Warning: It's Not So Easy to Win

No one said this would be easy. In new products warfare, one always faces a dilemma: On the one hand, you recognize that new products are critical to your business's long-term success. They keep your current product portfolio competitive and healthy, and in many companies, provide you with long-term and sustainable competitive advantage. The problem is that product innovation is fraught with dangers and pitfalls: Boasting a steady stream of successful new products is no small feat.

The hard realities are that the great majority of new products never make it to market. And those that do face a failure rate somewhere on the order of 25 to 45%. These figures vary, depending on what industry and on how one defines a "new product" and a "failure." Some sources cite the failure rate at launch to be as high as 90%. But these figures tend to be unsubstantiated, and are likely wildly overstated. According to Crawford, who has undertaken perhaps the most thorough review of these often-quoted figures, the true failure rate is about 35%.[19] Our own studies concur: We find the average *success rate* of developed products*

---

*That is, projects that emerged from the Development phase. Note that many projects are killed during Development or before.

to be about 67%. But averages often fail to tell the whole story: This success rate varies from a low of 0% to a high of 100%, depending on the company![20]

Other studies point to the difficult times faced by new product managers. Our most recent benchmarking study reveals that only 56% of new product projects meet their profit objectives, and that only 51% get to market on time.[21] A PDMA study reveals that new products have had a success rate of only 59% at launch over the last five years.[22] The Conference Board reports a median success rate of 66% for consumer products and 64% for industrial goods (defined as success in the marketplace after launch).[23] Booz-Allen & Hamilton cite a 65% success rate for new product launches.[24]

Regardless of whether the success rate is 55% or 65%, the odds of a misfire are still substantial. Worse, the figures cited above don't include the majority of new product projects that are killed along the way, long before launch, yet involve considerable expenditures of time and money.

The attrition curve of new products tells the whole story. One study reveals that for *every 7 new product ideas, about 4 enter development, 1.5 are launched, and only one succeeds.*[25] Another investigation paints an even more dismal picture: For every 11 new product ideas, 3 enter the development phase, 1.3 are launched, and only one is a commercial success in the marketplace.[26] The most recent PDMA survey reveals a seven-to-one ratio (see Exhibit 1.7).[27] The bad news continues. An estimated 46% of all the resources allocated to product development and commercialization by U.S.

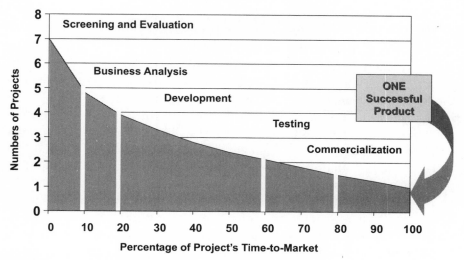

Exhibit 1.7   The Attrition Rate of New Product Projects

firms is spent on products that are cancelled or fail to yield an adequate financial return.[28] This is an astounding statistic when one considers the magnitude of human and financial resources devoted to new products. But a minority of firms (30%) does achieve an enviable 80% success rate: That is, 80% of the resources they spend on innovation goes to new product winners. These few firms show that it is possible to outperform the average, and by a considerable margin.

Notes for Senior Management

How well is your business doing in the product innovation war? Do you even know? Most senior executives cannot provide fact-based statistics from their business on success, fail, and kill rates; on the proportion of resources spent on winners versus losers; or on how profitable their new products are. In any war or game, serious contenders keep score!

The following chapter provides you with a list of metrics that you can use to keep score in this war, and also some data so that you can compare your performance with that of other businesses.

Next question: If your business is not winning this innovation war, do you know why? Have you identified some of the causes? Or have you figured out what winners do differently from you? If you seek these answers, again read on . . . for that's what the rest of this book is about.

The Role of Senior Management

The Generals Must Lead

This book is for you, the generals of industry: the CEOs, general managers, managing directors, VPs, and directors who aspire to lead their businesses to victory in the product innovation war. Your duty as a member of the leadership team of your business is to *lead*. And what could be more important these days than to lead the new product charge? More than most business endeavors today, this effort will shape your business strategy, and will determine your company's fortunes.

The trouble is that some generals have not been trained for the new products war. And that's where this book provides guidance. From Chapter 3 on, I outline the critical success factors in product innovation—those factors that our research finds consistently distinguish successful businesses, the victors, from unsuccessful businesses in the new products war.

Another problem is that too many business leaders seem not to be terribly interested in their responsibility to product innovation: They take a "hands-off" management approach. They talk the talk, about how important product development is, but often fail to walk the talk—for example, they fail to make the needed resource commitments, or distance themselves from key new product decisions. Perhaps it is because senior people are so focused on short-term, day-to-day issues; or perhaps your business is so financially driven that you simply don't have the personal time or the company resources to commit to product innovation; or maybe you view product development as a bit of a mystery; or perhaps you assume that product development is "an R&D thing," and "those techies" or scientists will take care of it.

Wrong on all counts! Fast-paced, successful product development is perhaps the *most important challenge faced by today's companies*. So it is essential that you leaders get involved; you must understand the critical success factors and how you manipulate each; and, most important, you must indeed lead! I am always surprised when I see senior management failing here.

> *An example:* A senior management meeting had been called to discuss product development and portfolio management—making the right product investment decisions—in a division of a major European automotive company. Management had proclaimed that new products and services were the key to the future in their competitive truck markets. And yet five of the vital senior people failed to show up, including the heads of both marketing and R&D. Some fairly lame excuses were made for most absentees. My response to this dismal showing was direct: "What on earth could be more important than your future . . . more important than making decisions about what your product and service offerings will be—in effect, decisions about the future of your company in the marketplace?" There was silence, because everyone in the room knew that *nothing was more important*, that some senior people had become sidetracked on urgent, but not important issues. And they were shirking their leadership responsibilities.

Fact-Based Management

Military principles are based on facts—facts gathered by military historians and strategists who have studied countless wars and battles since the beginning of time. This book and its prescriptions are also very much fact-based. Since the 1970s, my colleagues* and I have investigated over 2000 new product launches, and have studied almost 1000 companies' new

---

*I do not claim credit for all the research work. My colleagues, whom I have worked with, and whose research findings are part of this book, include my immediate colleagues and co-researchers, namely, Professor Elko Kleinschmidt and Dr. Scott Edgett; and others I have worked with (in alphabetical order), namely, Professors Ludwig Bstieler, Roger Calantone, Ulrike de Brentani, Chris Easingwood, and Chris Storey.

product efforts. The goal: to uncover what winners do differently from losers; what the common denominators of successful new products and businesses are; and what distinguishes the top performers.

▶ Some of our studies look at the entire business or company and ask the broad question: Why are some businesses so much better at product innovation than others? We call these the *benchmarking studies*.[29] And the quest is always for the identification of the critical success drivers and best practices—those practices that distinguish the top performers. Our most recent benchmarking study is the APQC study. See Box 1.1.

▶ Many of our studies have focused on *individual new product projects*— we call these the *NewProd®* project studies.[30] Typically we study groups of new product projects—some successes and some failures— and try to discern what separates the winners from the losers. In this way, we are able to pinpoint best practices and key success drivers. See Box 1.2.

Depending on the type of study—at the project level, or a study of businesses—the success factors uncovered are somewhat different. However, regardless of the study, the fundamental question was always the same: What makes for a winner?

These studies have been widely published (they have resulted in over 90 publications in leading journals); they have an international focus; and together they represent the most comprehensive set of studies on new

---

Box 1.1   Our Research in Support of the Prescriptions for Performance

In August 2002, a group of sponsor businesses met at the American Productivity and Quality Center (APQC) in Houston to begin the search for the answer to why some businesses are so much better at NPD—the quest for the "secrets to new product success." Some eight months later, after an investigation of 125 companies' NPD practices and performance, the sponsor firms of this study had gained valuable new insights into what makes winners win in product innovation. For example, a group of best-performing businesses were identified—businesses whose new product efforts were profitable, efficient, and high impact, and that also opened up windows of opportunity. These companies' methods and practices were compared to a group of poorer-performing businesses. From these comparisons, a number of best practices—practices and methods that really drive new product results—were identified. Many of my prescriptions on how to excel in the product innovation war are based on this major benchmarking study. See note 29.

Box 1.2   More Research Evidence

Our APQC study, whose results are cited throughout this book, is not the only benchmarking study we have undertaken. Indeed, this 2003 investigation is one of many in a long tradition of studies which had a common theme: how to win at new products.

Such investigations began with the *NewProd®* projects studies in the late 1970s that looked at individual new product projects and posed the question: Why are some new products so much more successful than others? See note 30. The *NewProd®* studies continued through the 1980s and 1990s, and to date, the *NewProd®* database contains over 2000 new product launches. Many critical success factors were identified in these *NewProd®* studies—factors that have helped to shape how many firms now undertake their new product projects.

Beginning in the 1980s, we also focused on *businesses* (rather than individual new product projects) as the unit of analysis. See note 29. Here we asked: why are some businesses more successful at NPD? These benchmarking studies revealed many secrets to new product success. Our current APQC study, cited in this chapter, simply continues and confirms these ongoing studies.

---

product management practices undertaken to date.[31] It is upon this research foundation that the current book has been constructed.

Moving at Lightning Speed

In product innovation, as in warfare or war games, the goal is victory—a steady stream of profitable and successful new products. On this new product battlefield, the ability to mount lightning attacks—well-planned but swift strikes—is increasingly the key to success. *Speed is the competitive weapon.* The ability to accelerate products to market ahead of the competition and within the window of opportunity is more than ever central to success. And so this book is about more than success; it's about how to get successful products to market in record time.

There are major payoffs to speeding products to market:

- *Speed yields competitive advantage.* The ability to respond to customers' needs and changing markets faster than the competition, and to beat competitors to market with a new product, often is the key to success. But too much haste may result in an ill-conceived product, which has no competitive advantage at all!
- *Speed yields higher profitability.* The revenue from the sale of the product is realized earlier (Money has a time value, and deferred revenues

are worth less than revenues acquired sooner.) Additionally, the revenues over the life of the product are higher, given a fixed window of opportunity and hence limited product life.

▶ *Speed means fewer surprises.* The ability to move quickly to market means that the original commercial assumptions are still probably valid, and that the product as originally conceived is more likely to meet market requirements. The short timeframe reduces the odds that market conditions will dramatically change as development proceeds. Then consider the *seven-year development effort* incurred by some U.S. and German auto companies: Here, market requirements, market conditions, and the competitive situation are likely to have changed considerably from beginning to end of the project.[32]

There is a dark side to speed, however. Too many senior managers have become *speed demons*, where getting to market fast has become the ultimate objective. One of the most frequent questions I am asked is: How can we do it faster?

> *An example:* A major company had identified a number of potential breakthrough new projects that promised to have huge impacts on the corporation. At a meeting between the president of the company and the project leaders, the CEO spoke about how vital these projects were, and how all eyes were on these select project leaders. When it came to the Q&A period, rather than asking how he could help these project leaders do a better job, his one telling challenge was: "How can you cut the time to market . . . we really need these fast!" I sensed that some of these project leaders were being set up for failure before they were even out of the starting gate.

Our studies of hundreds of new product winners and losers show that there is a strong and positive connection between speed and profits, but the connection is anything but one-to-one. Many of the actions that project teams take in the interest of saving a little time often have the exact opposite effect, and in some cases, destroy the profitability of the venture. Witness the case of Mega Bloks, where moving quickly and without discipline actually resulted in going slower! So, I will never recommend cutting corners in haste or executing in a sloppy fashion in order to save time—it just doesn't pay off. In short, speed is important, but it is only one component of your all-important goal of profitable, big new product winners.

Senior Management in Winning Businesses

As the generals in this product innovation war, you face many challenges, and sometimes it's difficult to know where to begin. But one thing is clear: Businesses whose senior managements are *strongly committed to* and *very much involved* in their new product efforts do much better, according to our benchmarking studies.[33] Such businesses with greater senior management involvement in new products boast much more successful new product efforts overall—more profitable and higher impact.

From our studies of hundreds of new product projects, one conclusion is that top management support is critical to getting individual new product projects to market. Without top management support, there is much less hope of securing the needed resources and approvals to proceed. This comes as no surprise. Perhaps more provocative is that top managers support failures with almost equal frequency as they do successes! That is, executive-sponsored "pet projects" don't do so well: They get to market alright, but their success rates are below average.

A very clear picture for senior management emerges from our research: You must lead, but not micro-manage. Don't get caught up in the trap of over-involving yourselves in the day-to-day management of individual new product projects, or of driving your own "pet projects" to market. It's often tempting to do this, but *that's not leadership* and *it's not your role!*

Rather, your role is very much that of an enabler—to set the stage, but not necessarily be an actor, front and center; to be a behind-the-scenes facilitator; and to create an environment that fosters product innovation.[34] This sounds like a worthwhile personal goal, but what does this mean in practice? Here are the key ingredients of new product success that studies have uncovered and that have a direct bearing on your actions and your leadership:

1. **You must embrace a long-term commitment to product innovation as the engine of growth and prosperity in your business.**[35] This is especially difficult in a world where a short-term financial focus seems to dominate. Look beyond a one-year time horizon and ensure that resources are committed for the longer term (not off again, on again), and that your development portfolio contains a certain proportion of longer-term and platform projects (not just quick hits or "low hanging fruit" projects).

2. **Then, develop a vision, objectives, and strategy for product innovation in your business,** driven by (and linked to) your business's objectives and strategy. Most business leaders have new product goals alright (for example: "By the year 2006, 32% of our revenue will come from new products"), but they don't have a clue how they'll achieve this goal—there is no product innovation strategy for the business!

3. **Install a systematic, high-quality idea-to-launch framework in your business,** and practice discipline, following the principles of the

process. Many firms do indeed have systematic new product processes, such as *Stage-Gate®* (over 70% of firms that develop new product have!).* Move toward a *third-generation* new product process (15% of firms have).[36] But most important, demonstrate that you're committed to the process by your actions, not just your words. Ironically, time and time again, the first to "break discipline" are usually the senior people! They circumvent the process with their executive-sponsored projects; they consistently miss gate meetings; and they fail to make timely Go/Kill decisions or ignore the gate criteria altogether.

4. **Next, make available the necessary resources.** Again, this is difficult given the desire to boost short-term profitability. Recognize that if new product success is the goal, there is no free lunch here: Our studies clearly show that businesses that commit the money and people on average are blessed with much higher new product performance— profitability, high success rates, and reduced time to market.[37]

5. **Practice effective portfolio management.** Make sure that you focus your scarce resources on the right development initiatives. And pay special attention to resource deployment or allocation—where the money is spent. For example, do you have the right mix and balance of projects in your development portfolio? And resist the temptation to try to undertake too many projects for your business's limited resources.

6. **Finally, foster innovation in your organization.** Create the right climate and culture for product innovation—one that supports, rewards, and recognizes new product efforts in your business. And support and enable effective cross-functional teams—empowering project teams, supporting committed champions, and acting as godfathers, sponsors, or executive champions for major new product projects.

We will revisit each of these themes as this book unfolds, providing practical direction for you and your leadership team here. But note these six themes—they are how leaders lead in businesses that achieve superlative new product results.

What's New About a New Product

Serious players keep score in new products warfare. But in order to keep score, one first must have a definition of what counts as a new product. One

---

*The term *Stage-Gate®* was coined by the author in the 1980s, and is a trademark of the Product Development Institute, Inc. (PDI): www.prod-dev.com.

Box 1.3 Another Way to Define a "New" Product

When keeping score, it's important to have an operational definition of "what counts as a new product." An alternate definition of a "new product"—and one effectively used by a number of firms—relies on the notion of **commercial risk**. Thus, any change to the product that is **visible** to the customer or user, and hence creates a risk to the brand, business, or franchise, is considered to be a new product. ITT Industries also adds the caveat that the project must have entailed a minimum amount of development or engineering time ($50,000).

Such a definition includes genuine new products, significant modifications and improvements, line extensions, line additions, and repositionings. However, it excludes cost reductions (that are invisible to the customer), process or manufacturing improvements, fundamental research, and maintenance projects.

---

of the problems with some of the scores cited above is that they include different types of new products: For example, the attrition rates for truly innovative new products are much higher than for extensions and modifications of existing company products. And not all new product projects are the same—there is a huge difference in the way one handles a product line extension versus an entirely new product to your business. And so you must develop some *categories of new products*, so that you can keep score better and handle different types of projects more effectively.

Defining a "New Product"

How does one define a "new product"? There are many different types of "new" products; indeed "newness" can be defined in terms of two dimensions:

- *new to the company*, in the sense that your business has never made or sold this type of product before, but other companies might have. Nonetheless, you must still incur the costs of development and launch, and face all the risks associated with a new initiative.
- *new to the market*, or "a true innovation": The product is the first of its kind on the market. This is the traditional definition of "new product"; but if you adhered to this definition alone, you'd exclude much of the product development effort that takes place within your business.

Categories of Newness

Viewed on a two-dimensional map as shown in Exhibit 1.8, six different types or classes of new products are identified.

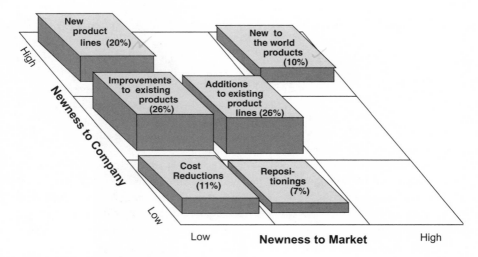

Exhibit 1.8   Categories of New Products

1. *New-to-the-world products*: These new products are the first of their kind and create an entirely new market (upper right corner of Exhibit 1.8). This category represents only 10% of all new products.[38] Well-known examples include the Sony Walkman, Pfizer's Viagra, Apple's original iPod, and 3M's Post-It Notes.
2. *New product lines*: These products, although not new to the marketplace, nonetheless are quite new to the particular firm. They allow a company to enter an established market for the first time. For example, Canon was not the first to launch an office version of a laser printer; Hewlett-Packard was, with its LaserJet™. When Canon did introduce its version, it was clearly not an innovation, but it did represent a new product line for Canon, with all the investment that entailed. About 20% of all new products fit into this category.
3. *Additions to existing product lines*: These are new items to the firm, but fit within an existing product line that the firm makes. They may also represent a fairly new product to the marketplace. An example is Hewlett-Packard's introduction of its next generation or model in its *LaserJet*™ line, a more up-to-date and more powerful version of its laser printers. Its added features and resolution make it somewhat novel or "new to the market." Such new items are one of the largest categories of new product—about 26% of all new product launches.
4. *Improvements and revisions to existing products*: These "not-so-new" products are essentially replacements of existing products in a firm's product line. They offer improved performance or greater perceived

value over the "old" product. These "new and improved" products also make up 26% of new product launches. For example, Exxon-Mobil Chemical produces modified polyolefin plastics. A significant percentage of its R&D effort goes into product "tweaks"—that is, modifying existing polymers in order to respond to a changing customer requirement or a competitive threat.

5. *Repositionings*: These are essentially new applications for existing products, and often involve retargeting an old product at a new market segment or for a different application. Repositionings account for about 7% of all new products. For years, Bayer's Aspirin (or ASA, as it is known in some countries) was the standard headache, pain, and fever reliever. Superseded by newer, safer compounds, Aspirin was in trouble. But new medical evidence suggested that Aspirin had other benefits. Now Aspirin is positioned, not as a headache pill, but as a blood clot, stroke, and heart attack preventer.

6. *Cost reductions*: These are the least "new" of all new product categories. They are new products designed to replace existing products in the line, but yield similar benefits and performance at lower cost. From a marketing standpoint, they are not new products; but from a design and production viewpoint, they could represent significant technical undertaking. They make up 11% of all new product launches.

Most firms feature a *mixed portfolio* of new products. The two most popular categories, additions to the existing line and product improvements or revisions, are common to almost all firms. By contrast, the "step-out" products—new-to-the-world and new-to-the-firm product lines—constitute only 30% of all new product launches, but represent 60% of the products viewed as "most successful."[39] Best-performing businesses appear to undertake a much higher proportion of such innovative projects: They represent over 40% of these firms' development portfolios.[40] In Chapter 3, which focuses on developing a product innovation strategy, we gain more insight into the right balance and mix of projects.

An Introduction to the Product Innovation War

In this chapter, you've seen that winning the product innovation war plays a critical role in determining your business's fortunes. It's innovate or die! You've also had a quick glimpse at some success drivers and best practices employed by senior managers in the Mega Bloks story. And I've challenged you and your leadership team to play the role of generals and to

---

Notes for Senior Management

Arrive at an agreed definition of "what is a new product" in your business. Most businesses count at minimum the top four types of products in Exhibit 1.8. Another popular definition is "any change in the product that is visible to the customer and hence creates risk to the business"—see Box 1.3. Now that you've defined a new product, you can start keeping better and more consistent scores in the product innovation war.

Having defined some new product categories for your business (and what counts as a new product), begin to categorize existing development projects currently in your pipeline. And then ask the question: Is this the right mix or balance of projects? Too often this simple exercise yields provocative "No" answers—too many tweaks and minor projects, and not enough game-changers that promise real growth for the business!

---

lead here, much like management at Mega Bloks led the way. Some of the key elements of your leadership role were outlined.

You have also witnessed the risks in product innovation: the high odds of failure and significant rates of attrition. But recall that when successful, winning at new products has major payoffs. Keeping score is an important facet of your war plan, so I laid out methods to help categorize new products in order that the scores can be more comparable.

In the following chapter, we begin to take a hard look at the evidence. Here you'll see the first of the benchmarking results so that you can compare your own business's performance. And you'll gain insights into what metrics business leaders use to keep score in this war. Finally, I introduce the *Innovation Diamond* as a framework to visualize the success drivers or the *four points of performance* in this innovation war.

Chapter 3 considers a critical, but often overlooked, driver of new product performance, namely *developing a product innovation strategy for your business*. It's fine to have all the tactics in place—for example, a solid idea-to-launch new product process. That's how one moves the ball down the field (in Chapter 7). And it's proper to speak about resources and their allocation: how many players to commit and what tasks they're assigned to (in Chapters 4 and 5). But the battle plan must begin with answers to strategic questions: What are your business's new product objectives? In which arenas should you play the game? And how do you plan to enter each or attack each arena?

Sufficient resources and *effective resource allocation* is a second driver of new product performance and a second key point in the *Innovation Diamond*. Chapters 4 and 5 focus on resource issues and on resource allocation decisions. Here senior management has a vital role, since you *are* the resource allocators. Chapter 4 considers the question: How much is enough?—how to decide how many resources to commit to the innovation war. Chapter 4 also introduces *strategic portfolio management*, dealing with broad strategic allocation decisions—about where you should deploy your development resources.

Making the right investment decisions and picking the right projects is the topic of Chapter 5. This chapter focuses more on the *tactical portfolio management decisions*, and offers a number of approaches and methods that promise more effective project selection and prioritization decisions. Portfolio management looks at all development projects together as a *portfolio of investments*.

Chapters 6 and 7 focus on one of the critical drivers of superior performance, namely, the *new product process* itself. Here, the *Stage-Gate®* idea-to-launch framework, developed by the author and implemented successfully in hundreds of leading firms worldwide, is outlined. Before you say, "but we already have a new product process in our company," wait! Most such processes either are poorly designed (they lack the vital ingredients of a high-quality process), or they simply haven't been installed well. In these chapters, you'll find out what the requirements and ingredients of a successful new product process are, and, without going into too much detail, gain a solid overview of the *Stage-Gate®* process—certainly enough to direct its implementation (or overhaul) in your own business.

The people side of the product innovation war is the topic of Chapter 8. Here you'll see how to foster the creation of effective cross-functional teams and how to instill a positive climate and culture for innovation in your business. And the role of senior management—and how you should lead here—is highlighted. Note that the leadership team of your business are the gatekeepers in the idea-to-launch framework; and so this chapter is also about how you can make your gates or Go/Kill decision-points on individual projects more effective.

The final chapter, Chapter 9, provides an executive summary and wrap-up: an overview of the entire book and a quick listing of the 25 key messages and calls to action.

So read on! Ready yourself for product innovation warfare: Witness the critical success factors, best practices, and the details of the *four points of performance* in the *Innovation Diamond*, and how they can and should be built into your business so that you too can be a *big winner* in the product innovation war.

Notes

1. "New, Smaller, Flashier iPod Sells Out Fast," *USA Today,* March 5, 2004, 1B.

2. F. M. R. Armbrecht, Jr., & R. L. Whitely, "Industrial Research Institute's 5th Annual Leaderboard," *Research-Technology Management,* November–December 2003.

3. OECD, MSTI (Main Science & Technology Indicators) database, May 2003.

4. C. F. von Braun, *The Innovation War.* Upper Saddle River, NJ: Prentice Hall, 1997.

5. This paragraph taken from a book co-authored by the author: R. G. Cooper, S. J. Edgett, & E. J. Kleinschmidt, *Portfolio Management for New Products,* 2nd ed. Reading, MA: Addison-Wesley, 2001.

6. *Fast, Focused, Fertile: The Innovation Evolution,* Cheskin and Fitch:Worldwide, 2003: www.fitchworldwide.com.

7. PDMA best practices study: see A. Griffin, *Drivers of NPD Success: The 1997 PDMA Report.* Chicago: Product Development & Management Association, 1997.

8. A. S. Bean, M. J. Russo, & R. L. Whiteley, "Benchmarking Your R&D: Results from IRI/CIMS Annual R&R Survey for FY '98," *Research-Technology Management,* January–February 2000, 16–24.

9. PDMA study: see note 7. The PDMA is the Product Development and Management Association, the largest association of product developers in the United States and in the world—both business and technical people.

10. See R. G. Cooper & E. J. Kleinschmidt, "Performance Topologies of New Product Projects," *Industrial Marketing Management,* 24, 1995, 439–456; see also *NewProd® studies* in note 30.

11. Based on the *NewProd® studies,* unpublished results: see note 30.

12. B. O'Reilly, "Secrets of America's Most Admired Corporations: New Ideas, New Products," *Fortune,* March 3, 1997, 60–66.

13. F. M. R. Armbrecht, Jr., & R. L. Whitely: see note 2.

14. OECD, MSTI (Main Science & Technology Indicators) database, May 2003.

15. von Braun: see note 4.

16. Cheskin and Fitch:Worldwide, 2003: see note 6.

17. APQC benchmarking study, note 29; also: Booz-Allen & Hamilton, *New Product Management for the 1980s.* New York: Booz-Allen & Hamilton Inc., 1982.

18. von Braun: see note 4.

19. C. M. Crawford, "New Product Failure Rates—Facts and Fallacies," *Research Management,* September 1979, 9–13.

20. Failure rates taken from several of our studies: *NewProd® studies,* note 30; the recent APQC benchmarking study, note 29; and earlier benchmarking studies, note 29.

21. APQC benchmarking study: see note 29. The APQC is the American Productivity and Quality Center, located in Houston, TX; it is the premier benchmarking institute in the United States, and is member-company-sponsored and -supported.

22. PDMA study: see note 7.

23. D. S. Hopkins, *New Product Winners and Losers.* Conference Board Report #773, 1980.

24. Booz-Allen & Hamilton: see note 17.

25. Booz-Allen & Hamilton: see note 17.

26. A. L. Page, "PDMA New Product Development Survey: Performance and Best Practices," paper presented at PDMA Conference, Chicago, November 13, 1991.

27. PDMA study: see note 7.

28. Booz-Allen & Hamilton: see note 17.

29. The APQC study is the most recent of a series of major benchmarking investigations undertaken by the author and co-workers, Dr. Scott Edgett and Dr. Elko Kleinschmidt. See R. G. Cooper, S. J. Edgett, & E. J. Kleinschmidt, *Best Practices in Product Development: What*

Distinguishes Top Performers at www.prod-dev.com, and *Improving New Product Development Performance and Practices* at www.apqc.org.

Earlier benchmarking studies were undertaken by the author and his colleague, Professor Elko Kleinschmidt, and are reported in R. G. Cooper, "Benchmarking New Product Performance: Results of the Best Practices Study," *European Management Journal*, 16, 1, 1998, 1–7; R. G. Cooper & E. J. Kleinschmidt, "Winning Businesses in Product Development: Critical Success Factors," *Research-Technology Management*, 39, 4, July–August 1996, 18–29; R. G. Cooper, & E. J. Kleinschmidt, "Benchmarking the Firm's Critical Success Factors in New Product Development," *Journal of Product Innovation Management*, 12, 5, November 1995, 374–391; also R. G. Cooper & E. J. Kleinschmidt, "Benchmarking Firms' New Product Performance and Practices," *Engineering Management Review*, 23, 3, Fall 1995, 112–120; and R. G. Cooper & E. J. Kleinschmidt, "Winning Businesses in Product Development: Critical Success Factors," *Research-Technology Management*, 39, 4, July–August 1996, 18–29.

30. These *NewProd®* projects studies began in 1975. Good summaries are provided in R. G. Cooper, Chapter 1, "New Products: What Separates the Winners from the Losers," in *PDMA Handbook for New Product Development*, 2nd ed. New York: Wiley, 2004; R. G. Cooper, *Winning at New Products: Accelerating the Process from Idea to Launch*, 3rd ed. Reading, MA: Perseus, 2001; R. G. Cooper, "Doing It Right—Winning with New Products," *Ivey Business Journal*, July–August 2000, 54–60 (available at www.stage-gate.com); and R. G. Cooper, "New Product Development," chapter in: *International Encyclopedia of Business & Management: Encyclopedia of Marketing*, edited by M. J. Baker. London, UK: International Thomson Business Press, 1999, 342–355. *NewProd®* is a tradename of R. G. Cooper & Associates Consultants, Inc.

31. Based on a survey of the new product (R&D management) literature undertaken at Cranfield University (UK) in 1996. See L. T. Falkingham & R. Reeves, "Context Analysis—A Technique for Analyzing Research in a Field, Applied to Literature on the Management of R&D at the Section Level," working paper SWP-1197. Bedford, UK: Cranfield University, Research Office, School of Management.

32. R. G. Cooper, "Developing New Products on Time, in Time," *Research & Technology Management*, 38, 5, September–October 1995, 49–57.

33. Benchmarking studies: see note 29.

34. R. G. Cooper, *Winning at New Products: Accelerating the Process from Idea to Launch*, 3rd ed. Reading, MA: Addison-Wesley, 2000.

35. This list of prescriptions for senior management comes from our benchmarking studies: see note 29; see also Booz-Allen & Hamilton, note 17.

36. R. G. Cooper, "Third-generation New Product Processes," *Journal of Product Innovation Management*, 11, 1994, 3–14.

37. Benchmarking studies: see note 29.

38. Booz-Allen & Hamilton: see note 17.

39. Booz-Allen & Hamilton: see note 17.

40. APQC benchmarking study: see note 29.

2

What Distinguishes
the Best Performers

Those that cannot remember the past are condemned to repeat it.
—George Santayana, American philosopher

I am the master of my fate;
I am the captain of my soul.
—W. E. Henley, *Invictus*

Learning from Past Victories and Defeats

Some companies are consistent winners in the product innovation war—
they are the "best performers." These winning businesses comprise a
familiar club: companies such as Procter & Gamble, 3M, Intel, Johnson &
Johnson, Microsoft, GE, Nike, Apple, Pfizer, Dell Computers, and Kraft
Foods. And then there's all the rest, perhaps including your own company: They have no big new product winners; most "new products" are
merely line extensions or modifications of existing company products; and
profits and growth from product innovation are sadly lacking. What do
the winning businesses do so differently—what are the secrets to success
that separate the Best from the Rest?

The ExxonMobil Chemical Story

ExxonMobil Chemical is one of the winners.[1] In the late 1980s, senior
management recognized the need to *rethink the way product innovation was
undertaken*. Too many projects seemed to take forever to get to market;
many would-be projects were cancelled after substantial spending; and

even when launched, many new products failed to realize their sales and profit expectations.

The ExxonMobil task force, created by senior management, tackled the innovation process—the idea-to-launch new product system. Working with business groups around the world, the task force pinpointed deficiencies in the current process, identified best practices in the industry, and crafted what has evolved into ExxonMobil's best-in-class *Product Innovation Process* (PIP). This process, a company-wide *Stage-Gate®* framework, has become ingrained in the language and culture of the company.*

ExxonMobil's management also worked on strategy, and instituted a *new product development strategy* that guides which products it plans to develop. Next, ExxonMobil installed a *portfolio management system* to ensure effective resource allocation and project prioritization, and to enable its *Stage-Gate®* process to function even better. Other areas were also attacked: improving the *climate and culture for innovation*, complete with rewards and recognition; instituting a "Quality in R&D" process; and creating effective cross-functional teams.

The results of this multifaceted effort at ExxonMobil have been impressive. Since 1999, for example, the overall cycle-time of development projects has been reduced by 50%; the total of the economic values of projects has risen dramatically; and resource utilization is much improved, with more than 60% of Kill decisions now made before significant resources are spent.

The ExxonMobil case is not unique. Indeed, a number of leading firms have taken similar actions, and seen their new product results—profitability, success rates, cycle time reduction—double and even triple.

Reality Is More Sobering

Achieving these impressive NPD results remains an elusive goal for many businesses, however. Our extensive APQC study of product innovation practices and performance revealed some stunning conclusions:[2]

▶ Fact 1: Most businesses really struggle with product innovation. The stars one reads about are the exception. In fact, for the typical business, the success rate in NPD is just better than 50:50, with 44% of new product projects failing to meet their profit objectives and nearly half being launched late to market. As one executive put it: "We'd be

---

Stage-Gate® is a registered trademark of Product Development Institute, Inc.

better off taking our R&D dollars to Las Vegas and betting on black at the roulette table! That's how poorly we perform."

♦ Fact 2: Most business leaders are somewhat or very disappointed with their NPD results, with 79% revealing that their business's NPD effort overall did not meet its annual profit objectives.

♦ Fact 3: A handful of firms model the way and show that superior NPD performance is indeed possible. The best performers achieve dramatically better results: Two-thirds of their projects meet profit objectives, and 80% are considered commercial successes and are launched on time.

Notes for Senior Management

Is your business one of the stars that we read about in the product innovation war? Or are you simply not doing very well at product development? Have you ever speculated about what it takes to excel here—what really separates the best from the rest? If so, read on: Witness the performance results of the top performers, and most important, how they achieved these superb results.

Keeping Score—Performance Results Achieved

Keeping score is a basic first step on the path to improving NPD performance. That is, before you embark on a major effort to improve your new product results like ExxonMobil Chemical and Mega Bloks did, the first question you must ask yourself is: "How well is my business currently doing in this product innovation war? Are we winning or losing?"

Here is some help in answering this question: How businesses fare on a number of key performance metrics is highlighted in this section. I also show the *distribution of results*—the top 20% and bottom 20% of businesses on each metric. You can compare your own business's new product performance, noting your performance against both the average business and against the top 20% on each vital metric.

Percentage of Revenues and Profits from New Products

The most popular performance metric that businesses use to keep score is the *percentage of a business's sales revenue derived from new products* each year. Here is how businesses perform on this popular metric (Exhibit 2.1):

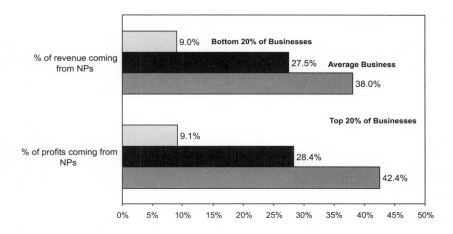

Percentage of the Business's Sales Revenues & Profits
Coming from New Products Launched in Last 3 Years

The average business gets 27.5% of its annual sales from new products launched in the last 3 years; the top 20% of businesses achieve 38% of sales from NPs; the bottom 20% see only 9% of sales from NPs.

Exhibit 2.1 Percentage of Revenues and Profits from New Products

	Average Business	*Top 20% of Businesses*	*Bottom 20% of Businesses*
Percentage of revenue from new products	27.5%	38.0%	9.0%
Percentage of profits from new products	28.4%	42.4%	9.1%

These percentages of sales revenues and profits are defined as follows: the percentage of the current business sales revenues (or the business's profits) derived from new products launched within the *last three years* (some businesses use two years or five years as the timeframe).

Overall, the average percentages are impressive for three-year new products. But most impressive are the results of top 20% performers on these two metrics: 38% of sales and an even higher percentage of profits (42.4%) coming from new products. Note that profit performance appears somewhat higher than sales performance for these top businesses.

Success, Fail, and Kill Rates

Another key metric is the new product success rate: What proportion of projects entering the Development stage become commercial successes?

Or become commercial failures? Or are killed after the critical "Go-to-Development" decision is made—the late kills? The average values, along with the top 20% and bottom 20% of businesses on this metric, are shown in Exhibit 2.2:

	Average Business	*Top 20% of Businesses**	*Bottom 20% of Businesses*
Success Rate	60.2%	79.5%	37.6%
Failure Rate	20.8	8.1	28.4
Late Kill Rate	19.0	4.3	25.7

*Note that these columns for the top and bottom 20% do not quite add up to 100%; this is because one is taking the top quintile and bottom quintile on three separate distributions (success, fail, and kill rates). Only the average success, fail, and kill rates necessarily add up to 100% (column 1 above).

What we witness is a respectable success rate of 60% on average. But note the huge difference between the top businesses and the bottom 20% on this success rate metric: The top businesses have *more than double the success rate* of the bottom 20%. And the bottom businesses have *more than three times the failure rate* of the top ones. These are *not small differences.* Indeed, this huge performance gap between the best and worst begs the question: What separates the best from the worst, and why do the top businesses do so exceptionally well?

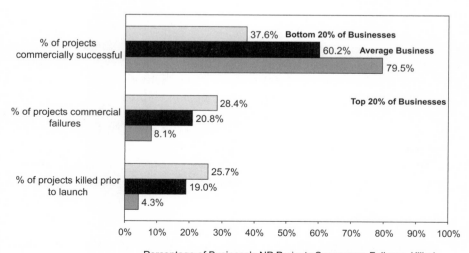

Exhibit 2.2   New Product Success, Fail, and Kill Rates

An example: One of the key metrics that ExxonMobil Chemical tracks is the "percentage of late kills." The company defines "late kills" as follows: "Late kills are any project that is killed after the Go-to-Development gate, the decision-point where significant investment decisions are made." Thus, kill decisions once past the Go-to-Development decision-point are an indication of poor performance. Each business's management tracks the percentage of late kills, and then takes steps to drive down the number.[3]

Time-to-Market

"Time-to-market" is a very topical performance metric, given the heavy emphasis placed on cycle time reduction in product innovation. The average product development—the time from idea generation through to launch—is 18.4 months. The breakdown by businesses is shown in Exhibit 2.3. Here, note that . . .

- slightly over one-quarter (28.4%) of businesses take longer than two years, on average, to get new products from idea to market
- almost one-quarter (23.6%) of businesses take one year or less

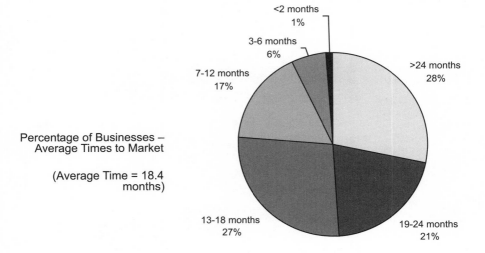

Percentage of Businesses –
Average Times to Market

(Average Time = 18.4 months)

<2 months 1%

3-6 months 6%

7-12 months 17%

>24 months 28%

13-18 months 27%

19-24 months 21%

28% of businesses take longer than 24 months to get their new products to market, on average (idea to launch time). But 6% get to market in 3–6 months.

Exhibit 2.3 Time-to-Market—Idea to Launch

On Time and On Budget

Yet another pair of performance metrics is the proportion of projects hitting their launch dates on time and on budget. Exhibit 2.4 provides the results:

	Average Business	*Top 20% of Businesses**	*Bottom 20% of Businesses*
Percentage of projects on time	51.1%	79.4%	20.5%
Percentage of projects on budget	57.1%	79.0%	15.5%

The fact that, on average, almost half the projects are launched behind schedule and that a considerable percentage (42.9%) are over budget raises serious concerns about scheduling, project management, and commitments to timelines. Admittedly, there is a small group of businesses that do much better than these average businesses: 79.4% of projects on schedule and 79.0% on budget. But the other extreme is the bottom businesses, whose performance is four times lower than the top 20%. The significant differences between the top and bottom businesses indicate that many firms have yet to achieve acceptable on-time and on-budget results, but that a handful of firms proves that this goal can be achieved.

But how late is late? The "slip rate" measures how late a project is as a percentage of its total scheduled time to market:

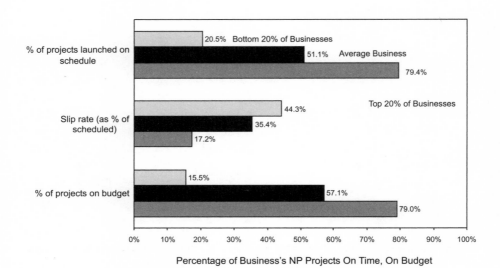

Percentage of Business's NP Projects On Time, On Budget

Exhibit 2.4   Percent of Projects on Time and on Budget

$$\text{Slip Rate} = \frac{\text{Actual Time} - \text{Scheduled Time}}{\text{Actual Time}}$$

On average, projects miss their time schedule (the slip rate) by 35.4%, as noted in Exhibit 2.4. That is, if a project is scheduled for 12 months time-to-market, the typical project gets there in 16.3 months, or 4.3 months late!

That's the data for the average business. The worst performers (bottom 20% on this metric) see their projects miss the time schedule by 44.3%, while the best drive their slip rates down to 17.2%.

New Product Projects Meeting Objectives

What portion of new product projects meet their objectives? Management measures the performance of projects on a number of objectives—profits, sales, market share. But just how do businesses rate on these metrics? Exhibit 2.5 shows the proportion of projects meeting profit, sales, and market-share objectives, and also the results for the top 20% and bottom 20% of businesses on these three metrics:

	Average Business	Top 20% of Businesses	Bottom 20% of Businesses
Percentage meeting profit objectives	56.0%	71.1%	26.9%
Percentage meeting sales objectives	55.4	74.5	29.6
Percentage meeting market-share objectives	54.3	73.4	29.3

These performance metric results are cause for concern. First, the fact that the average values are just better than 50% for all three metrics means that a sizable proportion of projects fail to meet objectives. This 50:50 hit rate should be unacceptable for most senior managements. Next, consider the distribution of results: The top businesses on these metrics achieve almost three times the performance of the bottom 20%, suggesting that many businesses have a long way to go to improve.

Performance Results on Other Metrics

There are many ways to measure a business's new product performance besides those cited in Exhibits 2.1 to 2.5. These include a number of qualitative metrics and comparative measures that are best captured on 0–10 scales. Exhibit 2.6 shows the results for those businesses with very positive

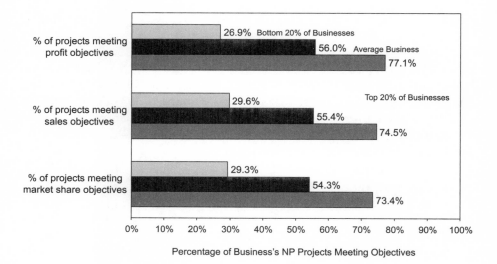

Exhibit 2.5   Percent of New Product Projects Meeting Objectives

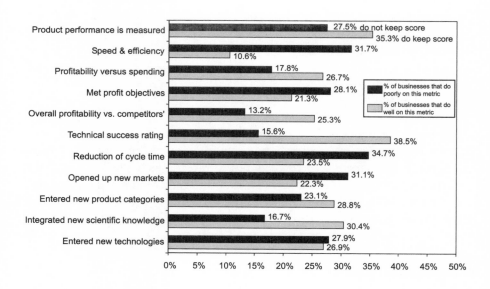

Exhibit 2.6   How Businesses Fare in Terms of Scaled Performance Metrics

results (scoring 8, 9, or 10 out of 10) and those with poor results (scoring 0, 1, 2, or 3 out of 10) on each performance metric. The results:

1. Some businesses (30.0%) actually do measure their overall new product performance. A surprising 27.5% *do not keep score*, however: More than one in four businesses do not measure their new product performance results overall.
2. The ability to get products to market quickly and efficiently is very weakly rated—the worst of all 10 performance metrics. Only 10.6% of businesses claim very good results here.
3. Businesses see their total NPD effort as moderately profitable relative to how much they spend on it. Only 26.7% see their NPD effort as very profitable.
4. The ability to meet profit objectives is more weakly rated. Only 21.3% of businesses' total NPD efforts meet their profit objectives.
5. Businesses rate the profitability of their NPD effort moderate versus competitors'. Just over one-quarter (25.3%) see their NPD effort as very profitable versus their competitors'.
6. Businesses are quite positive about the technical success of their NPD—this is the strongest performance metric. A total of 38.5% of businesses believe their NPD efforts to be highly technically successful.
7. Cycle time reduction is the goal in many businesses' NPD efforts. And so, the ability to reduce cycle time over the last three years is a key metric. Businesses rate poorly here, with only 23.5% of business claiming good results.

Four additional scaled metrics gauge the ability of the business's NPD effort to open new and longer-term opportunities to the business:

8. NPD generally does not open up new markets for businesses—markets that they have not served before; only 22.3% achieve very positive results here.
9. NPD efforts are relatively weak when it comes enabling businesses to enter new product categories, areas, or product types; only 28.8% of businesses are very positive here.
10. NPD is seen as somewhat enabling businesses to integrate (or build in) new technology or new scientific knowledge into their business. A somewhat higher proportion of business (30.4%) are very positive here.
11. NPD efforts are relatively weak in terms of getting businesses into new technologies: Only 26.9% of businesses are very positive here.

A quick glance at Exhibit 2.6 shows that a significant percentage of businesses fare quite poorly on almost all of these metrics—the average is *24% of businesses doing poorly* across these 11 scaled metrics. And with one exception (namely, technical success), less than one-third of businesses performs well on any of these performance metrics. The worst performance is on the two time metrics: speed and efficiency (the ability to get products to market quickly and efficiently), and the ability to reduce cycle time. Opening up new markets is also a very weak performance area. The two strongest performance metrics both deal with technical performance: the technical success rating of the NPD program, and the ability of the program to integrate new scientific knowledge into the business.

Notes for Senior Management

How is your business doing on some of these performance metrics?

- percentage of sales and profits coming from new products launched in last three years
- success, fail, and kill rates (or percentage of "late kills")
- time-to-market: actual versus scheduled (or the slip rate)
- on-budget performance (percentage of projects hitting targets)
- percentage of projects meeting sales, profit, or market-share objectives

If your performance is just average or below, start asking the question: Why? Why is your business's NPD performance substandard? Then read the rest of this chapter to find out the main drivers of successes. Much more detail is given on each of these success drivers in the following seven chapters, where the secrets to success—what the top-performing businesses do differently—are revealed.

What Separates the Best Performers from the Rest

What is it that best-performing companies do so differently than poorer performers? Or is it just that they're in the right industry or market at the right time? Or maybe it's blind luck—and a few years later, they aren't performing so well? Let's look more closely at those factors that really separate the best performers from the rest. Consider these two case histories:

How EXFO Engineering Got It Right

One of the top performers we investigated is a medium-sized firm engaged in the manufacture of fiberoptic test equipment, EXFO Electro-Optical Engineering, Inc. EXFO was begun in 1985 with a single new product idea—a cost-effective method and equipment for testing the integrity of fiberoptic cables. It has grown to a successful and profitable company, largely through a steady stream of successful new product launches. EXFO was singled out as one of the five benchmark firms by the APQC and coincidentally won the PDMA's Outstanding Corporate Innovator award in 2000. Here is how this company has won in the innovation war.[4]

According to EXFO's VP of R&D, "new product development is more than a process; it's a comprehensive system built on three axes":

1. portfolio management
2. the product development process (PDP)
3. the project environment

EXFO's first best practice is *portfolio management*, implemented in 1998. Until then, EXFO had experienced almost weekly changes in its project priorities, making it difficult to focus on any one project and to complete it on time. The old project-prioritization system was a reactive one (reacting to sales force requirements), rather than having a strategic focus. One of the results of moving to portfolio management was a decrease in time-to-market from 18 to 24 months down to 12 months, the result of more focus on the right development projects.

EXFO's *product development process* (PDP) is its second best practice, according to management. Through the 1990s, the PDP was driven by one department—first engineering and then marketing. Results were poor. The lesson learned is that NPD is not the sole domain of any one function. Additionally, as in so many businesses, the early process was so complicated and detailed that people stopped thinking—they just checked work items off on a list. The new process, implemented in 1998, is a simple yet robust four-stage, four-gate business process owned by all relevant departments; it focuses on the main deliverables and requirements necessary to move an idea through the stages and gates to full production, rather than on the details of the "how-to's."

EXFO's third best practice is its *project environment*. EXFO has moved beyond a functional orientation and has embraced a truly cross-functional team approach to NPD. Additionally, senior management has had a long history of strong commitment to product innovation, which has created a very positive environment for these project teams. As the CEO explained, the company was born because of a successful product innovation (created by him), and this continued emphasis on innovation and entrepreneurial spirit has come somewhat naturally.

As EXFO's story illustrates, there is no magic to getting superior NPD results. In EXFO's case, it boils down to:

- an effective portfolio management system, designed to pick the right projects and yield focus
- a superb idea-to-launch product development process to drive new product projects to market
- the right environment, including cross-functional teams and senior management commitment

The Cosmetics Business Story at Procter & Gamble

Procter & Gamble's cosmetics business is a case in point where a dramatic turnaround was achieved via a disciplined, holistic approach to new product management. The story begins when Procter & Gamble acquired the *Cover Girl* and *Clarion* cosmetics brands in 1989. Two years later *Max Factor* was acquired.

Procter & Gamble then applied its tried-and-true approach of leveraging scale and an innovation strategy consisting of a few, big new products. But there was no real business strategy: Efforts were scattered and unfocused as the business tried to do everything in many different product categories and segments. And so, by 1994, management was forced to retreat and retrench: They dropped the *Clarion* line, and through much of the 1990s, senior management wondered if they should be in the cosmetic business at all! A new cosmetics line, under the *Oil of Olay* banner, was attempted, but the new line failed, and the entire cosmetics business continued to decline.

The business turnaround started in the late 1990s, when management turned to Procter & Gamble's *Initiatives Diamond* philosophy. The first element of their diamond is *a product innovation strategy*. Indeed, the real breakthrough occurred when the leadership team began a rigorous business planning process leading to clearly defined objectives, goals, strategies, and measures. A much more *concentrated strategy* was elected, focusing on lips, face, and eyes, rather than the rest of the body. The battlefields had been decided! A second facet of strategy focused on getting the supply chain under control: *end-to-end supply chain management*. Management streamlined the supply chain so that production and shipments were tied to market demand; as a result, they were able to reduce the time in the supply chain, thereby eliminating much of the product obsolescence generated with each new product launch.

Next, management applied the second element of Procter & Gamble's *Initiatives Diamond*, their *SIMPL new product process*. Having a strategy is a solid first step, but the means of implementing strategy must be in place too. SIMPL is a methodology for driving new product projects from the idea phase through to launch, and incorporates many Procter & Gamble best practices. It is a rigorous product launch process using stage-and-gate decision making complete with clear Go/Kill criteria and timing requirements.

The SIMPL idea-to-launch model forced project teams to do their homework early in the project; for example, much consumer research work was done, and consumer insights were gained that led to winning new product concepts. One resulting big success is *Outlast*™ by *Cover Girl*. This 10-hour lipstick—a kiss-proof, long-lasting lipstick—uses a unique two-part application system (first a color and then a gloss) to produce an enduring lip color and gloss. A second winner—*Lipfinity*™ by *Max Factor*—was also introduced, again using the SIMPL idea-to-launch framework. Both new products have been huge successes not only in the United States, but around the world.

Portfolio management, a third element of Procter & Gamble's *Initiatives Diamond*, was employed to enable management to look at their entire portfolio of new product initiatives and secure the right balance and mix. Through portfolio management, the business built a pipeline of new and improved products that established the needed initiative rhythm for each product line (face, lips, eyes)—new products and upgrades that created news and excitement in the market. This "launch and sustain" portfolio approach was a key part of winning in the marketplace.

Today, Procter & Gamble's cosmetics business is a healthy, growing, and profitable enterprise. Performance results have significantly improved since the late 1990s, and the business is seen as a key growth engine for Procter & Gamble. But the turnaround did not happen by chance; one key to success was *getting new products right*—the development of an integrated *business and product innovation strategy*, coupled with an effective *idea-to-launch process (SIMPL)* and first-rate *portfolio management* to ensure a steady stream of the right new and improved products.

The *Innovation Diamond* and the *Four Points of Performance*

Compare and contrast the four case studies—the stories of ExxonMobil Chemical, Mega Bloks, Procter & Gamble, and EXFO Engineering. These companies are in very different businesses, and they range in size from medium-sized to corporate giants. But each has discovered the secrets to winning the innovation war. And there are common themes among the four cases. Indeed, these and other "secrets to new product success" are not only practiced by a number of better-performing businesses, but they're within the grasp of most business leaders.

These four companies' pathways to achieving dramatic new product results are not unique. Indeed, the *best performers* in our APQC benchmarking study report similar experiences. A number of best-performing businesses were identified in this study—see Box 2.1—and their practices were compared to those of average and poorer performers. Whenever we spotted the best-performing businesses doing something unique, we zeroed in on this practice: It's a potential *best practice.*

Box 2.1   Identifying the Best Performers

Which businesses are the best performers? And which are the worst? These are important questions, and lie at the basis of a valid benchmarking study. By comparing the practices used in best versus worst performers, one can zero in on best practices.

In the APQC study, in order to identify best and worst performers, we grouped the many metrics in Exhibits 2.1 to 2.6 into four main clusters or dimensions. Two of these dimensions proved particularly robust:

1. Overall NPD success and profitability—the overall profitability of the NPD effort, whether it meets its business objectives, success versus competitors, and whether it is time efficient.
2. Opening windows of opportunity—whether the NPD effort opens up new markets, technologies, and product categories to the business.

Best-performing businesses were selected on the basis of how well they did on both performance metrics or dimensions (about 20% of businesses studied were singled out as "best performers").

The best or top performers we identified do remarkably well in terms of the many performance metrics measured (Exhibit 2.7). Their results are overwhelming: clearly a powerful set of best or top performers has been identified. (There are 19 performance metrics in total in Exhibit 2.7; here we see that on all 19 metrics, the best performers score strongly higher than the worst.)

These best performers thus become our "benchmark businesses" on which we then lower the microscope in order to identify best practices.

Here, then, is a quick preview of the four areas of best practice that stand out as common denominators across the top-performing businesses

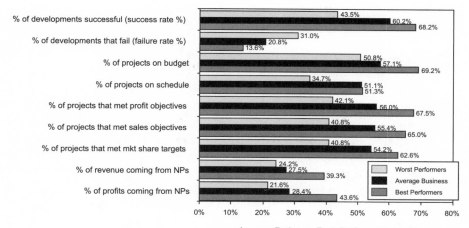

Worst Performers have a 43.5% success rate. Best Performers have a 68.2% success rate. The average business has a 60.2% rate on projects that entered the Development phase.

Exhibit 2.7   Performance Metrics—The Best Versus Worst Performers

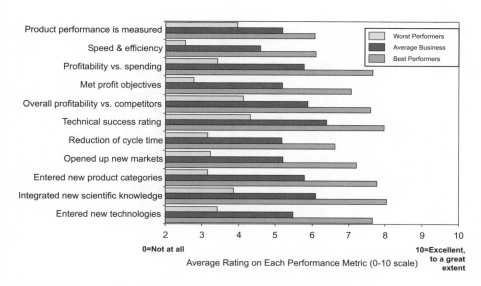

Exhibit 2.7 continued   More Performance Metrics—Best Versus Worst

(see Exhibit 2.8). I call these the *four points of performance* that comprise the *Innovation Diamond*:

1. *Product innovation and technology strategy*: Top performers put a product innovation and technology strategy in place, driven by the leadership team and the strategic vision of the business. This product innovation strategy guides the business's NPD direction and helps to steer resource allocation and project selection. Developing an innovation strategy is one key to success in Procter & Gamble's cosmetics business, and also at ExxonMobil Chemical.

2. *Resource investment and focusing on the right projects—portfolio management:* Top performers commit sufficient resources to undertake their new product projects effectively. They also boast an effective portfolio management system that helps the leadership team effectively allocate these resources to the right areas and to the right projects. A first-rate portfolio management system is EXFO Engineering's number one best practice, and is also a common denominator of success at Procter & Gamble, Mega Bloks, and ExxonMobil.

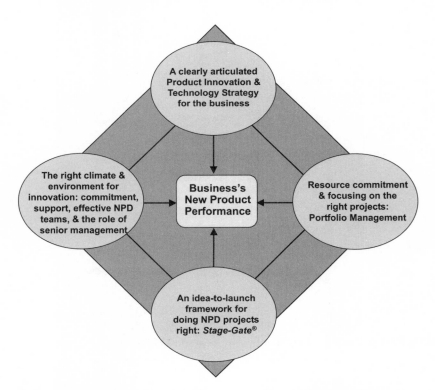

Exhibit 2.8 The *Innovation Diamond* and the *Four Points of Performance*

Notes for Senior Management

Take a close look at the *Innovation Diamond* in Exhibit 2.8. Each of the *four points of performance* of the diamond is a major driver of positive new product performance. Questions to ponder:

1. Does your business have a clearly articulated and communicated product innovation and technology strategy, complete with business goals spelled out for product innovation and clearly defined areas of focus? Do you have attack plans and a strategic roadmap in place?
2. Do you have an effective portfolio management system in place in your business that allocates and commits resources to development projects effectively, and yields a portfolio of high value-to-the-company projects? And have you committed sufficient resources to NPD to ensure that you'll achieve your goals?
3. Do you have a best-in-class idea-to-launch new product framework or process, such as *Stage-Gate®*? Is it really practiced, or is it just a "paper process"? And does it build in best practices such as tough gates (Go/Kill decision-points), voice-of-the-customer research, and solid upfront homework?
4. Do you have the right climate and environment for product innovation in your business—a climate that supports innovation, fosters effective cross-functional teams, and has senior management's committment to NPD?

If you are missing or deficient on any one of these four points or drivers, then chances are you're under-performing in the product innovation war. Why? Simple: The best performers typically have all four of the themes or practices—the *four points of performance* of the *Innovation Diamond* in Exhibit 2.8—in place in their businesses!

If you're not happy with your performance results, a good place to start is to find out the underlying causes. Begin by benchmarking your business—both your performance as well as your practices—versus the top performers. Use some of the metrics outlined in this chapter. And rate yourself on the four questions or points above. (Benchmarking tools exist to help you do this: see note 6.)

3. *An idea-to-launch framework for doing NPD projects right:* A best-in-class new product process or *Stage-Gate®* game plan exists in top-performing businesses—a framework that drives new product projects from the idea phase through to launch and beyond. This idea-to-launch framework emphasizes quality of execution, upfront homework, voice-of-the-customer input, and tough Go/Kill decision-points. This is a vital success driver in all four company case studies, and indeed for virtually all of the best performers in the APQC study.

4. *The right climate and environment for innovation:* Senior managers in top-performing businesses create a positive climate and culture for innovation and entrepreneurship, foster effective cross-functional NPD teams, and are themselves properly engaged in the NPD decision-making process. Mega Bloks excels here.

These are the principal practices that separate the best performers from the rest, as identified in our APQC study.[5] These four areas make up the *four points of performance* of the *Innovation Diamond* in Exhibit 2.8, and provide the framework for the rest of this book.[6] And they are the keys to winning the product innovation war.

Notes

1. This chapter is based in part on a major APQC benchmarking study undertaken by the author and co-workers Dr. Scott Edgett and Dr. Elko Kleinschmidt. The ExxonMobil case study, along with four other case studies from benchmark firms, is also reported in this benchmarking report. See note 29 in Chapter 1. Available as: *Best Practices in Product Development: What Distinguishes Top Performers* at www.prod-dev.com.

2. APQC benchmarking study: see note 1.

3. ExxonMobil Chemical case study: see note 1.

4. EXFO Engineering case study: see note 1.

5. APQC benchmarking study: see note 1.

6. You can benchmark your own business versus the best and the rest—your performance results as well as your practices. The benchmarking tool is called *SG-Benchmarker*™, and is available from the Product Development Institute at www.prod-dev.com.

3

A Product Innovation Strategy for Your Business: What Markets, Products, and Technologies?

I find the great thing in this world is not so much where we stand, as in which direction we are moving: To reach the port of heaven, we must sail sometimes with the wind and sometimes against it but we must sail, and not drift, and not lie at anchor.
—Oliver Wendell Holmes, *The Autocrat of the Breakfast Table*, 1858

Win the Battle, Lose the War?

What if . . .

- ▸ you had implemented a world-class idea-to-launch framework to guide projects to market, much like ExxonMobil Chemical did?
- ▸ you had a superb portfolio management system to help select projects, as EXFO Engineering has?
- ▸ you had created a very positive climate and culture for innovation within your business, as Mega Bloks has?

Would the result be a high-performing business? Not necessarily. One of the most important drivers of success in new product warfare is missing: one of the *four points of performance* of the *Innovation Diamond* from Chapter 2 (see Exhibit 3.1). And that driver makes the difference between winning individual battles and winning the entire product innovation war.[1]

The missing success driver is your *business's product innovation and technology strategy* (Exhibit 3.1). And it's lacking in too many businesses. The product innovation course charts the strategy for the business's entire new product effort. It is the master plan: It provides the direction for your

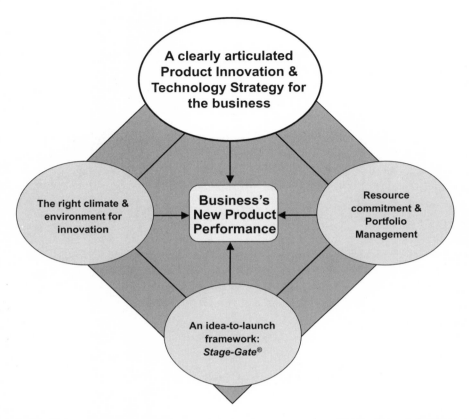

Exhibit 3.1 A Clearly Articulated Product Innovation Strategy Is One of the *Four Points of Performance* of the *Innovation Diamond*

enterprise's new product developments, and it is the essential link between your product development effort and your total business strategy.[2]

This chapter begins with a look at the hard evidence in support of strategy—facts that make it imperative that you and your leadership team develop a product innovation strategy for your business. The components of an innovation strategy are then defined, followed by a glimpse into some of the broad strategic options that your business might elect in product innovation. Next, approaches to developing a product innovation strategy are outlined—approaches where you define and elect arenas of strategic thrust for your new product efforts and possible attack strategies. So let's move forward and play the role of the general, looking at strategy and direction for the business's entire new product effort. Let's go win the innovation war!

What Is a Product Innovation Strategy?

A product innovation strategy is a strategic master plan that guides your business's new product war efforts. But how does one define or describe a product innovation strategy? The term "strategy" is widely used in business circles today. The word is derived from an ancient Greek word meaning "the art of the general." Until comparatively recently, its use was confined to the military. In a business context, *strategy* has been defined as "the schemes whereby a firm's resources and advantages are managed (deployed) in order to surprise and surpass competitors or to exploit opportunities."[3] More specifically, *strategic change* is defined as "a realignment of firm's product-market environment."[4] Strategy is closely tied to product and market specification: Corey argues that strategy is about choosing your *markets to target*, and choosing the *products to target them with*.[5]

Business strategy here refers to the *business's* overall strategy; *product innovation strategy* is a component of that business strategy.[6] And by *business and product innovation strategy*, I do not mean a vaguely worded statement of intent, one that approaches a vision or mission statement. Rather, I mean operational, action-specific strategies that include defined goals, arenas of strategic focus, deployment decisions, and attack and entry plans.

Why Have a Product Innovation Strategy at All?

Developing a product innovation strategy is hard work. It involves many people, especially top management. Why, then, go to all the effort? Most of us can probably name countless companies that do not appear to have a master plan for their new product effort. How do they get by?

Doing Business Without a Strategy

Running an innovation program without a strategy is like running a war without a military strategy. There's no rudder, there's no direction, and the results are often highly unsatisfactory. You simply drift. On occasion, such unplanned efforts do succeed, largely owing to good luck or perhaps brilliant tactics.

A new product effort without a strategy will inevitably lead to a number of ad hoc decisions made independently of one another. New product and R&D projects are initiated solely on their own merits and with little regard to their fit into the grander scheme (portfolio management is all but impossible, for example). The result is that the business finds itself in unrelated or unwanted markets, products, and technologies: There is no focus.

Goals and Role—The Necessary Link to Your Overall Business Strategy

What types of direction does a product innovation strategy give a business's new product efforts? First, the goals of your product innovation strategy tie your product development effort tightly to your overall business strategy. New product development, so often viewed in a "hands-off" fashion by senior management, becomes a central part of the business strategy, a key plank in the business's overall strategic platform.

The question of spending commitments on new products is dealt with by defining the role and goals of the new product effort. Too often the R&D or new product budget is easy prey in hard economic times. Development and new product marketing spending tend to be viewed as discretionary expenditures, something that can be slashed if need be. If you establish product innovation as a central facet of your business's overall strategy, and firmly define the role and goals of product innovation, cutting this R&D budget becomes much less arbitrary: There is a continuity of resource commitment to new products.

The Strategic Arenas—Guiding the War Effort

A second facet of the product innovation strategy, the definition of arenas, is critical to guiding and focusing your new product efforts. The first step in your idea-to-launch new product process is *idea generation.* But where does one search for new product ideas? Unless the arenas are defined, the idea search is undirected, unfocused, and ineffective.

Your business's product innovation strategy is also fundamental to project selection and portfolio management. That's why I show strategy as the top box in the portfolio management system of Exhibit 4.5: Strategy drives the entire project selection process. Without a definition of your playing fields—the arenas of strategic thrust—you will have little luck in trying to make effective screening decisions!

The definition of arenas also guides long-term resource and personnel planning. If certain markets are designated top-priority arenas, then the business can acquire resources, people, skills, and knowledge to enable it to attack those markets. Similarly, if certain technologies are singled out as arenas, the business can hire and acquire resources and technologies to bolster its abilities in those fields, or perhaps even seek alliances with other firms. Resource building doesn't happen overnight. One can't buy a sales force on a moment's notice, and one can't acquire a critical mass of key researchers or engineers in a certain technology at the local supermarket.

Putting the right people, resources, and skills in place takes both lead time and direction.

The Evidence in Support of Strategy

The argument in favor of a product innovation strategy, although logical, may be somewhat theoretical. One can't help but think of all those companies that have made it without a grand strategy. Further, the notion of deciding what's in versus out of bounds is foreign to many businesses: After completing his large sample study on innovation charters, Crawford notes that "the idea of putting definitive restrictions on new product activity is not novel, but the use of it, especially sophisticated use, is still not widespread."[7]

So where's the evidence in support of having a product innovation strategy? The studies that have looked at businesses' new product strategies have a clear and consistent message: A product innovation strategy at the business unit or company level is critical to success, and some strategies clearly work better than others. Consider these facts:

▶ Ten best practices were identified by management in a study of 79 leading R&D organizations.[8] Near the top of the list is "use a formal development process," an endorsement of the use of stage-and-gate processes. Even higher on the list is "coordinate long-range business planning and R&D plans"—a call for a new product or R&D plan for the business that meshes with the business plan. Although adoption of these best practices varies widely by company, the study revealed that high performers tend to embrace these best practices more than do low performers.

▶ Booz-Allen & Hamilton's study of new product practices found that businesses that are most likely to succeed in the development and launch of new products are those that implement a company-specific approach, driven by business objectives and strategies, with a *well-defined product innovation strategy* at its core. The product innovation strategy was viewed as instrumental to the effective identification of market and product opportunities.[9] The authors of this study explain why having a product innovation strategy is tied to success:

A product innovation strategy links the new product process to company objectives, and provides focus for idea or concept generation and for establishing appropriate screening criteria. The outcome of this strategy analysis is a set of strategic roles, used not to generate specific new product ideas, but to help identify markets for which new products will be developed. These market opportunities provide the set of product and market requirements from which new product ideas are generated. In addition, strategic roles provide guidelines for new product performance measurement criteria. Performance thresholds tied to strategic roles provide a more precise means of screening new product ideas.

▶ Our APQC benchmarking study also reveals that having an articulated product innovation strategy for the business is one of the four important drivers of new product performance (see Exhibit 3.1). Businesses with a defined product innovation strategy—one that specifies goals and the role of new products, defines arenas of strategic thrust and their priorities, outlines a product roadmap, and has a longer-term orientation—achieve better new product results: These businesses meet their new product sales and profit objectives more often; their new product effort has a much greater positive impact on the business; and they achieve higher success rates at launch.

▶ Nystrom and Edvardsson studied how various new product strategies are tied to performance in a number of industrial product firms.[10] Strategies emphasizing the synergistic use of technology, a responsive R&D organization, and an externally oriented R&D effort are generally more successful. While the study was limited to a handful of strategy dimensions, the message is clear that strategy and performance are closely linked.

▶ The *performance impact of product innovation strategies* in 120 businesses was investigated in one of my own earlier studies.[11] This study is one of the first investigations undertaken on a large number of businesses that considers many strategy dimensions, and how the strategy of the business's entire new product effort is tied to performance results. The overriding conclusion is that product innovation strategy and performance are strongly linked. The types of markets, products, and technologies that firms choose, and the orientation and direction of their product innovation efforts, have a pronounced impact on success and profitability. Strategy really does count. Here are some strategy-types uncovered in this study:

  • The strategy yielding the best performance results is the *differentiated strategy*—a technologically sophisticated and aggressive effort, very focused, and with a strong market orientation. In this strategy, the business targets attractive high-growth, high-potential markets with premium-priced, strongly differentiated, superior and high-quality products. This strategy leads to the highest percentage of sales by new products (47% versus 35% for the other businesses); the highest success rates at launch; a higher profitability level; and greater new product impact on the business's sales and profits.

- The next best strategy is the *low-budget conservative strategy*—low relative R&D spending with copy-cat, me too, undifferentiated new products.

  Thus strategy entails a highly focused and a "stay-close-to-home" approach, with new products matching the business's production and technological skills and resources, fitting into the business's existing product lines, and aimed at familiar and existing markets. Such a strategy achieves respectable results: The business's new product effort is profitable relative to spending, but yields a low proportion of sales by new products and has a low impact on the business's sales and profits. This conservative strategy results in an efficient, safe, and profitable new product effort, but one lacking a dramatic impact on the business.

A number of companies do develop innovation strategies. For example, *product innovation charters* were described by Crawford in his study of 125 firms.[12] He notes that managements are now beginning to pull *all the multifunctional elements together* in one document, which specifies the types of markets, products, technologies, and orientation the company will pursue with its product innovation strategy.

The Elements of a Product Innovation Strategy and Their Impacts

Do you have a clearly articulated product innovation strategy for your business?[13] If so, you're in the minority. But businesses that boast such a strategy do better, according to our APQC benchmarking study.[14] Six ingredients of a solid product innovation strategy strongly distinguish the top-performing businesses in NPD (see Exhibit 3.2).[15]

These strategy elements also provide insights into how to go about developing a product innovation strategy for your business: They are the basis for the ideal logical flow or "thought process" to guide your leadership team in developing an insightful product innovation strategy (see Exhibit 3.3 for the pathway or flow). So let's look at each of these elements, what they are and why they are so critical:

1. Goals and role: Begin with your goals! The business's product innovation strategy specifies the goals of the new product effort, and it indicates the role that product innovation will play in helping the business achieve its business objectives. It answers the question: How do new products and product innovation fit into your business's overall plan? A statement such as "By the year 2007, 30% of our business's sales will come from new products" is a typical goal. Performance goals can also be stated, such

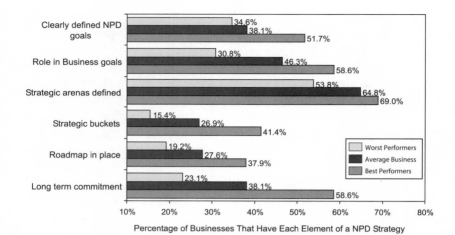

Percentage of Businesses That Have Each Element of a NPD Strategy

38.1% of businesses have clearly defined NPD goals for their business (meaning that 62% do not!). This practice is more prevalent among the best performers—51.7% of top performers and only 34.6% of the worst define their NPD goals.

Exhibit 3.2 Innovation Strategy and Its Elements—Impact on Performance

as the desired number of major new product introductions, expected success rates, and desired financial returns from new products.

This ingredient of strategy—having clear goals—would seem to be fairly basic. What is surprising is how many businesses lack clear, written goals for their overall new product effort. Note the mediocre scores in Exhibit 3.2: Only 38.1% of businesses proficiently define such NPD goals. By contrast, 51.7% of best performers do spell out their NPD goals; and the worst performers are quite weak here, with only 34.6% defining goals. Having clearly articulated NPD goals for your business is thus a mandatory best practice.

Another key best practice is to ensure that the role of new products in achieving the business's goals is clear and communicated to all (also highlighted in Exhibit 3.2). The whole point of having goals is so that everyone involved in the activity has a common purpose—something to work toward. Yet, far too often, personnel who work on new product projects are not aware of their business's new product objectives, or the role that new products play in the total business objectives. What we witness here are very mediocre practices: Only 46.3% of businesses define and communicate the role of NPD in achieving their business goals. However, 58.6% of best performers do define this role (versus only 30.8% of the worst performers), and this element of an innovation strategy is the most strongly correlated with NPD performance. It's clearly a best practice.

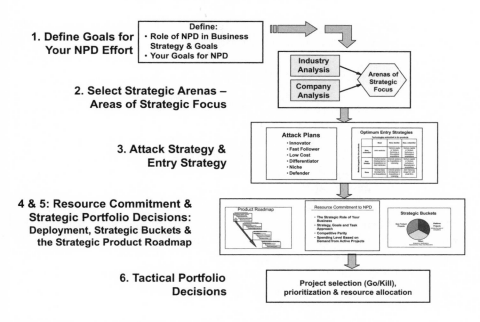

1. Define Goals for Your NPD Effort

Define:
• Role of NPD in Business Strategy & Goals
• Your Goals for NPD

2. Select Strategic Arenas – Areas of Strategic Focus

Industry Analysis

Company Analysis

Arenas of Strategic Focus

3. Attack Strategy & Entry Strategy

Attack Plans
• Innovator
• Fast Follower
• Low Cost
• Differentiator
• Niche
• Defender

Optimum Entry Strategies

4 & 5: Resource Commitment & Strategic Portfolio Decisions: Deployment, Strategic Buckets & the Strategic Product Roadmap

Product Roadmap

Resource Commitment to NPD
• The Strategic Role of Your Business
• Strategy, Goals and Task Approach
• Competitive Parity
• Spending Level Based on Demand from Active Projects

Strategic Buckets

6. Tactical Portfolio Decisions

Project selection (Go/Kill), prioritization & resource allocation

Exhibit 3.3   The Major Steps in Defining Your Product Innovation Strategy

2. Arenas and strategic thrust: Focus is the key to an effective NPD strategy. Your product innovation strategy specifies where you'll attack, or, perhaps more important, where you won't attack. Thus the concept of *strategic arenas*—the markets, industry sectors, applications, product types, or technologies on which your business will focus its new product efforts—is at the heart of a new product strategy. The *battlefields* must be defined!

Here, businesses on average do a solid job, with 64.8% identifying and designating strategic arenas in order to help focus their NPD efforts (Exhibit 3.2). Best performers define strategic arenas more so than do worst performers—69.0% versus 53.8%—and this strategy element is again strongly correlated with NPD performance.

The specification of these arenas—what's "in bounds" and what's "out of bounds"—is fundamental to spelling out the direction or *strategic thrust* of the business's product development effort. It is the result of identifying and assessing product innovation opportunities at the strategic level. Without arenas defined, the search for specific new product ideas or opportunities is unfocused. Over time, the portfolio of new product projects is likely to contain a lot of unrelated projects, in many different markets, technologies, or product types—a scattergun effort. And the results are predicable: a not-so-profitable new product effort:

> *An example:* One DuPont polymers business faced exactly this problem: much money spent on R&D, but no focus because there was no strategy or defined arenas. Senior management recognized the deficiency. Management first identified a number of possible arenas (product-market-technology areas) that might be "in bounds"; assessed each in terms of their market attractiveness and the opportunity for leveraging the business's core competencies; selected several arenas; and then began to focus their new product initiatives within these chosen arenas.

3. Attack strategy and entry strategy: The issue of *how to attack* each strategic arena should also be part of your business's product innovation strategy. For example, the strategy may be to be the industry innovator, the first to the market with new products; or the attack strategy may be to be a "fast follower," rapidly copying and improving upon competitive entries. Other strategies might focus on being low cost versus a differentiator versus a niche player; or on emphasizing certain strengths, core competencies, or product attributes or advantages. Additionally, entry plans should be outlined and can include internal product development, licensing, joint venturing, and even acquisitions of other firms.

4. Deployment—spending commitments, priorities, and strategic buckets: *Strategy becomes real when you start spending money!* Your product innovation strategy must deal with how much to spend on product innovation, and it should indicate the relative emphasis, or strategic priorities, accorded each arena of strategic focus. Thus an important facet of a product innovation strategy is *resource commitment* and *allocation*. And earmarking buckets of resources (funds or person-days targeted at different strategic arenas or project types) helps to ensure the strategic alignment of NPD with your business goals.[16]

Many best-in-class companies use the concept of *strategic buckets* to help in this deployment decision. But the use of strategic buckets is a decidedly weak area overall, with only 26.9% of businesses doing this well. Strategic buckets is clearly a best practice, with 41.4% of best performers employing this strategic buckets approach (and only 15.4% of worst performers). More on how to develop strategic buckets in Chapter 4.

5. The strategic product roadmap—the major initiatives and platform developments: A strategic roadmap is an effective way to map out a series of major initiatives in an attack plan. A roadmap is simply a management group's view of how to get where they want to go or to achieve their desired objective.[17]

The product innovation strategy should map out the planned assaults—*major new product initiatives* and their timing—that are required in order to succeed in a certain market or sector in the form of a *strategic product roadmap*.* This roadmap may also specify the platform developments required for these new products. Additionally, the development or acquisition of new technologies may be mapped out in the form of a technology roadmap.

The use of roadmaps is a weak area generally, with only 27.6% of businesses developing product roadmaps proficiently. About twice as many best performers (37.9%) use product roadmaps than do worst performers (19.2%). Roadmaps are also a topic of Chapter 4.

Once these five strategy steps are completed, management can then deal with the next level of decision making: translating strategy into reality, namely, the *tactical decisions*:[18]

6. Tactical decisions—individual project selection: Tactical decisions focus on individual projects, but obviously follow from the strategic decisions. They address the questions: What specific new product projects should you do? And what resources should be allocated to each—what are their relative priorities? Even when a strategic product roadmap has been sketched out strategically (above), it tends to be conceptual and directional; one still must look at each and every project and decide whether it is really a Go. And while resource spending splits (buckets), decided above, are useful directional guides, Go decisions on specific projects must still be made.

When selecting projects, an important best practice is to make sure that your new product effort has a long-term thrust and focus—that your portfolio includes some longer-term projects (as opposed to just short-term, incremental projects). This is a fairly weak ingredient of the six elements in Exhibit 3.2, with only 38.1% of businesses having a longer-term new product strategy. Indeed, this short time horizon of businesses' new product efforts has been a widely voiced criticism. Ironically, this one ingredient is *the one of the most important* of the six strategy elements: A longer-term orientation separates top performers from the worst, with 58.6% of the best (and only 23.1% of the worst) adopting a longer-term approach.

Strategy items 1, 2, and 3 above—defining goals, selecting strategic arenas, and developing attack strategies—are the topics of the rest of this chapter. Strategy items 4 and 5—resource commitment and deployment,

---

*The term "product roadmap" has come to have many meanings in business. Here I mean a *strategic* roadmap, which lays out the major initiatives and platforms envisioned into the future—as opposed to a tactical roadmap, which lists each and every product, extension, modification, tweak, and the like.

and the product roadmap—are strategic portfolio management topics covered in the following chapter. Finally item 6, picking the right development projects, is about tactical portfolio decisions, the topic of Chapter 5.

Notes for Senior Management

Doing business without a strategy is like sailing a ship without a rudder. Our APQC benchmarking study's results strongly support this adage. So do other investigations. Clearly, those businesses that lack goals for their total new product effort, where arenas of strategic focus have not been defined, and where the strategy is little more than a short-term list of projects (no strategic product roadmap) are at a decided disadvantage.

Do what the top performers do. *Set goals* for your business's product innovation effort (e.g., percentage of sales from new products). Tie your goals for product innovation firmly to your business's goals. And make these goals clear to everyone involved in your organization.

Emulate the best performers by *specifying strategic arenas*: areas of strategic focus defined in terms of markets, technologies and product types or categories. And map out *your attack strategies:* how you plan to enter and win in each arena.

Then consider going several steps further. Move toward *strategic buckets* and decide priorities and spending splits across these arenas, and spending splits across other strategic dimensions: your deployment decisions. And develop *strategic product roadmaps*, laying out your major development initiatives over the next few years.

In the rest of this chapter, we'll see how to develop some of these strategic ingredients, and how to craft them into a winning product innovation strategy for your business. . . so read on!

Setting Goals for Your New Product Effort

A few years ago, I boarded an early morning flight on a major airline. The captain began his announcement: "Welcome aboard flight 123 en route to . . . ah . . . ah . . ." There was a long pause. The pause was punctuated by laughter and wisecracks from the passengers; the captain didn't know where the flight was going! Fortunately, within 30 seconds, he remembered our destination. If he hadn't, the plane probably would have emptied. Who would stay on a plane if the captain didn't know his destination? Many of us, however, seem content to stay onboard a new product effort that has no destination.

Defining goals for your product innovation strategy is essential. Most of us accept that premise. But my earlier strategy study and our APQC benchmarking investigation both reveal that many organizations lack written and measurable goals for their innovation effort.

What types of goals should be included in an innovation strategy? First, the goals should be measurable so that they can be used as benchmarks against which to measure performance. Second, they should tie the business's new product initiatives tightly to its business strategy. Finally, they must give you, your leadership team, and project teams a sense of direction and purpose and be criteria for project selection and investment decision making.

Goals That Describe the Role of New Products

One type of new product goals focuses on the role that the new product effort will play in achieving the business goals. Some examples:

- The percentage of your business's sales in Year 3 that will be derived from new products introduced in that three-year period. (Three years is a generally accepted time span in which to define a product as "new," although given today's pace, two years may be more appropriate for many businesses.) Alternately, one can speak of absolute sales—dollars in Year 3 from new products—rather than percentages.
- The percentage of your business's profits in Year 3 that will be derived from new products introduced in that time span. Again, absolute dollars can be used instead of percentages.
- Sales and profits objectives expressed as a percentage of business growth. For example: 70% of growth in your business's sales over the next three years will come from new products introduced in this period.
- The strategic role, such as defending market share, exploiting a new technology, establishing a foothold in a new market, opening up a new technological or market window of opportunity, capitalizing on a strength or resource, or diversifying into higher-growth areas.
- The number of new products to be introduced. (There are problems with this type of objective, however: products could be large-volume or small-volume ones, and the number of products does not directly translate into sales and profits.)

An example: One general manager of an ITT business has a very succinct NPD goal: "five in five," which translates into "five major new product introductions in each of the next five years." And this simply stated goal has become the battle cry of everyone within his business, and has provided a very clear and measurable purpose for the organization.

The specification of these goals gives a strong indication of just how important new products are to the total business strategy. The question of resource allocation and spending on new product efforts can then be more objectively decided.

Performance Goals

A second type of goals deals with the expected performance of the new product effort. Such goals are useful guides to managers within the new product group. Examples include:

- success, failure, and kill rates of new products developed
- number of new product ideas to be considered annually
- number of projects entering development (or in development) annually
- minimum acceptable financial returns for new product projects

Many of these performance goals flow logically from the role goals. For example, if the business wants 70% of sales growth to come from new products, how does that figure translate into number of successful products; number of development projects; success, failure, and kill rates; and number of ideas to be considered annually?

How to Set Goals

Setting these goals is no easy task. The first time through, the exercise is often a frustrating experience. Yet these goals are fundamental to developing an innovation strategy, not to mention a logically determined R&D spending figure.

New product goal setting usually begins with a strategic planning exercise for the entire business. The business's growth and profit goals are decided, along with the business's overall strategy. These business goals and thrusts then are translated into new product goals, often via *gap analysis*.

In gap analysis, one creates two plots:

- what you desire your business's sales (or profits) to be over the next three to five years, based on your overall business goals

▶ what the expected sales (or profits) will likely be, assuming the current product lines and status quo strategy. This amounts to making forecasts of current products and lines, and their life cycle curves

Usually there is a gap between the two projections. And this gap must be filled—by new products, new markets, new businesses, market development, or market share increases. In such a way, the goals are decided for each of these efforts, including product development.

> *An example:* Senior management at Guinness (Ireland) developed a strategic plan for their brewing business. Ambitious growth and profit goals were decided. A review of current products and markets revealed that a gap would exist between projected sales and the goals. That is, current products and markets were projected into the future, and expected revenues and profits were compared to the desired level of sales and profits (the business goals). The gap must be filled by new markets, new products, or new businesses. From this, a set of new product goals is determined.

> *Another example:* Lucent Technologies goes through a process similar to Guinness's, mapping out sales projections from current products and product categories (see Exhibit 3.4). From this exercise, Lucent's management is able to spot shortfalls, which leads to the need for new products to fill the gaps, and hence their goals for new products for the business.[19]

Goals by type of business: Here are the types of goals most often used by various types of businesses for their new product efforts, and which might prove a useful guide in setting your new product goals.[20]
Innovator businesses most often use:

- percentage of profits from new products
- percentage of sales from new products
- ability to open up new windows of opportunity

Fast-follower enterprises look to:

- ROI from development efforts
- whether the innovation effort fits or supports the business's overall strategy
- percentage of profits from new products
- success/failure rates

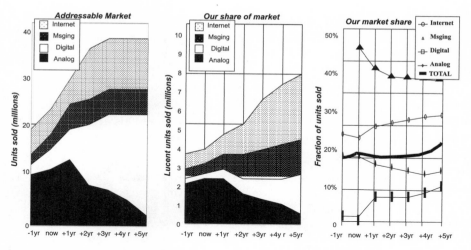

Exhibit 3.4 Setting NPD Goals for Your Business—Sample Market Share and Growth Charts

Source: R. Albright, Lucent Technologies. See note 17.

Defender organizations have goals such as:

- ROI from development efforts
- fit with or support of the business's strategy

Reactor businesses rely on:

- ROI from development efforts
- success/failure rates
- fit with or support of the business's strategy

Defining Target Arenas for Your Business

The specification of strategic arenas or battlefields provides an important guide to your product innovation efforts. As Day notes, "what is needed is a strategy statement that specifies those areas where development is to proceed and identifies (perhaps by exclusion) those areas that are off limits."[21] The arenas provide direction for resource commitment and deployment. They guide the search for new product ideas and help in idea screening and project selection. Finally, delineation of where the business wishes to focus its new product efforts is critical to long-term planning, particularly for resource and skills acquisition.

Defining the target arenas answers the question: On what business, product, market, or technology areas should your business focus its new product efforts? Conceptually, the task is one of *opportunity identification* followed by *opportunity assessment.*

Two issues immediately arise. First, one may question the need for focus at all. Note, however, that new product focus has been found to be an important ingredient of successful innovation strategies.[22] Focus provides direction for idea generation, criteria for project selection, and targets for resource acquisition. A second criticism is that focus will inhibit creativity: Some of the best ideas, which may lie outside the target arenas, might be rejected. The counter-argument is that focus improves creativity by targeting energies on those areas where the payoff is likely to be the greatest.[23] Further, significant new product breakthroughs outside the bounds of the new product strategy statement can usually be readily accommodated in an ongoing project screening process, or via free-time or scouting projects. Finally, inevitably there will be products that "got away" in any new product effort, just as there will be the proverbial "fish that got away." But there will continue to exist ample opportunities within the defined arenas for the business to exploit, provided senior management has done a credible job at arena delineation.

There are three steps to defining the target arenas. The first is assessing your marketplace as well as your own company (strategic analysis). The second is developing a comprehensive list of possible arenas (opportunity identification). The third is paring the list down (assessment of the opportunities to yield a choice of the target arenas).

Strategic Analysis

The purpose here is to identify possible "hot" or interesting arenas—markets, technologies, or product areas—which might become candidate arenas on which to focus your NPD efforts. Key actions include:

Assess your industry and market: Analysis begins with an assessment of your marketplace and your customers' industry. Some approaches:

- Map your value chain, identifying the key players, including rivals. Assess their futures and possible changing roles. Who is gaining and who might be disintermediated (cut out)? And why?
- Look at your industry structure—your direct and indirect competitors. Who is winning and who is losing? And why? Are there opportunities here for you?

▶ Identify your customers' industry drivers and any shifts in these drivers. Assess what factors make your customers profitable and successful. Look at how these factors and drivers are changing in a way that might open up opportunities for you. Are there opportunities for you to provide new solutions here to help your customers?

▶ Assess where the profits are to be found in your industry and in your value chain (and why your business may be missing its fair share of profits). For example, develop profit pool maps and market maps that illustrate who makes the money in your industry, market, or value chain. (Exhibit 3.5 provides an illustration of a market map from the financial services sector.[24])

An example: A major manufacturer of high-end synthetic kitchen countertops undertook an analysis of its downstream value chain. Numerous players are involved in the installation of countertops: the manufacturer, the fabrication shop, the kitchen designer, the retailer, and the installer. To its surprise, the manufacturer discovered that the bulk of the profits was going to other members of the value chain. For

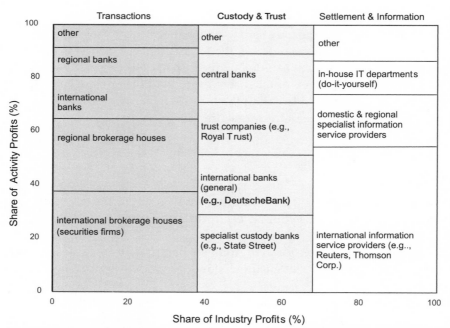

Example is Financial Institutions: the Custody, Trust and Settlements business (i.e. stocks & bonds trades) The chart reveals the distribution of an industry's profits along 2 dimensions—activities and type of player

Exhibit 3.5 Use Market Maps to Identify Attractive Sectors in an Industry

Source: From a major North American bank (disguised); method based on a chart in note 4.

example, the fabricator not only cuts the countertop to size, but often adds edging in the form of multiple layers, which is then machined to a contoured edge—a highly desired feature for high-end installations, but also very pricey. Strategically the manufacturer made a commitment to get control of the distribution channel, obtain its fair share of the profit pool, and also introduce new molded products to move some of the fabricator value-add to the manufacturer.

▶ Undertake a market and industry trend analysis. Analyze historical trends and estimate future trends; forecast market size and shifts. Look at qualitative trends that are occurring: Spell out a scenario (or alternate scenarios) of where your market and industry are headed. Look for possible disruptions in your industry and in your customer's industry. And look for opportunities (or threats) that can be exploited.

▶ Look for niches or holes in the marketplace: areas that may be under-served or have been missed altogether. Use Porter's Five Forces model to assess the attractiveness of these areas,[25] checking
  - the strength of suppliers
  - the strength and intensity of potential competitors (rivals)
  - the power of the customers
  - the ease with which players can enter and exit the area
  - the threat of substitutes

This strategic analysis should not only identify possible new opportunities—arenas that are emerging and on which your business might focus—but also provide quality data so important to evaluating and selecting the right arenas.

Assess the impact of disruptive technologies: Disruptive technologies present difficult challenges in terms of industry trend analysis.[26] The one thing that is certain in forecasting the size of such markets or impact of the technology: The forecast will be wrong, and often by orders of magnitude.

What is a disruptive technology? Most new technologies result in improved performance, which can come from incremental innovations, or from those that are more radical in character. Most technological advances in industry are sustaining, but "Occasionally disruptive technologies emerge: innovations that result in worse performance, at least in the near term."[27] These innovations may be inferior to the existing technology when measured on traditional performance metrics, but they bring a new performance dimension or a new value proposition to the market. For example, the first digital cameras actually produced a poorer picture (lower resolution) than traditional 35 mm film cameras, and were considered inferior products by most camera users. But for a handful of users—most notably those who wanted the picture in digital format so that they could modify or electronically transmit the photo, such as real estate agents—there was new value in the digital camera.

In your industry and market analysis, be sure to identify potential disruptive technologies and radical or step-change innovations. Assess the probability and timing of each, the potential impact, and whether this represents an opportunity (or a threat) for your business. And most important, ask, "So what?"—what can and should you do about this technology?

Identify your core competencies: The next component of this strategic analysis is an internal assessment, namely, looking at your own business. The old adage "attack from a position of strength" rings true in product development. Many studies repeat the message: Leveraging your strengths and competencies increases success rates and new product profitability.[28] So take a hard look at your business, and undertake a core competencies assessment. This means looking at strengths and weaknesses in all facets of your business, and relative to your competitors:

> ▶ your marketing and sales force strengths
> ▶ your products and their technology
> ▶ your operations or production capabilities, capacities, and technology

Assess yourself on each item, especially relative to your direct and indirect competitors. Use the list of items in Exhibit 3.6 as a guide. Or use a chart like the example in Exhibit 3.7 from Lucent Technologies to plot your position versus that of competitors.[29] Then identify areas where you are better than the rest: your core or distinctive competencies. These are your strengths, so look for arenas that can leverage these to advantage.

Defining the Arenas . . . But What Is a New Product Arena?

How does one define a new product opportunity or arena? Corey proposes building two-dimensional matrices, with the dimensions labeled "products" and "markets," in order to identify new business arenas.[30] He notes that markets, together with the products that can be developed in response to needs in these markets, define the opportunities for exploitation: the arenas.

> *An example:* Telenor, the Norwegian telephone system, uses a product-market matrix to help visualize strategic choices and to define arenas

- Rate your marketing and sales force strengths versus competitors:
  - the loyalty of your key customer groups and customer relationships
  - your brand name or franchise in the marketplace
  - your product – quality, reliability and value reputation
  - your distribution and channels (e.g., access to key customer groups)
  - your sales force (e.g., coverage, skills, reputation)
  - your advertising, communications and public relations
  - your service, support and technical service
  - your market shares, presence in certain markets or segments, and reputation overall.

- Rate your products and their technology versus competitors:
  - areas of product leadership, technologically (e.g., features, functionality, product performance)
  - your technological capabilities
  - your access to new technologies
  - your unique technologies or technological skills
  - your intellectual property and proprietary positions
  - your technology skill base, in-house.

- Your operations or production capabilities, capacities and technology versus competitors
  - your production or operations resources, facilities and capacities
  - your unique skills or abilities here
  - your technological capabilities in production or operations
  - your unique production technologies, intellectual property and protection
  - your access to raw materials
  - your work force – their skills, knowledge and availability.

Exhibit 3.6   Assess Your Business Strengths and Core Competencies

Competitor (Market Share)	Strengths (+) weakness	Core Competency	Strategic Goals	Customer-perceived Value Proposition
Lucent (%)				
Competitor A				
Competitor B				
Competitor C				
Competitor D				

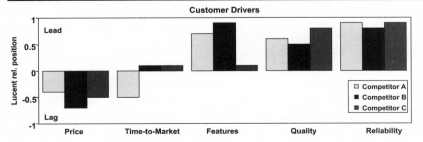

Exhibit 3.7   Sample Chart to Assess Your Competencies Versus Competitors' Competencies

Source: R. Albright, Lucent Technologies. See note 19.

Markets	Voice	Data	Internet	Wireless	Long Distance
Small - Home Office			★	★	★
Medium Business		★		★	
Large Business		★		★	
Multinationals		★		★	★
Residential	★			★	

Products

The axes of the diagram are "Products" and "Markets." Each cell represents a potential strategic arena.

Arenas are assessed for their potential and the company's business position. Stars designate top priority arenas—where new product efforts will be focused.

Exhibit 3.8 The Product-Market Matrix Defines the Strategic Arenas

on which to focus its new product efforts. One dimension of the matrix is *market segments*: Home Office; Small Business; Residential; and so on (Exhibit 3.8). The other dimension is the *product offering* or product categories: voice, data, Internet, wireless, and the like. The roughly 10 by 10 matrix identifies 100 cells or possible arenas; some are ruled out immediately as nonfeasible. The remaining cells are evaluated, and priorities are established. The top priority or "star" arenas are singled out for more intensive product development efforts.

In *Defining the Business,* Abell takes this matrix approach one step further by proposing that a business be defined in terms of *three* dimensions:[31]

1. *Customer groups served.* For a computer manufacturer, customer groups might include banks, manufacturers, universities, hospitals, retailers, and the like.
2. *Customer functions served.* These might include hardware applications, support and services, software, data storage, and the like.
3. *Technologies utilized.* For data storage, several existing and new technologies might have application.

The result is a three-dimensional diagram, with new product arenas defined in this three-dimensional space.

Finally, Crawford's study of innovation charters points to several ways in which managers define new product arenas in practice.[32] Arenas are specified by:

- product type (e.g., high-pressure industrial pumps)
- end-user activity (e.g., plants or factories that process chemicals or liquids)
- type of technology employed (e.g., rotary hydraulic; centrifugal)
- end-user group (e.g., oil refineries)

On its own, each of these arena definition schemes has its problems. For example, a product-type definition is limiting: Product classes or product types die. Similarly, an end-user group definition could lead the business into a number of unrelated technologies, products, and production systems.

A review of these and other schemes for defining a business arena reveals that a single-dimension approach is likely too narrow. A two- or three-dimensional approach, variants of Corey's or Abell's, probably will suit most business contexts.[33] For example, a new product arena can be defined in terms of:

1. *Who:* the customer group to be served (markets or market segments)
2. *What:* the application (customer need to be satisfied)
3. *How:* the technology required to design, develop, and produce products for the arena

These three dimensions—who, what, and how—provide a useful starting point to describe new product arenas. Sometimes, the last two dimensions—what and how—can be simply combined into a single dimension, product type.

Defining Arenas: A Blow-by-Blow Illustration

Let's look more closely at some of the details of this process of searching for and prioritizing arenas. A two- or three-dimensional diagram can be used for this search and evaluation. You might also use the product-market matrix of Exhibit 3.8, or any other convenient dimensions that define arenas for your business. Here I use the three dimensions of customer groups, applications, and technologies, which are shown as the X, Y, and Z axes of the diagram (Exhibit 3.9). Home base is located, and then other opportunities are identified by moving away from home base in terms of other (but related) customer groups, applications, and technologies.

> *An example:* Chempro is a medium-sized manufacturer of blending and agitation process equipment for the pulp and paper industry. The company's major strength is its ability to design and manufacture rotary hydraulic equipment. The market served is the pulp and paper

industry. The application is agitation and blending of liquids and slur-ries. The company's current or home base is shown as the cube in Exhibit 3.9.

What new product arenas exist for the company? Clearly, the home base is one of these, and indeed the firm is active in seeking new prod-uct ideas for agitation equipment in the pulp and paper field. Most of these opportunities, however, are limited to modifications and improvements.

One direction that senior management can take is to develop new products aimed at alternative customer groups. These customer groups include the chemical, food-processing, petroleum-refining, and hydro-metallurgical fields. The options are shown on the X, or hori-zontal, axis of Exhibit 3.9.

Similarly, new products in related applications can be sought. These related applications include the pumping of fluids, fluid aeration, and refining and grinding, as shown on the Y, or vertical, axis of the arena matrix.

Considering these two dimensions—different applications and dif-ferent customer groups—management now proceeds to define a num-ber of new arenas. Working with a two-dimensional grid (Exhibit 3.10), recognize that, besides the home-base arena, there are 12 other arenas that the company can consider for its new product focus. For example, Chempro can develop blending and agitation equipment (same appli-cation) aimed at the chemical or petroleum industries (new customer

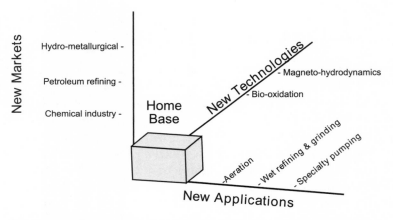

"Home Base" is current markets, current technologies, current applications—the cube.
One can move away from home base in any direction—new markets, new technologies, and new applications for the business.

Exhibit 3.9   A Three-Dimensional Map Defines Possible Arenas

	Pulp & Paper (home base)	Chemical Process Industry	Petroleum Refining	Hydro-Metalurgical
Agit ation & Blending	HOME BASE: Agitators & blender for P&P industry	Chemical mixers & blenders	Blenders for petroleum storage tanks	Hydro-metal-urgical mixers, agitators
Aeration	Surface aerators for P&P: waste treatment	Aerators for chemical waste treatment plants	Aerators for petroleum waste treatment plants	Aerators for floatation cells
Wet Refining & Grinding	Pulper, repulpers & refiners			Wet refining equipment
Specialty Pumping	High density paper stock pumps	Specialty chemical pumps	Specialty petroleum pumps	Slurry pumps

Chart is similar to the product-market matrix, Exhibit 3.8.

Exhibit 3.10   Chempro's Arenas—Applications and Customer Types

groups). Alternatively, the business can develop aeration devices (new application) targeted at its current customers, namely, pulp and paper companies. Each of these possibilities represents a new arena for Chempro.

Chempro might also be able to change its third dimension by moving from its home base of rotary hydraulic technology to other technologies. If the alternatives are superimposed along the third dimension atop the matrix, the result is a much larger number of possible arenas. (This third dimension expansion is not shown in Exhibit 3.10, as it's a little hard on the eyes!) Possible alternative arenas along the "new technologies" axis include magneto-hydrodynamic pumps and agitators for a variety of end-user groups, bio-oxidation reactors for the food industry, and many others.

Selecting the Right Arenas

The task now is to narrow down the many possible arenas to a target set that will become the focus of the business's innovation strategy. To a certain extent, a prescreening of these arenas has already occurred: the arenas have been identified as being related to the base business on at least one of the three dimensions.

The choice of the right arenas is based on a single "must-meet" criterion and two "should-meet" criteria. The must-meet criterion is an obvious one: Does the arena fit within the business's mission, vision, and overall strategy? The other two criteria were identified in my studies of successful new product strategies. These criteria are *arena attractiveness* and *business strength* (Exhibit 3.11).

Arena attractiveness: This strategic dimension captures how attractive the external opportunities are within that arena. Is this strategic arena an oasis—lush and fertile with ample opportunities for profitable new products? Or is it a sterile desert, offering few opportunities for innovation and growth? This dimension, *arena attractiveness*, consists of:

- *market attractiveness:* the size, growth, and potential of market opportunities within the arena
- *technological opportunities:* the degree to which technological and new product opportunities exist within the arena

In practice, *arena attractiveness* is a composite index constructed by rating the arena on a number of detailed criteria that capture market growth, size, and the potential for new products in that arena. Typically, the leadership team of the business scores each arena on these criteria, and scores are added to yield an *index of arena attractiveness*. Arenas that feature large, growing, and high-potential markets that are characterized by

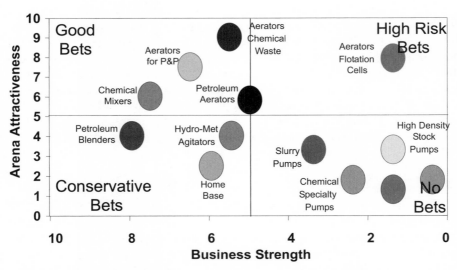

Exhibit 3.11   Strategic Map—Arenas Plotted on Two Dimensions

technological elasticity (large bang for R&D buck spent*), dynamic technologies, and many new product introductions score high on the *arena attractiveness* dimension.

Business strength: The other strategic dimension focuses on the business's ability to exploit the arena successfully. In other words, what does your business bring to the table that suggests that you will be successful in this arena? The ability to leverage your business's resources and skills to advantage in the new arena is a key concept here. Business strength is again a composite dimension or index, consisting of three factors:

- ability to leverage the business's technological (development and operations) competencies
- ability to leverage its marketing and sales competencies
- strategic leverage: the potential to achieve product advantage and product differentiation

Arenas that build on the business's core and distinctive competencies, fit the business's marketing and technological strengths and resources, and offer the business a solid opportunity to gain product advantage or achieve product differentiation are the ones that score high on the business strength dimension.

Mapping the Strategic Arenas

How the various arenas score on the two criteria can be shown pictorially in the arena assessment map of Exhibit 3.11. *Arena attractiveness* is shown as the vertical, or north-south, dimension, and *business strength* as the horizontal, or east-west, axis. The result is a four-sector diagram, not unlike traditional business portfolio models, but with different dimensions and different components to each dimension.

Each sector represents a different type of opportunity:

- ▶ The arenas shown in the northwest sector (upper left), which feature high *arena attractiveness* and *business strength,* are clearly the most desirable. These are called the "good bets."
- ▶ Diagonally opposite, in the southeast (lower right) sector, are the "low-low" arenas—those arenas that neither build on the business's

---

*Technological elasticity captures the slope of the technology S-curve: the curve that plots product performance versus development money spent to achieve this. Technological elasticity answers the question: Will a dollar spent on product development in this arena yield products with significant performance advantage?

strengths nor offer attractive external opportunities. These are the "no bets."

▶ The "high-risk bets" are in the northeast (upper right) sector. They represent high-opportunity arenas where the business has no exploitable strengths.

▶ Finally, the southeast (lower left) sector houses the "conservative bets"—arenas where the business can utilize its strengths to advantage, but where the external opportunity is not so attractive. These opportunities can be pursued at little risk, but offer limited returns.

Using such a map, senior management can eliminate certain arenas outright (those in the "no bet" sector), and select a reasonable balance of arenas from the other three sectors. The "good bets" in the northwest sector are usually the top-priority ones.

> *Assessing the arenas at Chempro:* At Chempro, strategic arena assessment is simplified by recognizing the company's technological and financial resource limitations. Chempro's main asset is its ability to design and engineer rotary hydraulic equipment. Embarking on new and expensive technologies, such as bio-oxidation, is deemed out of bounds. Moreover, having identified its current technology as a field of particular strength, and recognizing that there are many opportunities that can build on this strength, senior management elects to stay with its current technology. Management chooses to *attack from a position of strength*, and so the third dimension, alternative technologies, is deleted. The result is the two-dimensional grid in Exhibit 3.10.
>
> Next, the 12 new arenas plus the home base are rated by senior management on the two key dimensions of *arena attractiveness* and *business strength*. A list of rating questions is employed, with each arena rated on each question. The ratings are added, and both a *business strength* and *arena attractiveness index* are computed for each of the 13 possible arenas. Using these two indexes for each arena, the 13 arenas are plotted as bubbles on an *X-Y* grid. The results for Chempro are shown in Exhibit 3.11.

Selecting the Arenas

The choice of arenas depends on the risk-return values of management. Selecting only those arenas in the top half of the arena assessment diagram—the good bets and the high-risk bets—emphasizes the attractiveness of the external opportunity. This choice places no weight at all on the business-strength dimension: It is a high return, but a higher-risk strategy. The other extreme is selecting only those arenas on the left of the vertical, the good bets and conservative bets. This is a low-risk, low-return strategy:

selection of only those arenas in which the company possesses a good business position. Ideally, one looks for a combination of the two:

▶ arenas in which the market attractiveness and the business strength both are rated high—the good bets in the northwest sector of Exhibit 3.11
▶ some balance of arenas: some attractive but riskier arenas, some lower risk but less attractive ones

For Chempro, six arenas are rated positively on both dimensions. In order to quantify or rank-order the arenas, a cutoff or 45-degree line is drawn on Exhibit 3.11 (not shown). Arenas to the left of and above this line

---

Notes for Senior Management

The place to begin is with the *strategy of your business,* and flowing from it, *your product innovation and technology strategy.* After defining the overall goals for your business, spell out your *new product goals*: for example, what percentage of sales or profit or growth new products will contribute. Use gap analysis as Guinness and Lucent do.

Then move to mapping your battlefields: that is, identify arenas of strategic focus. Undertake a strategic analysis—first on your industry, marketplace, and your customers' industry; next on yourself—then search for strengths and core competencies that you hope to leverage.

Next draw an arena diagram for your business. Use two dimensions (products and markets, as does Telenor) or perhaps three dimensions (customer groups, applications, and technologies, like Chempro). Locate your home base, and then move out on each of the three axes, identifying other customer groups, applications, and technologies. This exercise should help you display a number of new but related possible arenas, as in Exhibit 3.10.

Now that you've identified a list of possible arenas, rate each on the two key dimensions of *arena attractiveness* and *business strength.* Develop a list of rating questions for each dimension, and score each arena on these questions. Draw an arena assessment map (similar to Exhibit 3.11) to see where your arenas lie. And then select and prioritize these arenas, looking for those in the desirable northwest sector (upper left), but perhaps seeking a balance by including some from the sure-bets and the high-risk bets sectors. You now have decided your areas of focus for NPD!

are positive; those to the right and below are negative. The distance of each arena from that line is measured: the greater the distance, the more desirable the arena. Based on this exercise, three good bets and one conservative bet are defined as target arenas for Chempro:

- aerators for the chemical industry (waste water treatment)
- blenders for the petroleum industry
- agitators and mixers for the chemical industry
- surface aerators for the pulp and paper industry

Management decides to continue seeking new products in the home-base arena as well.

Developing the Attack Strategies

The goals have been decided, and the strategic arenas mapped out and prioritized. Now it's time to determine the *new product attack strategy*—that is, how you plan to win on these selected battlefields or arenas. These attack strategies tend to be fairly industry- and company-specific. However, there exist a number of frameworks that help guide this effort.

Strategy Types Based on Innovativeness

One way of looking at strategy is via a typology based upon the way that an organization responds to changing market and external conditions. There are four strategy types, according to Miles and Snow,[34] and you may wish to elect one as the strategy or vision for your own business. Which one are you? And which one should you be?[35]

▶ *Innovators:* These businesses are the *industry innovators* or *prospectors*. They value being first in with new products and are first to adopt new technologies, even though there are risks and not all such efforts are profitable. Innovators respond rapidly to early signals that point to emerging or new opportunities. In the automobile business, Honda and Chrysler are considered to be innovators.

▶ *Fast Followers*: These businesses are the *analyzers*. By carefully monitoring the actions of major competitors, and by moving quickly, they often are able to bring a superior product to market—more cost-efficient or with better features and benefits—than the innovator's product. But analyzers are rarely first to market. Toyota and Ford are analyzer companies.

- *Defenders*: Defenders attempt to locate and *maintain a secure position* or niche in a relatively stable product or market area. They protect their domain by offering higher-quality, superior service or lower prices. These businesses ignore industry changes that have no direct influence on their current operations. General Motors, Nissan, and Mazda are defenders.
- *Reactors*: These firms are not as aggressive in maintaining established products and markets as competitors. They respond only when forced to by strong external or market pressures.

These four strategy types are useful descriptors when your leadership team is trying to envision which type of product developer you aspire to be. There are pros and cons to each strategic approach above. You must weigh your own situation—your marketplace's dynamics, your competition, and your own capabilities and competencies—and decide. But do make a choice: Don't just let it happen by default!

Other Ways of Visualizing Strategy Types

Numerous ways to describe and portray your attack strategy (or how you plan to win) exist. Some options you might wish to consider, perhaps in combination:[36]

- *The low-cost provider:* This strategy emphasizes your low manufacturing and delivery costs, which are reflected in lower pricing to achieve market share. This strategy can often be combined effectively with the *analyzer* or fast-follower strategy above: waiting and watching for competitors to launch a new product, and then rapidly copying the product but more cost-effectively.
- *The differentiator:* This approach builds on the very successful strategy identified in my strategy study, outlined earlier in the chapter. The goal is to develop unique, superior products—ones that meet customer needs better than competitive products and deliver real value to the customer. A combination of a strong market orientation (spotting market trends, listening to the voice-of-the-customer) and technological prowess are keys to success here.
  An example: Black and Decker power tools aimed at the consumer market are the result of this strategy. The business has had a steady stream of differentiated new products from the early days with its *Workmate*™ bench through to more recent combination tools, always boasting new features, functionality, and design, and always in tune with consumer wants and needs.

▶ *The customer-friendly strategy:* Here your business is highly reactive to customer desires, but in a positive way. You respond to specific requests from customers, handling them quickly and effectively. A proficient sales force, solid relationships with key customers, and a fast-paced, responsive development organization and process are fundamental to success here.

An example: One major consumer paper company (toilet paper, facial tissues) operates this way, catering closely to the needs and wishes of its major retailer customers. Most of its product developments are in fact responses to major retailer requests. And the company has designed an organizational structure and a new product process that enables handling these retailer requests in an effective and fast manner.

▶ *The niche player:* The idea here is to focus on one segment or type of user in the marketplace. And you orient your entire product development effort (and your marketing effort) to satisfying that target user's needs and desires. Market knowledge and customer intimacy are keys to success here, along with technological capability.

An example: Kenworth trucks, a U.S. manufacturer of heavy-duty highway trucks, has traditionally elected this niche or focused strategy. From the beginning, Kenworth has focused on the owner-operator, the independent truck driver who owns and drives his or her own rig. Everything, from the traditional and macho truck exterior through to the ability to custom-design and custom-outfit a truck for the discriminating owner, is done to serve this type of buyer.

▶ *The low-budget conservative strategy:* Here, you develop copy-cat, me too, undifferentiated new products, remain highly focused on one or a few product-market areas, and stay close to home (not venturing into new areas). You make sure your new products match your business's production and technological skills and resources, fit into your business's existing product lines, and are aimed at familiar and existing markets for you. R&D spending is usually quite low relative to that of competitors.

Chempro's attack strategy: Chempro's management elects a general attack strategy that is the same across all arenas, namely, a differentiated approach, focusing on delivering superior products with unique product features and improved performance for customers. This strategy requires a marriage of Chempro's core technology competency (prowess in the field of rotary hydraulic equipment design) coupled with a customer-orientated, market-driven approach to defining product requirements. Thus the strategy is really a combination of the *fast-follower strategy* and the *differentiated strategy*.

Deciding Your Entry Strategies

This chapter so far has dealt with the questions: Which new product arenas should your business focus on, and how? Another equally important question is: By what mechanism *should you enter these arenas* to avoid failure and maximize gain? Although these questions are fundamentally different, note that they should not be answered independently of one another.[37] Entering a new business arena may be achieved by a variety of mechanisms, such as internal development, joint ventures, and minority investments of venture capital. And each of these mechanisms makes different demands upon your business.[38]

Roberts and Berry propose an entry-strategy selection framework based on their popular market and technological newness and familiarity dimensions (see Exhibit 3.12):[39]

1. *Technology newness:* how new that technology is to the company—the degree to which the technology is different from that found in the products that the company currently produces

Technologies Embodied in the Products

		Base	New, familiar	New, unfamiliar
Market Targeted by the Products	**New, unfamiliar**	Joint Ventures	Venture Capital or Venture Nurturing or Educational Acquisitions	Venture Capital or Venture Nurturing or Educational Acquisitions
	New, familiar	Internal Market Development or Acquisitions (or Joint Ventures)	Internal Ventures or Acquisitions or Licensing	Venture Capital or Venture Nurturing or Educational acquisitions
	Base	Internal Base Developments (or Acquisitions)	Internal Product Development or Acquisitions or Licensing	Joint Ventures (large firm with small firm)

Exhibit 3.12 Optimum Entry Strategies
Source: E. B. Roberts & C. A. Berry. See note 37.

2. *Market newness:* how new that market is to the company—the degree to which the company's products are not sold to that particular market
3. *Technology familiarity:* the degree to which knowledge of the technology exists within the company, but is not necessarily found in its current products
4. *Market familiarity:* the degree to which a market is known by the company, but not necessarily as a result of selling into that market

If a business in which the firm currently competes is defined as its *base business,* then market factors associated with the new business may be characterized as *base, new familiar,* or *new unfamiliar.* The same is true for technological factors.

The thesis underlying this framework is that the newer or more unrelated an arena is to the base business, the poorer the results to the firm. This leads to the logical conclusion that *entry strategies requiring high corporate involvement* should be reserved for *new arenas with familiar market and technological characteristics.* Similarly, entry mechanisms requiring low corporate input seem best for unfamiliar arenas.

Various entry strategies are shown in the matrix in Exhibit 3.12 for different degrees of market and technological newness and unfamiliarity. Roberts and Berry support their matrix approach with actual case histories, showing the success-failure patterns across the matrix. Various entry strategies and their appropriateness are outlined below, and the advantages of each are summarized in Exhibit 3.13.

Internal development: Internal development exploits internal resources as a basis for establishing a new business or entering a new arena for the company: a "do it yourself" approach. Lack of familiarity with markets and technologies in the new business arena often leads to major errors, and is one reason for poor performance.[40] Internal developments are recommended only for base business arenas and those involving new but familiar markets using base technologies, or new but familiar technologies targeted at base markets (bottom left part of Exhibit 3.12).

Acquisitions: Acquisitions may be attractive not only because of speed of execution, but also because they might offer a much lower cost of entry into a new arena. Acquisitions are appropriate for new but familiar arenas, as shown in Exhibits 3.12 and 3.13. But words of warning: Not all acquisitions end up as profitable as initially projected, and many prove difficult and costly to integrate into the culture and operations of the acquiring company.

Licensing: Acquiring technology through licensing represents an alternative to acquiring a complete company. Licensing avoids the risk of product development by exploiting the experience of firms which have already

Entry Strategy	Advantages	Disadvantages
Internal Development	Uses existing resources Familiar markets & technology – fewer surprises, more experience	Resources may be tied up on other projects Time lag to break-even may be long Unfamiliarity with some markets may lead to business errors
Acquisition	Rapid market entry	New business area unfamiliar to parent Acquisitions are often costly Merging two cultures can be problematic, time-consuming & costly
Licensing	Rapid access to proven technology & product designs Reduces financial exposure	Not a substitute for internal competence Not propriety technology – dependent on licensor
Internal Venture	Uses existing resources Enables company to retain/foster talented entrepreneurs	Mixed success record Company's internal climate often unsuitable, non-supportive
Joint Venture or Alliance	Technology/marketing unions can exploit large company/small company synergies Distributes risk	Potential for conflict between partners Sometimes surprises about each other's capabilities & commitment
Venture Capital & Nurturing	Can provide window in new technology or market	Unlikely to be a major stimulus for company growth
Educational Acquisitions	Provides window & initial staff	Higher initial financial commitment than VC Risks the departure of entrepreneurs

Exhibit 3.13   Advantages and Disadvantages of Various Entry Strategies
Source: E. B. Roberts & C. A. Berry. See note 37.

developed and marketed the product.[41] Licensing is particularly appropriate when entering new but familiar technology arenas.

Internal ventures: Many companies adopt new venture strategies in order to meet ambitious plans for diversification and growth.[42] In this strategy, a firm attempts to enter different markets or to develop substantially different products from its base businesses by setting up a separate entity within the existing corporate body. The concept is to establish small businesses—entrepreneurial, venture businesses—within the large corporation, taking advantage of the corporation's resources, but freeing the venture team from the usual corporate barriers to entrepreneurial behavior.

Joint ventures or alliances: When projects get larger, technology too expensive, and the cost of failure too large to be borne alone, joint venturing becomes increasingly viable.[43] Often the joint venture occurs where a large company and a small company join forces to create a new entry in the marketplace (upper left cell in Exhibit 3.12). In these efforts of "mutual pursuit," usually without the formality of a joint venture company, the small firm provides the technology, the large enterprise provides the marketing capability, and the venture is synergistic for both parties. Large-company/small-company alliances, called strategic partnering, often involve the creative use of corporate venture capital.[44]

Venture capital and nurturing: The venture strategy that permits some degree of entry, but has the lowest level of corporate commitment, is that associated with external venture capital investment. Major corporations invest venture capital in developing or start-up firms in order to become involved in the growth and development of such firms, and may eventually acquire them outright. The motivation is to secure a "window on technology" by making minority investments in young, growing, high-technology enterprises. When the investing company provides managerial assistance as well as venture capital to the small firm, the strategy is classed as "venture nurturing" rather then pure venture capital. This nurturing strategy appears a more sensible entry in achieving diversification objectives as opposed to simple provision of funds, but it also needs to be tied to other company diversification efforts.[45]

Educational acquisitions: Targeted small acquisitions can fulfill a role similar to that of a venture capital minority investment and, in some circumstances, offer significant advantages. In such an acquisition, the large firm acquires a small firm, usually with an "interesting technology" at the early stage of development. The acquisition is made, but not so much for financial return reasons, but to acquire know-how and familiarity at minimal cost. The acquiring firm immediately obtains people familiar with the new technology area, whereas in a minority investment, the parent company relies on its existing staff to build familiarity by interacting with the investee. Acquisitions made for educational purposes may

---

Notes for Senior Management

You have selected one or more strategic arenas as a target. Now, how are you going to win in that arena? Develop the outline of your attack strategies:

- Your strategic stance: innovator, fast follower, defender, low-cost provider, differentiator, customer-friendly, niche player, or low-budget conservative
- How you plan to enter the arena, perhaps alone, or via an acquisition, licensing, or with alliance partners or a joint venture

With arenas defined and with attack strategies in place, it's time to turn to the challenging issue of resources. Translating your strategy into reality means *deployment of resources*: how many resources, and where to allocate them. And that's the topic of the following chapter on strategy.

therefore represent a faster route to familiarity than the venture capital "window" approach, and are recommended as one possible entry strategy for new, unfamiliar arenas (top right cell in Exhibit 3.12).

Some Thoughts on Your Product Innovation Strategy

With the increasing importance of new product warfare also comes a desire to manage product innovation effectively, hence the wish to

---

Notes for Senior Management

Reflect on Chempro's strategic exercise outlined in this chapter for a moment. There are several positive facets to note:

1. First, *senior management leads the way here.* It is the senior people of the business who took up the challenge and mapped out this business's new product strategy. This task is not left to a Marketing or R&D group to do: This is not the time or place for "hands-off" management!

2. This strategy goes beyond vision and mission and nice-sounding words. It is translated into goals and prioritized arenas (for Chempro, defined by application and customer groups). And an attack plan is developed: how management intends to win on these battlefields. In Chempro's case, it is to adopt a fast-follower-with-better-products and differentiator strategic stance, coupled with internal development; for your business, there exist many other options (outlined in this chapter).

3. Next, strategy becomes real when you start spending money, so strategy must be translated into spending decisions, the topic of the following chapter. Decisions must be made on resource commitment (how much is enough?), on deployment (strategic buckets), and on major development initiatives (the strategic product roadmap).

4. This strategic exercise—for example, selecting arenas, deciding resource commitments, and determining the split in resources across arenas—although top-down and strategically driven, also considers opportunities within each arena. This is not a sterile strategic exercise, but rather an *iterative one* between a top-down, strategic approach, and a bottom-up approach that takes into account active and as well as proposed projects and opportunities.

develop product innovation strategies. Developing such a strategy for your business is not easy. In spite of the challenge, however, a product innovation strategy is a must for all businesses that are serious about building new products into their long-range plans. Many businesses operate without such a strategy, and the senior managements know the problems only too well. There is no direction to the Discovery stage or to idea search, or there is no discovery at all. Much time is wasted in screening proposed projects and agonizing over the same question: Should we be in this business? Portfolio management is almost impossible, and there are difficulties in making a long-term, sustained budget commitment for new products. And personnel, resource, and technology acquisition planning is hit-and-miss.

Methods for developing your product innovation strategy have been outlined in this chapter. I began with a recognition of the need for and payoffs of having such a strategy. Goals are defined that give the business's new product effort a sense of purpose, and tie it firmly to the business's overall objectives. Strategic arenas—the target battlefields or arenas of strategic thrust—are identified and pared down to a set of top-priority fields for exploitation. These arenas give the new product effort direction and focus, ingredients that are critical to a successful innovation strategy. Attack strategies are then defined for the arenas: how you plan to enter and win in each.

These arenas are also prioritized, and from these priorities, spending splits—the strategic buckets—must be decided, as the business's new product strategy begins to drive portfolio management (in the following chapter). Strategic product roadmaps are developed to yield a map showing the major initiatives. And so the product innovation strategy evolves to guide your business's product innovation war effort.

Notes

1. APQC benchmarking study: see note 29 in Chapter 1. Available as: *Best Practices in Product Development: What Distinguishes Top Performers* at www.prod-dev.com.

Parts of this chapter appeared in R. G. Cooper, "Product Innovation & Technology Strategy," reprinted in *Succeeding in Technological Innovation*. Washington, DC: Industrial Research Institute, May 2001, 14–17; parts are taken from R. G. Cooper, *Winning at New Products: Accelerating the Process from Idea to Launch*, 3rd ed. Reading, MA: Perseus, 2001.

2. APQC benchmarking study: see note 1.

3. D. J. Luck, & A. E. Prell, *Market Strategy*. Englewood Cliffs, NJ: Prentice Hall, 1968, 2.

4. I. H. Ansoff, *Corporate Strategy*. New York: McGraw-Hill, 1965.

5. R. E. Corey, "Key Options in Market Selection and Product Planning," *Harvard Business Review*, September–October 1978, 119–128.

6. Some sections in this chapter are taken from a recent book, where the author was one of the co-authors: R. G. Cooper, S. J. Edgett, & E. J. Kleinschmidt, *Portfolio Management for New Products*, 2nd ed. Reading, MA: Perseus, 2002.

7. C. M. Crawford, "Protocol: New Tool for Product Innovation," *Journal of Product Innovation Management*, 2, 1984, 85–91.

8. M. M. Menke, "Essentials of R&D Strategic Excellence," *Research-Technology Management*, 40, 5, September–October 1997, 42–47.

9. Booz-Allen & Hamilton, *New Product Management for the 1980s*. New York: Booz-Allen & Hamilton, Inc., 1982.

10. See H. Nystrom, "Company Strategies for Research and Development," in *Industrial Innovation*, edited by N. Baker. New York: Macmillan, 1979; H. Nystrom, *Company Strategies for Research and Development*, Report S-75007. Uppsala, Sweden: Institute for Economics and Statistics, 1977; H. Nystrom & B. Edvardsson, *Research and Development Strategies for Swedish Companies in the Farm Machinery Industry*, Uppsala, Sweden: Institute for Economics and Statistics, 1978; and: H. Nystrom & B. Edvardsson, *Research and Development Strategies for Four Swedish Farm Machine Companies*. Uppsala, Sweden: Institute for Economics and Statistics, 1980.

11. The Cooper strategy studies: R. G. Cooper, "Industrial Firms' New Product Strategies," *Journal of Business Research*, 13, April 1985, 107–121; and R. G. Cooper, "Overall Corporate Strategies for New Product Programs," *Industrial Marketing Management*, 14, 1985, 179–183.

12. C. M. Crawford, "Defining the Charter for Product Innovation," *Sloan Management Review*, 1980, 3–12.

13. Paragraph taken from R. G. Cooper, "Benchmarking New Product Performance: Results of the Best Practices Study," *European Management Journal*, 16, 1, 1998, 1–7.

14. APQC benchmarking study: see note 1.

15. APQC benchmarking study: see note 1.

16. See note 6; also R. G. Cooper, S. J. Edgett, & E. J. Kleinschmidt, "Optimizing the *Stage-Gate® Process*: What Best Practice Companies Are Doing—Part II," *Research-Technology Management*, 45, 6, November–December 2002.

17. See R. E. Albright & T. A. Kappel, "Roadmapping in the Corporation," *Research-Technology Management*, 46, 2, March–April 2003, 31–40; also A. McMillan, "Roadmapping—Agent of Change," *Research-Technology Management*, 46, 2, March–April, 2003, 40–47; and M. H. Myer & A. P. Lehnerd, *The Power of Product Platforms*. New York: The Free Press, 1997.

18. Parts of this section are taken from an article by the author: R. G. Cooper, "Maximizing the Value of Your New Product Portfolio: Methods, Metrics and Scorecards," *Current Issues in Technology Management*, published by Stevens Alliance for Technology Management, 7, 1, Winter 2003, 1.

19. R. E. Albright, "Roadmaps and Roadmapping: Linking Business Strategy and Technology Planning," *Proceedings, Portfolio Management for New Product Development*, Institute for International Research and Product Development & Management Association, Ft. Lauderdale, FL, January 2001.

20. A. Griffin & A. L. Page, "PDMA Success Measurement Project: Recommended Measures for Product Development Success and Failure," *Journal of Product Innovation Management*, 13, 6, November 1996, 478–495.

21. G. S. Day, "A Strategic Perspective on Product Planning," *Journal of Contemporary Business*, Spring 1975, 1–34.

22. Strategy studies: see note 11.

23. Day: see note 21.

24. Based on maps in O. Gadiesh & J. L. Gilbert, "How to Map Your Industry's Profit Pool," *Harvard Business Review*, May–June 1998, 3–11.

25. M. E. Porter, *Competitive Advantage: Creating and Sustaining Superior Performance*. New York: The Free Press, 1985.

26. See C. M. Christensen, *The Innovator's Dilemma*. New York: HarperCollins, 2000.

27. See note 26.

28. See success drivers in, for example, M. M. Montoya-Weiss & R. J. Calantone, "Determinants of New Product Performance: A Review and Meta Analysis," *Journal of Product Innovation Management* 11, 5, November 1994, 397–417; and R. G. Cooper, Chapter 1, "New Products: What Separates the Winners from the Losers," in *The PDMA Handbook of New Product Development*, 2nd ed. New York: Wiley, 2004; also the *NewProd® studies*: see note 30 in Chapter 1.

29. Albright: see note 19.

30. Corey: see note 5.

31. D. F. Abell, *Defining the Business.* Englewood Cliffs, NJ: Prentice Hall, 1980.

32. Crawford: see note 7.

33. Based on R. G. Cooper, "Defining the New Product Strategy," *IEEE Transactions on Engineering Management,* EM-34, 3, 1987, 184–193; R. G. Cooper, "Identifying and Evaluating New Product Opportunities," in G. S. Day, B. Weitz, & R. Wensley, *The Interface of Marketing and Strategy,* vol. 4 of the series: *Strategic Management Policy and Planning: A Multivolume Treatise.* Greenwich, CT: JAI, 1990. See also R. G. Cooper, "Product Innovation & Technology Strategy," reprinted in *Succeeding in Technological Innovation.* Washington, DC: Industrial Research Institute, May 2001, 14–17.

34. R. E. Miles & C. C. Snow, *Organizational Strategy, Structure and Process.* New York: McGraw-Hill, 1978.

35. These definitions are taken from an article by Griffin and Page, who provide a breakdown of project types by strategy elected: see note 20.

36. These strategy types are based on concepts from several sources: M. E. Porter, note 25, and R. G. Cooper, note 11.

37. E. B. Roberts & C. A. Berry, "Entering New Businesses: Selecting Strategies for Success," *Sloan Management Review,* Spring 1983, 3–17.

38. E. B. Roberts, "New Ventures for Corporate Growth," *Harvard Business Review,* 1980, 3–17.

39. See note 37.

40. See success factors: note 28.

41. J. P. Killing, "Diversification through Licensing," *R&D Management,* 1978, 159–163.

42. See note 38.

43. See note 41.

44. See note 38.

45. See note 38.

4

Product Innovation Strategy to Portfolio Management—Resource Commitment and Deployment

Plans are nothing. Planning is everything.
—Dwight D. Eisenhower

If a man look sharply and attentively, he shall see Fortune;
for though she is blind, she is not invisible.
—Francis Bacon, *Of Fortune*, 1623

Optimizing Your New Product Investments

Much like stock market portfolio managers, senior executives who manage to optimize their R&D investments—to commit the right resources, to focus these resources on the right arenas, to select winning new product projects, and to achieve the ideal balance and mix of projects—will win in the long run. There are two facets to NPD resource optimization:

1. Determining the right level of NPD investment: Have you committed sufficient resources to achieve your business's NPD goals? Or are you heavily under-resourced, and face tough decisions regarding resource commitment for the future? This is the *NPD investment* question, and is a major topic of this chapter.

Many executives struggle with the issue: How much is enough? And with today's business pressures to cut expenditures of all types, R&D spending comes under scrutiny. Too many companies fail to recognize that *development spending is an investment* (and not an expense), and hence create a resource crunch in NPD in their businesses. So the question of *determining the optimal investment level* for NPD or R&D is the topic for the first half of this chapter.

2. Portfolio management: A vital and related question is this: Are you allocating your scarce and valuable NPD resources in the right way—to the right markets, product types, and projects? That is what *portfolio management* is all about: resource allocation and investment decisions to achieve your business's new product objectives.[1] Portfolio management is also a topic of this and the following chapter.

Resource Commitment—A Decisive Factor in the Innovation War

You cannot win games without players on the field! Or as one executive succinctly put it: "You gotta spend money to make money!" Committing sufficient resources for NPD, and then allocating the resources effectively, is one of the *four points of performance* of the *Innovation Diamond* (Exhibit 4.1). And how astutely and aggressively you and the leadership team of your business commit and allocate your development resources is one of the main differences between the best and poorer performers, according to our APQC benchmarking study.[2]

Insufficient Resources Cripple Businesses' Product Innovation Efforts

The resource sufficiency issue is a major problem in too many businesses, and it's a problem that senior management seems loathe to deal with. So serious is the problem that I call it "the resource crunch in product innovation."[3] A close examination of the many reasons for new product failure, coupled with results from recent benchmarking studies, shows that many of these failure modes are themselves interlinked, and are traceable to a much more fundamental cause, namely, *major resource deficiencies* in key areas.[4] For example, poor quality of execution and leaving out important tasks (such as voice-of-the-customer work) is often not so much due to ignorance or a lack of willingness. It's more often because of a lack of time and people. As one senior project leader declared: "We don't deliberately set out to do a bad job on projects. But with seven major projects underway, on top of an already busy 'day job,' I'm being *set up for failure*. . . there just isn't enough time to do what needs to be done to ensure that these projects are executed the way they should be. . . and so I cut corners."

This project leader is not alone in her concern. Our benchmarking studies reveal that the NPD resource deficiency is perverse and widespread. A lack of focus and inadequate resources surfaces as *the number one weakness* in businesses' product innovation efforts in our APQC benchmarking

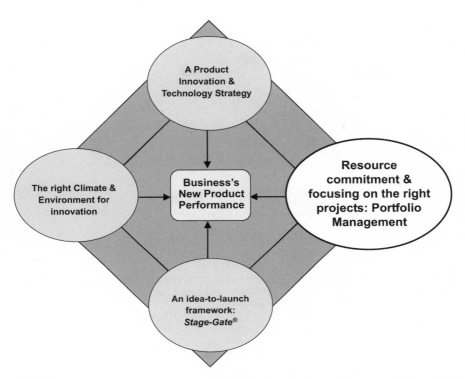

Exhibit 4.1 Resource Management Is One of the *Four Points of Performance* in the *Innovation Diamond*

study—project teams working on too many projects or not sufficiently focused on NPD work (Exhibit 4.2):[5]

- Only 10.7% of businesses indicate that adequate resources are available to projects and project teams to enable them to do a quality job—meaning that almost 90% believe that resources are inadequate!
- Only 11.4% of businesses indicate that project team members are coping with about the right number of projects (but almost 90% confess that project teams are spread too thinly over too many projects). Multi-tasking is fine up to a point, but clearly the point of multi-tasking for optimum efficiency has been far exceeded in many businesses.
- Only 21.9% of businesses boast having the correct balance between NPD demands and other work that project team members are assigned. But for the great majority—almost 80% of businesses—team members are doing far too many "other tasks" as well as struggling to work on new product projects.

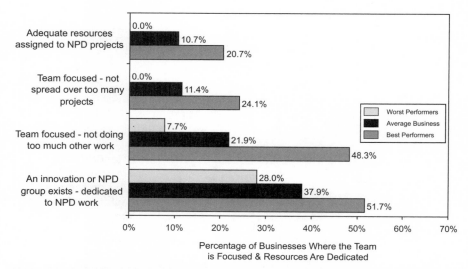

Exhibit 4.2 Project Team Focus and Dedicated Resources—Impact on Performance

A lack of resources devoted to product innovation is not just an R&D or one-function problem: It's pervasive within the corporation, cutting *across all functional boundaries* (see Exhibit 4.3).[6] The weakest areas are marketing resources (only 15.2% of businesses have sufficient marketing resources devoted to new product projects), followed by manufacturing and operations resources for NPD (only 24.3% with sufficient resources for NPD). Ironically, R&D or technical resources is the strongest area, with 31.4% of businesses indicating sufficient technical resources are in place—still weak, but better than the other functions.

Best Performers Dedicate Resources to Product Innovation

Best-performing businesses are *much more resource-rich in NPD* than other businesses. Simply stated, top performers have more players on the field; they commit the necessary resources to product innovation to get the job done. And more: Best performers' project teams are much more focused and dedicated to NPD. Indeed, *having the necessary resources in place*, and ensuring that these resources are *properly dedicated and focused*, is one of the strongest discriminators between the best-performing businesses and the rest.[7] Look at the results in Exhibit 4.3:

▶ *Adequate resources* are assigned to NPD project teams in best-performing businesses—about twice likely as for the average business.

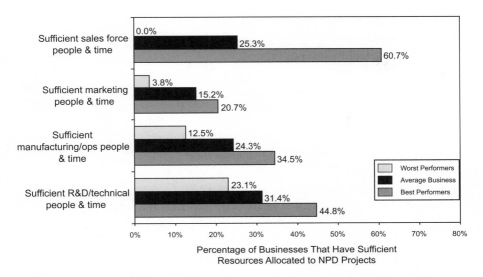

Exhibit 4.3 Resource Availabilities by Functional Area—Impact on Performance

‣ Best performers are more than twice as likely to assign *dedicated resources*—that is, their project teams are not spread too thinly over too many projects.

‣ Project team members in best-performing businesses are much *more focused*—not doing a lot of other work in addition to their new product projects—than those in average and in poor-performing businesses.

‣ Best performers tend to use dedicated *innovation groups* to undertake NPD. Such cross-functional group focus 100% of their time on NPD.

Resource commitment is also more *cross-functional* in top-performing business, much more so than in other businesses: It's not just a matter of R&D players on the field. Exhibit 4.3 reveals that top performers are much more likely to commit sufficient resources from marketing, sales, operations, as well as R&D. Note that the greatest difference between best and worst businesses is for salesforce resources: In top-performing businesses, the sales force makes salespeople available to work on NPD project teams; poor performers do not.

This impact of resource commitments confirms an earlier study, where resource deficiencies in all areas—R&D, marketing, sales and operations—were identified as significantly and seriously deficient when it came to NPD.[8] Further, adequate resources devoted to new product development was identified as one of the *three strongest drivers* of new product performance. Indeed, the *strongest single driver* of the most commonly used performance metric, percentage of sales from new products, is how much the business spends on R&D (also as a percentage of sales).

When You Don't Have Sufficient Resources in Place

A lack of new product resources leads to many common ailments in product innovation efforts. How many does your business suffer from?

1. Quality of execution suffers: When resources on projects are tight, corners are cut as project teams scramble to meet timelines with minimal resources. Thus, essential market studies are truncated, upfront home-work is short-circuited, field trials are overly accelerated, and launch plans are thrown together and under-resourced. As one frustrated executive put it: "We're so busy just getting the projects done—marching to a timeline—that we don't have the time for any of this important upfront work. We have a 'heads down' rather than a 'heads up' mentality."

Box 4.1   More Research Evidence: The Portfolio Management Investigations

Two studies cited here are on the topics of resource allocation and portfolio management methods and results. The first study probed major firms and their portfolio management approaches. The second investigation, done with the help of the Industrial Research Institute (IRI, Washington, DC) looked at a much larger sample of businesses, and in particular, on what portfolio and project selection techniques they used, and what performance results they achieved. See notes 13 and 14.

Research into NPD practices reveals *poor quality of execution* of project tasks from idea right through to launch.[9] Only 34.4% of businesses on average proficiently execute the key activities from idea through to launch—fairly dismal performance overall.[10]

Poor quality of execution ultimately results in serious new product costs. Quality of execution drives new product success rates, so that success rates and profitability at launch suffer.[11] Then there's the hidden cost of "fix and repair" work: Activities done in haste come back to haunt the project team, and end up taking twice as long via rework, as the project team gets caught in an almost endless "build-and-fix" spiral.

2. Time-to-market lengthens: With not enough resources to handle the many projects in the pipeline, queues begin to build. The "time to get things done" is not so much execution time, it's waiting or queuing time—waiting for people to get around to doing the work. And thus time-to-market suffers. One estimate is that in many businesses, the waiting time is 30 to 50% of the project cycle time.[12] Get rid of the queues and you could cut time-to-market by up to 50%!

3. Game-changers are lacking: New product failures and being late or slow to market are the *measurable costs* of poor or untimely execution, often brought on by insufficient resources. A far greater cost is unmeasurable, because it's an *opportunity cost.* How many projects are simply not done due to a lack of resources? Given a limited resource base, human nature dictates that it be spent on lower-risk initiatives that don't cost very much. As one executive exclaimed: "My business has a limited R&D budget. I can't afford to risk a major percentage of that budget on a handful of big projects. I've got to *hedge my bets*, and pick the smaller and lower-risk ones. Besides, many of these smaller projects have to be done—they're needed to respond to a customer request or to keep the product line up-to-date. If I had a larger R&D budget, then I might tackle some more venturesome projects."

Lacking the resources to do an effective job, technical and marketing executives start to favor smaller, easier-to-do, and faster projects—the "low hanging fruit" projects. The trouble is, they're often of *low value to the company*. The immediate result is the lack of blockbuster or game-changer projects in the pipeline. Indeed, 45% of executives confess to too many low-value projects in their development portfolios, and 69% indicate a poorly balanced portfolio of projects.[13]

Most businesses also have projects that must be done in order to keep the product line up-to-date, respond to a major customer's request, or simply fix a problem. But lacking adequate development resources, often these "must do" projects end up taking the lion's share of the limited resources. The result is a very unbalanced portfolio—too many tweaks, modifications, and fixes—and a lack of projects that promise significant growth and profitability.

4. The active projects are "dumbed down": Another occasional result of resource deficiencies is that projects are "dumbed down" or de-scoped. One R&D leader described the resource deficiency this way: "Heroic efforts can only compensate for the resource gap for so long. So they [the project teams] make the projects simpler: They de-scope the project, and de-feature the product. . . they simply don't build in all the product features and functionality that they know they should." And so de-scoping and de-featuring take their toll on potentially great new products.

5. The project team's morale suffers: Inadequate resources also impact the project team. Faster time-to-market and cycle time reduction are paramount themes in many businesses. But lacking the necessary personnel and their time commitments from functional bosses, the project team is stretched. Deadlines are missed, pressure mounts, people are blamed, and team morale starts to deteriorate. Crawford identified team morale problems as one result of an over-emphasis on cycle time reduction; I continue to see much evidence of moral problems, brought on by a combination of too few resources and time pressures:[14]

> *An example:* In one business investigated, the morale of project teams was so bad that no one wanted to be on future teams. Being put on a product development team *was viewed as a punishment.* The reason: There was so much time pressure on these teams to accomplish the impossible, and so few resources to do the work, that teams were destined to fail. And they were being chastised by management.

Notes for Senior Management

Do these ailments beset your new product programs:

- poor quality of execution and missing key activities, such as voice of customer studies
- too long to get to market
- too many trivial, low value projects and a lack of game-changer projects in your portfolio
- de-scoped and de-featured products
- morale problems?

If so, perhaps the culprit is not so much unwilling or unable project teams or a lack of a sense of urgency. The underlying cause is far more likely to be too many projects for the limited resources available: a resource crunch! And the problem appears to be getting worse, as firms try to develop even more new products with the same or fewer resources.

So read on to better understand how to solve the resource crunch problem, and to determine what resources your business should devote to NPD.

How Much Is Enough—Deciding the Investment Level for Your Product Innovation Effort

Four fundamental approaches are available to help you, the leadership team of the business, decide how many resources to commit to product development or how much to invest in R&D in your business. They are:

1. investment level based on the strategic role of your business
2. strategy, goals, and task approach
3. competitive parity
4. investment level based on demand created by new product opportunities.

These methods are not mutually exclusive and can be used in conjunction with each other. Let's now look at each approach in more detail:

1. Investment Level Based on the Strategic Role of Your Business

Here, investment in product innovation is decided by the *strategic role* of your business. This top-down method is premised on the simple tenet that *your business strategy should drive your product innovation or R&D spending.* It is a particularly useful approach when your business is part of a much larger corporation.

First, recognize that not all businesses are the same when it comes to resource commitment to NPD. True, some businesses face limited prospects in product development, and thus few development resources should be allocated here. But others have many opportunities and merit much more spending.

Sadly, the emphasis on short-term operating results has caused some corporate headquarters to treat all business units much the same—a cookie-cutter approach to planning. Planners have lost sight of strategy and have become scorekeepers instead: The short-term numbers are all-important. This is wrong. Setting R&D spending levels equally across businesses, perhaps using some financial formula or magic percentage, fails to recognize the opportunities and potential for growth that some businesses face, and that others lack.

It's time to reintroduce a good dose of strategic thinking into your corporate planning exercise. Let's get back to the fundamentals of strategic planning, where differences between businesses and their opportunities were recognized. Recall the Boston Consulting Group (BCG) or McKinsey-GE portfolio model for business units.[15] This strategic model was a good model in its day: It plotted businesses on a two-dimensional grid with "market attractiveness" and "business position" as the axes (much like the arena map in Exhibit 3.11). Business units were then classified as Stars, Cash Cows, Dogs, and Wildcats; and the model defined different goals, strategic roles, and even NPD emphases for each business type. This model made a lot of sense, so perhaps it's time to dust it off and update it.

Star businesses merit more spending on product innovation than the average business, and an aggressive NPD effort. A "harvest and/or divest" strategy is usually elected for Dog businesses; Cash Cows see average or modest R&D spending, with NPD designed to keep the product line up-to-date. And Wildcats or Question-marks see selective R&D spending, depending on the magnitude of the opportunity and track record to date.

One more point: For Star businesses, be sure to change the performance metrics! Measuring all businesses with the same metrics assumes that all businesses are the same: again, wrong! For example, your Star businesses should be treated as Stars and, most important, *be measured as Stars*. Thus, instead of relying on *traditional short-term operating profits,* apply more *growth-oriented metrics* to gauge their performance, such as:

- percentage of sales from new products[16]
- growth in revenue
- growth in profits

Note that these growth metrics may not be appropriate for every business unit—just for the designated ones.

> *An example:* At Air Products & Chemicals (a global supplier of industrial gases, equipment, and chemicals), each global business unit is assigned its own growth and profitability targets, depending upon the type of industry and markets that each is in, and the level of importance of the business to the corporation. This approach recognizes that *each business unit is different,* and as such, should have different targets set for it. Each business unit thus has its own NPD strategy and corresponding spending level that matches its own unique business needs.[17]

2. Strategy, Goals, and Task Approach

This top-down method attempts to ensure that your *new product resources are consistent with the tasks needed to achieve your business's strategy and goals.* Begin by taking a hard look at your business's goals, business strategy, and product innovation strategy. If there are stretch growth goals, and the strategy is to expand dramatically via new products (as is typical in a Star business), then the resources must be in place. For example, since the metric "percentage of revenue from new products" is driven by R&D spending,[18] then NPD goals expressed in terms of sales from new products must be reflected in appropriate levels of R&D spending.

Next, translate your business growth or new product sales goals into new product launches: how many major, medium, and minor product launches per year? Then convert these launches over time into resource requirements—how many people and dollars will be required to undertake all the development projects you need to do? This is the demand side, and is usually measured in full-time equivalent people or dollars. For more detail on this method, see Box 4-2.

Now look at the supply side. Undertake a resource capacity assessment—how many people are available to work on projects.[19] Be sure to subtract the time they must spend on day-to-day work just to keep the business going. This is the supply side.

Each time we undertake such a resource analysis, a gap between demand (based on goals and strategy) and supply is identified. And the result is predicable: The goals won't be achieved and the strategy will not be realized. Senior management then has three choices: set more realistic goals; put the resources in place; or reallocate the existing resources. This resource analysis is an excellent way to decide whether you should be spending more or less you currently are on R&D and NPD.

3. Competitive Parity

A simpler approach to deciding the correct level of resource commitment to NPD is by benchmarking your business against others in your industry. This competitive parity approach assumes that the "average competitor" in an industry is close to optimal—that some competitors probably overspend on R&D and others underspend; but on balance the average of the group is just about right.

Currently, the average R&D spending in the United States is about 2.8% of GNP (that is, 2.8% of industry output). This figure has remained remarkably constant over the years. On a per industry basis, the average spending varies widely, however—from a low of 0.6% of sales in mature, commodity businesses (such as petroleum and coal) to a high of 12.1% of sales in fast-paced higher-technology industries, such as telecommunications equipment. Exhibit 1.5 provides the industry breakdown.

If you use this competitive parity approach, here are a few caveats. First, recognize that not all R&D spending goes to new products. Some goes to process developments and manufacturing improvements, and

---

Box 4.2   Your Business's New Product Goals— Resource Demand Versus Resource Capacity

Determine resource demand:
- ▶ Begin with your new product goals—what sales or percentage of sales you desire from new products.
- ▶ Translate these goals into numbers of major, medium, and minor new product launches annually.
- ▶ Then, determine the number of projects per year you need moving through each stage. (Use your attrition curve, as in Exhibit 1.7, which shows how many Stage 1, Stage 2, Stage 3, etc. projects it takes to yield one successful launch.)
- ▶ Next, consider the person-days and dollar requirements in each stage, broken down by function or department. The numbers of projects per stage combined with the person-days requirements per project yield the resource demand—namely, the person-days and personnel requirements to achieve your business's new product goals, again by department.

What is your resource capacity?
- ▶ Next, look at the capacity available—how many work-days each department has available in total. (These work-days look at all people in that function or department, and what proportion of their time they have available for new products. Be sure to consider their "other jobs" in this determination—for example, the fact that a marketing group likely has 90% of their time eaten up by day-to-day assignments.)
- ▶ Then compare your resource capacity available with your resource demand, and note any gap.

This exercise can be done either with person-days (people x days) or dollars as the measure of resources.

One outcome is the determination of the size of the demand-versus-supply resource gap. Another outcome is the determination of the ideal resource commitment (or spending level) needed to achieve your NPD goals.

---

some is spent on ongoing technical work required to maintain the product line. Our APQC benchmarking study revealed that the median spending on R&D is 3.6% of sales for companies engaged in NPD (this number is higher than the 2.8% cited above for the entire economy, as not all firms undertake NPD). Of this R&D spending, the median proportion going to NPD is exactly 50%, for a median NPD spending rate of 1.65% of sales.

Second, your product innovation strategy might not be totally consistent with "the average competitor" or its spending level. Thus, you might decide to spend somewhat more than competitive parity if your strategy is more aggressive than the average competitor—for example, being the industry innovator; or somewhat less than the average, if you elect a follower or low-cost strategy.

> *An example:* The annual report of one firm in the instrument industry boasted that the company's strategy is to "be a leader in the field of product innovation in its industry." A closer look at actual spending on R&D showed that the company spent about *half the industry average* as a percentage of sales. Clearly there was a strong disconnect between stated strategy and spending level.

Finally, note that while most companies measure and report R&D spending, there are certainly resources other than just R&D required to develop new products. These "other resources" include marketing, sales and operations people, time and expenses, and capital costs, for example, for new equipment. One study estimates that for every dollar you spend on the technical (or R&D) side for NPD, you spend two dollars on "other items."[20]

4. Investment Level Based on Demand Created by NPD Opportunities

The final approach assumes that your investment level should be determined by the demand in your development pipeline. It is a bottom-up approach (rather than top-down and strategically driven), and it is *need- and opportunity-based*. The argument here is that development projects are proposed, assessed, and screened; assuming that your assessment and screening process is a good one, the resource demands created by approved projects—namely, the active and on-hold development projects in your pipeline—is a good gauge of what resources you should devote to NPD. For example, if many excellent projects are on hold awaiting resources, this signals a needed increase in overall resource commitments—you're probably suboptimizing and not spending enough on NPD!

This demand-based exercise is similar to the resource demand-versus-capacity analysis introduced above in item 2, except the analysis here is based on *resource demands of active and on-hold projects* in your development pipeline, rather than the projects needed to achieve your strategic goals. This approach poses the question: *Do you have enough of the right resources to handle projects currently in your pipeline? And what about proposed projects that are on hold due to no resources?* The analysis attempts to quantify your projects' demand for resources (usually people, expressed as person-days of work) versus the availability of these resources. For more detail on this method, see Box 4.3.[21]

You will likely learn several things from this exercise. First, if you are typical, you have far too many projects in your development pipeline, often by a factor of two or three. Next, you can spot the departments that are the bottlenecks. Finally, you realize that either you must devote more resources to NPD, or suboptimize and put some very attractive projects on hold.

Deploying Your Development Resources—Portfolio Management

Strategy and new product resource allocation must be intimately connected. And the link is *portfolio management*. Remember: *Strategy becomes real when you start spending money!* Until one begins allocating resources to specific activities—for example, to specific development areas or to major initiatives—strategy is just words in a strategy document. The mission, vision, and strategy of the business is made operational through the portfolio decisions it makes on *where to spend money*. For example, if a business's strategic mission is to "grow via leading-edge product development," then this must be reflected in the mix of new product projects underway— projects that will lead to growth (rather than simply to defend) and products that really are innovative.

What Is Portfolio Management?

Portfolio management is about resource allocation in the business. That is, which new products and development projects from the many opportunities the business faces should it fund? And which ones should receive top priority and be accelerated to market? It is also about business strategy, for today's new product projects decide tomorrow's product-market profile of the firm. Finally, it is about balance: about the optimal investment mix between risk versus return, maintenance versus growth, and short-term versus long-term new product projects.

Portfolio management is formally defined as follows:[22]

> Portfolio management is a dynamic decision process, whereby a business's list of active new product (and development) projects is constantly up-dated and revised. In this process, new projects are evaluated, selected and prioritized; existing projects may be accelerated, killed or de-prioritized; and resources are allocated and re-allocated to active projects. The portfolio decision process is characterized by uncertain and changing information, dynamic opportunities, multiple goals and strategic considerations, interdependence among projects, and multiple decision-makers and locations.

Box 4.3 Your Active Projects—
Resource Demand Versus Capacity

Determine resource demand:

- Begin with your current list of active and on-hold development projects, prioritized from best to worst (use a balanced scorecard to prioritize projects, or financial approaches such as NPV or ECV with the productivity index—explained in the following chapter).
- Develop a prioritized-list-of-projects table, as shown below (here Alpha is the top priority project; Foxtrot is the least attractive).
- Then consider the detailed plan of action for each project (use a timeline software package, such as MS-Project). Such a timeline and project plan should have been submitted at the most recent gate by the project team.
- For each activity on the timeline, note the number of person-days of work (or work-months), and what function or department will do the work. Again, this information should be provided as part of the deliverables package to each gate by the project team.
- Record these person-days requirements in the prioritized-list-of-projects table—these are shown in the "Person-Days" columns. Show the person-days per project and also the cumulative person-days down the column, as shown in the table below.
- Develop such a table for each month for the next six months (or whatever your resource planning cycle is).

Resource Demand Versus Capacity Chart—Example

Project	Product Mgmt Person-days	Cumulative	Marketing Person-days	Cumulative	Research Group A Person-days	Cumulative	Research Group B Person-days	Cumulative
Alpha	3	3	2	2	10	10	5	5
Beta	4	7	2	4	10	20	5	10
Gamma	3	10	2	6	15	35	5	15
Delta	5	15	3	9	15	50	8	23
Epsilon	6	21	3	*12*	5	55	8	31
Foxtrot	6	*27*	2	*14*	5	60	5	36
Demand		27		14		60		36
Available Person-days		20		10		60		40
% Utilization		*135.00%*		*140.00%*		100.00%		90.00%

Source: Portfolio Management for New Products, note 1.

What is your resource capacity?

- ❯ Next, look at the capacity available (much the same as for the resource-versus-demand analysis earlier in this chapter). Determine how many person-days each department or function has available in total. Look at all people in that department, and what proportion of their time they have available for NPD work.
- ❯ Then mark the point in your prioritized-list-of-projects table where you run out of resources—where demand exceeds capacity (numbers in bold italics indicate where the resource limit is reached in the table above)
- ❯ Determine the "percent utilization": the cumulate resources (down a column) divided by the resources available ("available person-days" row).

This analysis identifies resource gaps and potential bottlenecks. It also yields a target spending level for NPD based on resources demanded by attractive opportunities.

> The portfolio decision process encompasses or overlaps a number of decision-making processes within the business, including periodic reviews of the total portfolio of all projects (looking at all projects holistically, and against each other), making Go/Kill decisions on individual projects on an on-going basis, and developing a new product strategy for the business, complete with strategic resource allocation decisions.

New product portfolio management sounds like a fairly mechanistic exercise of decision making and resource allocation. But there are many unique facets of the problem that make it perhaps the most challenging decision making faced by the modern business:

- ❯ First, new product portfolio management deals with *future events* and opportunities; thus much of the information required to make project selection decisions is at best uncertain, and at worst very unreliable.
- ❯ Second, the decision environment is a very *dynamic* one: The status and prospects for projects in the portfolio are ever changing, as markets change and new information becomes available.
- ❯ Next, projects in the portfolio are at *different stages* of completion, yet all projects compete against each other for resources, so that comparisons must be made between projects with different amounts and "goodness" of information.
- ❯ Finally, *resources* to be allocated across projects are limited: A decision to fund one project may mean that resources must be taken away from another; resource transfers between projects are not totally seamless.

Notes for Senior Management

Do you have enough players on the field to win games consistently? Or is your business like far too many—attempting to undertake new product projects with serious resource deficiencies: a resource crunch? Resource deficiencies in NPD is one of the most serious challenges that senior management faces, and it has significant negative effects on product innovation performance.

Four methods are offered that provided guidance to the question: How much is enough—how much should you spend? They are:

1. The strategic role of your business—Stars, Cash Cows, Dogs, and Question-Marks—which provides directional guidance for your spending decisions
2. Strategy, goals, and task approach, which translates your goals and strategy into spending levels
3. Competitive parity, which determines spending based on what competitors are spending
4. Spending level based on demand from active projects, which determines the spending level based on the projects in your development pipeline

None of these approaches is perfect, nor can I recommend any one over the others. Indeed, the use of several of these methods together—a triangulation exercise—is best. But one thing is clear: A conscious effort to determine the appropriate spending level on R&D or NPD is better than the default option, which usually boils down to "what you spent last year" or some automatic percentage of sales.

The Vital Role That Portfolio Management Plays

Portfolio management and the prioritization of new product projects is a critical management task. Roussel, Saad, and Erikson in their widely read book claim that "portfolio analysis and planning will grow to become the powerful tool that business portfolio planning became in the 1970s and 1980s."[23]

Here's why portfolio management—the ability to pick the right projects and make the right investments—is vital to winning the product innovation war:

1. A successful product innovation effort is *fundamental to business success*. This logically translates into portfolio management: the ability to select today's projects that will become tomorrow's new product winners.
2. New product development is the *manifestation of your business's strategy*. One of the most important ways you operationalize strategy is through the new products you develop. If your new product initiatives are wrong—the wrong projects, or the wrong balance—then you fail at implementing your business strategy.
3. Portfolio management is about *resource allocation*. In a business world preoccupied with value to the shareholder and doing more with less, technology and marketing resources are simply too scarce to waste on poor projects. The consequences of poor portfolio management are evident: You squander scarce resources on the wrong projects, and as a result, starve the truly deserving ones.

Specific reasons for the importance of portfolio management, cited by managers and derived from a best practices portfolio study, are noted in Box 4.4.[24]

Box 4.4　Portfolio Management is Important Because. . .

There are **eight key reasons** why portfolio management is a **vital management task**, according to managers in a survey of 205 firms (see note 13):

1. Financial—to maximize return; to maximize R&D productivity; to achieve financial goals
2. To maintain the competitive position of the business—to increase sales and market share
3. To allocate scarce resources properly and efficiently
4. To forge the link between project selection and business strategy: The portfolio is the expression of strategy; it must support the strategy
5. To achieve focus—not doing too many projects for the limited resources available; to resource the "great" projects
6. To achieve balance—the right balance between long- and short-term projects, and high- and low-risk ones, consistent with the business's goals
7. To better communicate priorities within the organization, both vertically and horizontally
8. To provide better objectivity in project selection—to weed out bad projects

Notes for Senior Management

Does your business have a formal and systematic system for new product portfolio management? That is, do you have an effective method for allocating development resources, and selecting and prioritizing projects? And does your method ensure that you have the optimum set of development projects in your pipeline—the right balance, mix, timing, and emphasis?

If not, one action item you must consider is to install a first-rate portfolio management system. Companies that have done so report very positive impacts, as you'll see next.

The Impact of Portfolio Management on Business Performance

The impact of portfolio management and practices on performance cannot be understated: Effective portfolio management is one of the top best practices in NPD! This is one overriding conclusion of our APQC benchmarking study into NPD practices and performance.[25] Exhibit 4.4 reveals the results; here is what the top performers possess that distinguishes them from the rest:

1. Top performers have a formal and systematic portfolio management system in place. This portfolio system is designed to select the right projects and to optimally allocate development resources to projects or types of projects: A large proportion of businesses (44.2%), however, report *no such portfolio system at all*, and only 21.2% have a proficient portfolio management scheme. But having a portfolio management system does make a big difference: Note that best performers are *eight times as likely* as poor performers to have such a system.

> *An example:* EXFO Engineering boasts a very disciplined project ranking and prioritization portfolio process. Senior management at EXFO rates their approach to portfolio management to be the company's *strongest best practice* and attributes a reduction in time-to-market from 18 to 24 months to 12 months to their portfolio system.
>
> The portfolio process session is held quarterly, takes about five days, and is undertaken by a portfolio team comprised of the executives. The session begins with a strategy review, followed by a technology overview. Subsequent steps in the process include the project post-mortem recommendations; a quick review of ongoing projects; and gate review presentations for upcoming or new projects. The portfolio

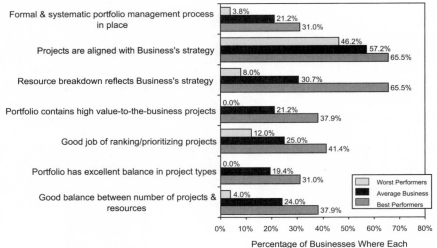

Percentage of Businesses Where Each
Portfolio Management Practice is in Place

21.2% of businesses have a systematic portfolio management process in place (meaning that 79% do not!). Best performers are better here, with 31.0% having such a system, while only 3.8% of poor performers do.

Exhibit 4.4 Portfolio Management Practices—Impact on Performance

team then undertakes a project prioritization exercise using scorecard criteria. This prioritization exercise parallels EXFO's gating process and enables the portfolio team to kill a project if necessary. Next, the portfolio team performs a final prioritization, but this time *with loadings* (that is, resource determination per project). The final step in EXFO's portfolio review process is staff feedback.

2. Best performers' portfolios are aligned with the business's objectives and strategy. This practice is the one strength of the seven portfolio practices highlighted in Exhibit 4.4, with the majority of businesses (57.2%) achieving strategic alignment. This practice is also a strong discriminator between best and worst performers, and is correlated strongly with NPD performance.

3. In top performers, the breakdown of spending (resources) in the portfolio truly reflects the business's strategy. This is another practice designed to achieve strategic alignment—ensuring that spending splits across project types, markets, and business areas mirror the strategic priorities of the business. If there are disconnects between stated business strategy and where the resources are spent, the portfolio is in trouble and strategic alignment is missing. This facet of strategic alignment is a weak area: Only 30.7% of businesses claim good alignment between business strategy and resource splits. Again, this practice is a significant discriminator between best and worst performers (with only 8.0% of worst performers achieving this strategic resource split, versus a relative high 65.5% for best performers).

> *An example:* Fluid Handling Systems, an ITT business unit in Detroit, develops pie charts that show where its R&D resources are going. These pie charts are by *project type* and also by *industry sector*, and capture current resource commitments to development projects. The two pie charts are then compared to the business's strategy and strategic direction. If there are disconnects, corrections are made to the mix of projects at periodic portfolio reviews.

4. Best performers' portfolios contain high-value new product projects for the business—profitable, high-return projects with solid commercial prospects. Picking the winners—the high-value-to-the-business projects—is no easy task. And only a small minority of businesses (21.2%) claim to have achieved this ability to load their portfolios with high-value projects. But many more businesses—38.5%—indicate that their portfolios contain low-value projects. Best performers fare better here, with 37.9% indicating high-value projects in their portfolios; not one worst performer makes this claim! Seeking high-value projects is the most strongly correlated with performance of all elements listed in Exhibit 4.4.

> *An example:* Air Products & Chemicals achieves positive results by using a standardized *project impact analysis* across all projects. Each project is assessed using a *leverage-profitability index*, which is determined by dividing the project's NPV by its cost. This leverage-profitability index is then used to compare all projects against each other and to prioritize them. Air Product's goal is to see the day where new product development teams will perform their own impact analyses, and compare projects across platforms based on their total projected expectations. In this way, the value of the portfolio will be maximized.

5. Top performers rank and prioritize new product projects well— management strives to focus its product development efforts, and does kill projects. This is rated a weak area, however, with only one-quarter of businesses indicating proficient project prioritization, while 30.8% confess to extremely weak project prioritization and a great reluctance to kill projects. Best performers do a much better job here (41.4% achieving proficient prioritization), and indeed this practice is strongly correlated with NPD performance.

An example: In EXFO Engineering's prioritization exercise (cited above), projects are rank-ordered by the portfolio team (the executives) using a scorecard approach with five criteria:
- strategic fit
- ability to increase revenue
- ability to increase market share
- degree of product differentiation
- technology advancement

Resource requirements are determined per project, and projects are selected until there are no more resources. The result is a prioritized list of the best projects, consistent with the firm's resource constraints.

6. Best performers have an excellent balance of projects in their portfolios in terms of long-term versus short-term, high-risk versus low-risk, and across markets and technologies. Here too businesses are weak, confessing to unbalanced portfolios of projects. A total of 36.9% of businesses indicate a very poorly balanced portfolio; only 19.4% have a well-balanced portfolio. Note that best performers again fare moderately well here, while not one poor performer has achieved the right balance. This is the second most strongly correlated practice with NPD performance in Exhibit 4.4.

An example: Bausch & Lomb balances its portfolio by controlling the mix of short-, medium-, and long-term projects. Currently about one-third of its projects are expected-to-launch within two years; half in three to four years; and the remainder farther out. The goal is to launch a new product every quarter. This split allows the portfolio team to judge balance in the portfolio, assessing whether it is too short-term-focused.

7. Top performers strike a good balance between the number of new projects undertaken and the resources available (people and money): Ideally, management tries to balance resource availabilities (usually people and time) with resource demand (the number of projects), and strives not to do more projects at a time than can be handled effectively. Seeking the right number of projects is a very weak practice in portfolio management: Only 24% of businesses achieve this resource-project balance, while 44.2% confess to serious deficiencies here. Again, best performers do much better, with 37.9% achieving resource balance (versus only 4.0% of worst performers).

An example: EXFO Engineering undertakes periodic portfolio reviews four times per year as one way to ensure the right balance between resource availability and demand. EXFO ranks its projects—best to worst—noting resource demands or "loadings" (person-days) for each one. When the resource demand exceeds the supply, a line is drawn: All projects below the line are put on hold.

Notes for Senior Management

In spite of the recent emphasis on new product portfolio management, the benchmarking evidence suggests that most businesses have a long way to go in terms of implementing best practices and achieving desired results from portfolio management. Simply stated, most businesses have not installed an effective and systematic portfolio management method to allocate development resources and pick the right projects. But top performers have such a system in place! Do you?

The only positive element or practice identified is achieving alignment between the projects selected and the business's strategy—that projects in the portfolio are generally "on strategy." This strategic alignment is a good first step, but there are other practices as well that must be built into a world-class portfolio management scheme: balancing resource demands and supply; ensuring good project prioritization; and seeking a portfolio of high-value projects. Seeking the right balance of projects and a project mix that mirrors strategic priorities are also important practices that are evidently missing in all but a small proportion of the businesses studied.

How does your business fare on each of the items in Exhibit 4.4? If you are deficient on some, you're in good company—many companies are weak on these elements of portfolio management.

Suggestion: Consider doing an assessment of your current portfolio management practices (use the items in Exhibit 4.4). Then compare your results to the average and top-performing businesses. This is a good way to begin the task of installing a first-rate portfolio management system in your business.

The Five Goals of Portfolio Management

How should you go about setting up a portfolio management system in your business? The items in Exhibit 4.4 give a clue—there are essentially five main goals that an effective portfolio management system should achieve. You might set your sights on at least some of these goals (according to our benchmarking results, very few companies achieve all five!):

1. To ensure strategic alignment: The main goal here is to ensure that, regardless of all other considerations, the final portfolio of projects truly reflects your business's strategy—that all projects are "on strategy," support your strategy, and/or are critical components of your strategy; and that the breakdown of spending across projects, business areas, and markets is directly tied to the business strategy (e.g., to areas of strategic focus that management has previously delineated).

2. To maximize the value of your portfolio: Here the goal is to allocate resources so as to maximize the value of your portfolio for a given spending level. That is, you select projects so as to maximize the sum of the values or *commercial worth* of all active projects in your pipeline in terms of some business objective (such as NPV, EVA, return-on-investment, likelihood of success, or some other strategic objective).

3. To seek the right balance of projects: The goal of seeking the right balance flows logically from point 1 above, strategic alignment. Here the principal concern is to develop a balanced portfolio—to achieve a desired balance of projects in terms of a number of parameters; for example, the right balance in terms of long-term projects versus short-term ones; or high-risk versus lower-risk projects; and across various markets, technologies, product categories, and project types (for example, new products, improvements, cost reductions, maintenance and fixes, and fundamental research).

Note: Although the focus here is on portfolio management for *new products*, because technology resources used in new products are also required for other types of projects, portfolio management also includes process developments, extensions and modifications, cost reduction projects, platform developments, and even fundamental research projects.

4. To ensure portfolio sufficiency versus your overall product innovation goals: Most businesses have growth goals, which can then be translated into specific goals for their new product effort—for example: "Twenty-five percent of sales shall come from new products next year." The sufficiency test or goal is to make sure that when you add up what your portfolio of projects will yield—for example, how many dollar sales they will generate next year—it meets or exceeds your stated goal.

5. To balance the number of projects with resources available—not overloading the pipeline: Most companies have too many projects underway for the limited resources available. The result is pipeline gridlock: Projects end up in a queue; they take longer and longer to get to market; and key activities within projects are omitted because of a lack of people and time. Thus an over-riding goal is to ensure a balance between resources required for the Go projects and resources available.

Begin with Strategic Portfolio Management

Portfolio management and resource allocation can be treated as a hierarchical process, with two levels of decision making. This hierarchical approach simplifies the decision challenge somewhat (see Exhibit 4.5):[26]

▸ **Level 1—Strategic portfolio management:** Strategic portfolio decisions answer these questions: Directionally, where should your business spend its NPD resources (people and funds)? How should you split your resources across project types, markets, technologies, or product categories? And on what major initiatives or new platforms should you concentrate your resources? Establishing *strategic buckets* and defining *strategic product roadmaps* are effective tools, which I outline below.

▸ **Level 2—Tactical portfolio decisions (individual project selection):** Tactical portfolio decisions focus on individual projects, but obviously follow from the strategic decisions. They address the question: What specific new product projects should you do? Such decisions are shown at the bottom part of Exhibit 4.5, and are the main topic of the following chapter.

Exhibit 4.5 Moving from Strategic Decisions to Portfolio Management—Resource Allocation Is a Hierarchical Decision Process with Two Levels of Decision Making

Establish Strategic Buckets

When translating your business's strategy into strategic portfolio decisions (middle left part of Exhibit 4.5), one major challenge faced is your *spending breakdown or deployment:* Where does senior management wish to spend its resources when it comes to product innovation—what types of projects, and in what product, market, or technology areas? And how much do they wish to spend in each area?

The *strategic buckets model* operates from the simple principle that *implementing strategy equates to spending money on specific projects*[*] Thus, operationalizing your strategy really means "setting spending targets."

The method begins with the business's strategy, and requires senior management of the business to make *forced choices* along each of several dimensions—choices about how they wish to allocate their scarce resources. This enables the creation of "envelopes of resources," or "buckets." Existing projects are categorized into buckets; then one determines whether actual spending is consistent with desired spending for each bucket. Finally, projects are prioritized within buckets to arrive at the ultimate portfolio of projects—one that mirrors management's strategy for the business.

> *An example:* A rather simple breakdown is used at Honeywell: their "Mercedes Benz star" method of allocating resources (Exhibit 4.6). The leadership team of the business begins with the business's strategy, and uses the Mercedes emblem (the three-point star) to help divide up the resources. There are three buckets:
> - fundamental research and platform development projects (which promise to yield major breakthroughs and new technology platforms)
> - new product developments
> - maintenance (technical support, product improvements and enhancements, etc.)
> Management divides the R&D funds into these three buckets. Next, the projects are sorted into each of the three buckets; management then ranks projects against each other within each bucket. In effect, three separate portfolios of projects are created and managed. And the spending breakdowns across buckets and project types mirror strategic priorities.

---

[*]Note that "resources" also includes dollars as well as people time, hence resource or money allocation is for fiscal expenditures as well as person-power allocation.

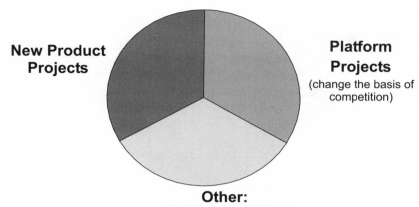

The business's strategy dictates the split of resources into buckets; projects are rank ordered within buckets, but using different criteria within each bucket.

Exhibit 4.6   Strategic Buckets—"Mercedes Benz Star" Method of Portfolio Management

Determining the Size of the Buckets

Sounds simple in theory. But how does one decide the size of these strategic buckets in the first place? Management typically goes through a modified Delphi process. This begins with a current-state assessment, including:

- a historical review—where the money was spent in the last 12 months (typically a review of pie chart splits across markets, business areas, project types, and perhaps geographies)
- a historical results analysis of major projects—how well have you done?
- a review of the current split in resources—the "what is"

The proposed strategy that management has previously agreed to is also highlighted, along with a listing and quick review of major projects underway. These are the inputs to the decision-making session (see Exhibit 4.7 for an outline). Some companies even consider splits for best-in-class companies as an input.

Next comes the Delphi voting, where each senior manager simply writes down what he or she believes the correct split of resources should be across several dimensions.

- **Historical Review**
  - Historical spending splits
  - Results from major projects

2. **Review Your Product Innovation Strategy & Current Spending Splits**

3. **Review Active Projects (and consider splits from best-in-class businesses)**

4. **Delphi Vote (senior management)**
   - Tally votes
   - Discuss & reach consensus

Exhibit 4.7   Deciding the Size of Your Strategic Buckets—The Major Steps

Some examples: In one major tool manufacturer, a dozen key executives take part in the strategic buckets session. The current splits in resources along with a list of current major projects is presented; so are the overall business strategy and the strategies for each of the firm's four major product lines. Then the executives vote by allocating resources as percentages across product lines, across project types, and across geographic regions of the world. These votes are immediately displayed on a large-screen Excel spreadsheet, are debated, and consensus is reached. The buckets are decided.

In another company, each executive is given 100 poker chips along with a "game board" that shows various categories of projects and business areas. He or she makes the necessary splits into buckets by placing the poker chips on the areas of the game board—much like placing one's bets at a roulette table. It's a very visual and effective method.

What Dimensions to Use for the Buckets

What dimensions should be used in the strategic bucket splits? One leading R&D planning executive exclaimed, "Whatever dimensions the leadership team of the business find most relevant to describe their own strategy." In other businesses, such as ITT Industries, the dimensions used in each business unit are prescribed: ITT uses two dimensions, namely, project types and business areas. And Honeywell uses only the single dimension, project types as in Exhibit 4.6. Some common dimensions you might consider are:

- *Strategic goals:* Management is required to split resources across the specified strategic goals. For example, what percent should be spent on Defending the Base? On Diversifying? On Extending the Base? and so on.

- *Across arenas:* The most obvious spending split is across the strategic arenas just defined and prioritized in the previous chapter. That is, having assessed the attractiveness of each arena in Exhibit 3.11, and having defined the priorities of each, move to deployment—that is, deciding how many resources each arena or battlefield should receive.

- *Product lines:* Resources are split across product lines: for example, how much to spend on Product Line A? on Product Line B? on C? A plot of product line locations on the product life cycle curve is used to help determine this split.

- *Types of projects:* Decisions or splits can be made in terms of the *types of projects* (as in Exhibit 4.6). For example, given its aggressive product innovation strategic stance, EXFO Engineering's management targets 65% of R&D spending to genuine new products; another 10% to platform developments and research (technology development for the future); and the final 25% to incrementals (the "supportfolio," namely, product modifications, fixes, and improvements).

- *Technologies or technology platforms:* Spending splits can be made across technology types (for example, base, key, pacing, and embryonic technologies) or across specific technology platforms (Platforms X, Y, and Z, etc.).

- *Familiarity matrix:* What should be the split of resources to different types of markets and to different technology types in terms of their *familiarity to the business?* You can use the popular "familiarity matrix"—technology newness versus market newness—to help split resources (similar to Exhibit 3.12).[27]

- *Geography:* What proportion of resources should be spent on projects aimed largely at North America? at Latin America? at Europe? at Asia-Pacific? or at the global marketplace?

- *By stage or phase of development*: Some businesses distinguish between early stage projects and projects in Development and beyond. Two buckets are created, one for development projects, the other for early-stage projects. One division at GTE allocates *seed corn money* to a separate bucket for early-stage projects.

Gap Analysis—Adding Up the Projects

Following the splitting or voting exercise comes a gap analysis. Existing projects are categorized by bucket and the total current spending by bucket is added up (the *"what is"*). Spending gaps are then identified between the *"what should be"* and *"what is"* for each bucket.

Finally, projects within each bucket are rank-ordered. You can use either a scoring model or financial criteria (to be described in Chapter 5) to do this ranking within buckets. Exhibit 4.8 shows an example of four buckets with projects ranked within each bucket. Three buckets are overspent, while the second bucket does not have enough projects. Portfolio adjustments are then made, either via immediate pruning of projects or by toughening up (or relaxing) the approval process for future projects.

Four of 12 Buckets with Spending Targets in Each Bucket

New Products: Product Line A Target Spend: $8.7M	New Products: Product Line B Target Spend: $18.5M	Maintenance of Business Product Lines A & B Target Spend: $10.8M	Cost Reductions: All Products Target Spend: $7.8M
Project A 4.1	Project B 2.2	Project E 1.2	Project I 1.9
Project C 2.1	Project D 4.5	Project G 0.8	Project M 2.4
Project F 1.7	Project K 2.3	Project H 0.7	Project N 0.7
Project L 0.5	Project T 3.7	Project J 1.5	Project P 1.4
Project X 1.7	**Gap = 5.8**	Project Q 4.8	Project S 1.6
Project Y 2.9		Project R 1.5	Project U 1.0
Project Z 4.5		Project V 2.5	Project AA 1.2
Project BB 2.6		Project W 2.1	

12 buckets or project categories are defined in this business; only 4 buckets are shown here. Projects are sorted according to bucket or column, and then rank-ordered within each column (using a financial or scorecard method for ranking). Numbers in each cell show the resources required to do each project, annualized ($M).

Note that Bucket 1—New Products for Line A—runs out of resources after Project L; whereas in Bucket 2—New Products for Line B—there is a shortage of good projects. Source: note 29.

Exhibit 4.8   Projects Prioritized Within Buckets

Notes for Senior Management

Strategic buckets is an excellent method for ensuring that your new product spending or deployment mirrors your business's strategic priorities. By breaking the decision process into two levels—first deciding the strategic breakdown of your resources via strategic buckets, and then deciding which projects to do—your portfolio mix and balance of projects will ultimately reflect your business's priorities in terms of project types, markets, and product types. And via strategic buckets, you take steps to prevent the problem that many firms suffer from, namely, an over-abundance of small, incremental, low-value projects, and a real lack of major innovations.

Thus:

- Define relevant strategic dimensions for your business—project types, markets, product types, or business areas (examples in Exhibits 4.6 and 4.11).
- Decide the right split in resources among the various buckets—use the management thought process outlined in Exhibit 4.7.
- Then sort your existing and on-hold projects by bucket.
- Prioritize the projects within each bucket. Note the resources required for each project—the "loadings." Add up resource demands in each bucket, looking for gaps.
- The prioritized list in each bucket (up to the point of each bucket's resource limits) yields your ultimate portfolio.

In effect, you now run multiple portfolios, one portfolio (or list of projects) per bucket.

The Right Split in Project Types

A major strategic question is: What's the best mix or balance of development projects—for example, incremental developments versus true innovations? Certainly, a business's new product strategy ideally should be reflected in the *breakdown of types of product developments* it undertakes—where the funds are invested. Additionally, breakdowns of new products and projects by type are a predictor of the business's NPD performance. For example, too much emphasis on short-term, small projects might point to an under-achieving business. Exhibit 4.9 shows breakdown results from

	Average Business	Best Performers	Worst Performers
Promotional developments & package changes	9.45%	5.89%	12.31%
Incremental product improvements & changes	32.74%	28.21%	40.42%
Major product revisions	21.97%	25.00%	19.15%
New to the business products	24.16%	24.11%	20.00%
New to the world products	10.23%	15.89%	7.42%

9.45% of development projects on average are "promotional developments & package changes". Best performers are more innovative—only 5.89% of their projects are package changes; but 12.31% of worst perfromers' projects are package changes.

Exhibit 4.9   Breakdown of Projects by Project Type—Best Versus Worst

Note: Does not add quite to 100% down a column due to a small percentage of "other" projects.

our APQC benchmarking study; you can benchmark your own business against this:

- Incremental product changes is the dominant category, representing 32.7% of all projects, on average.
- Next are new products to the business, accounting for 24.2% of projects.
- Then are major product revisions, making up 21.9% of projects.

What we witness is an even balance among projects across these three most popular categories. Note that on average, fairly non-innovative products—incrementals, revisions, and promotional developments— together account for about 64% of projects. By contrast, new-to-the-world products—true innovations—represent a minority of development projects (10.2%).

Do the best performers adopt a different mix of project types—is there an optimal portfolio of project types? Consider how the average business compares to the best- and worst-performing businesses in Exhibit 4.9. What is noteworthy is the shift toward much more innovative and bolder projects as one moves from worst to best performers. For example:

- More than half (53%) of worst businesses' projects are the small, incremental ones—promotional/package changes or incremental product improvements and changes.
- By contrast, just over one-third (34%) of best performers' projects are these small, incremental ones.
- Top performers take on a higher proportion of larger, more innovative projects: 40% of best performers' projects are either new-to-the-business or true innovations (new-to-the-world). By contrast, only 27% of worst performers' projects are these bolder projects.
- Best performers undertake twice as large a proportion of true innovations (new-to-the-world products) than do worst performers: 15% of their projects are true innovations (versus 7%).

I am not arguing that businesses should only undertake true innovations and genuine new products. Product improvements and modifications are certainly needed to keep the product line healthy and to respond to customer requests. But when these incremental projects dominate your portfolio, then take care—you're starting to look a lot like a poor-performing business.

Another way to look at the resource split across project types is by *type of business*. Innovator businesses undertake proportionately more new-to-the-world projects as a percentage of their total portfolio. Average breakdowns by project type are shown in Exhibit 4.10 for each of the four strategy types, and may provide a useful guide or point of comparison for your business.[28]

Notes for Senior Management

What proportion of your NPD resources are going to genuine new product projects and innovations versus just tweaks and extensions? And what should be the right split? You might want to examine just where your resources are going in terms of project types: platforms, genuine new products, and incremental projects.

One cannot prove cause-and-effect here—that doing more venturesome projects will lead to better performance results. But if you wish to benchmark the best performers in terms of project types, Exhibit 4.9 is a good guide. Be sure to note the tendencies when comparing worst versus best performers—the heavy shift from small and incremental projects to bolder and more innovative projects. Next consider your strategic stance—innovator versus fast follower versus defender—and look again at your current versus ideal split in resources by project type (use Exhibit 4.10 as a guide).

Project Type	Innovator or Prospector	Fast Follower or Analyzer	Defender	Reactor
Cost reductions	15%	17%	21%	12%
Reposition- ings	8%	8%	9%	11%
Improvements to existing products	11%	16%	11%	13%
Additions to existing product line	22%	42%	40%	48%
New to the company	15%	16%	17%	8%
New to the world (innovations)	30%	6%	7%	0%

15% of development projects that Innovators undertake are Cost Reductions; adds to 100% down a column.

Exhibit 4.10   Breakdown of Project Types by Strategy
Source: A. Griffin & A. Page. See note 16.

The Power of Strategic Buckets

The major strength of the strategic buckets approach is that it firmly links spending to the business's strategy. Over time, the portfolio of projects and the spending across strategic buckets will equal management's desired spending targets across buckets. Another positive facet is the recognition that all development projects that compete for the same resources should be considered in the portfolio approach.

Additionally, different criteria can be used for different types of projects. That is, one is not faced with comparing and ranking very different types of projects against each other—for example, comparing major new product projects to minor modifications. (When major and venturesome projects are compared against the smaller, lower-risk ones, invariably the latter always win out, which is one reason why most firms have an unbalanced portfolio.) Finally, because this is a two-step approach—first allocate money to buckets, then prioritize similar projects within a bucket—it is not necessary to arrive at a universal list of scoring or ranking criteria that fits all projects.

An example: In the Chempro's illustration from the previous chapter, management prioritizes the four new arenas, along with the existing arena, namely, home base. The arena map in Exhibit 3.11 provides a good guide for this prioritization exercise. Also considered are new product opportunities or possible projects that are proposed within each arena. After much discussion and analysis, spending levels are established for each arena (see Exhibit 4.11 for Chempro's deployments).

Additionally, Chempro's management develops strategic buckets for project types: genuine new products versus product improvements and cost reductions and versus platform developments (also in Exhibit 4.11). Here, the arenas chosen and the nature of the developments required in each arena help to decide the resource split by project types.

Notes for Senior Management

Strategic buckets is a simple concept, but it has profound implications for the way you mange your portfolio decisions. Instead of just letting the portfolio be decided by the projects you select, you've reversed the order—letting strategy decide what the mix and balance in the portfolio should be. It's like the difference between the amateur investor in the stock market, who buys stocks one at a time, versus the portfolio manager, who first decides what the strategic breakdown of her or his portfolio will be, and then makes investment decisions. I've outlined a number of examples, and even a proven method for developing your strategic buckets. Strategic buckets is a logical extension of translating your product innovation strategy into reality. So give strategic buckets a try—it's a powerful concept.

The Strategic Product Roadmap

The product roadmap is another strategically driven resource allocation method, and can be used instead of or along with the strategic buckets approach. This top-down approach is designed to ensure that the list of projects—at least the major ones—contributes to or is essential for the realization of the business's strategy and goals.[29] A strategic product roadmap is an effective way to map out this series of assaults in an attack plan.

What is a roadmap? It is simply management's view of how to get where they want to go or to achieve their desired objective.[30] The strategic roadmap is a useful tool that helps the senior management ensure that the capabilities to achieve their objective are in place when needed. Note that there are different types of roadmaps: the product roadmap and the technology roadmap.

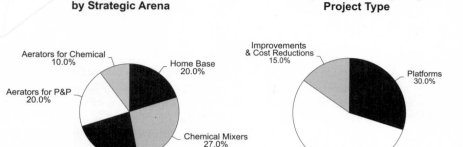

Exhibit 4.11 Deciding the Spending Splits—Strategic Buckets—at Chempro

From Strategy to Roadmaps

Let's use a military analogy: After all, the term "strategy" was first used in a military context, and much of what we know about strategy comes from the military field. You are a five-star general and are at war. You have clearly specified goals—presumably to win the war or to achieve certain ends. You may have identified certain key strategic arenas—fronts, major battlefields, or arenas on a map where you hope to attack and win. But as you chart your strategy, you see that there are some key assaults or initiatives along the way—individual battles that you must fight in order to see your strategy succeed.

Now let's translate this into a new product context:

- ▶ *Goals:* Goals your business has, including specific new product goals. For example, what percentage of your business's growth over the next three years will come from new products?
- ▶ *Arenas, fronts, and major battlefields:* These are the strategic arenas defined in your business and new product strategy (in Chapter 3). That is, which markets, technologies, and product types do you plan to attack? Where will you focus?
- ▶ *Deployment:* How many troops do you place on each battlefield or front—your strategic buckets?
- ▶ *Assaults and initiatives:* These are the major developments that you must undertake in order to implement your strategy—the major new product, technology, or platform developments: your strategic roadmap.

Your *strategic product roadmap* defines your major new product and platform developments along a timeline (see Box 4.5). An example is in Exhibit 4.12 for Chempro. Here the product roadmap not only also maps out the various major product introductions and their timing, it also defines the platforms and platform extensions needed to develop these new products. (Note that a *tactical roadmap* gets into more detail, and is essentially a list that outlines each and every product release, extension, improvement, and modification; it tends to be more short-term-focused, for example, one year.)

The *technology roadmap* is derived from the product roadmap. It also specifies how you will get there. That is, it lays out the technologies and technological competencies that are needed in order to implement (develop and source) the products and platforms in the product roadmap. The technology roadmap is a logical extension of the product road-map and is closely linked to it. Indeed, at Lucent Technologies, the two are combined

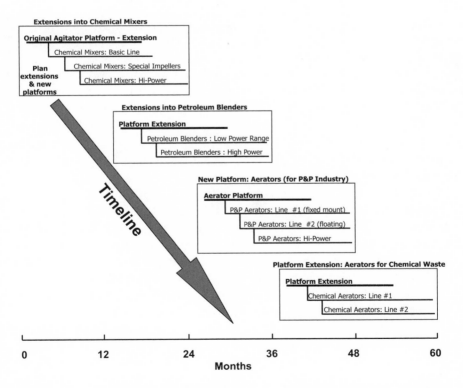

Exhibit 4.12   The Strategic Product Roadmap at Chempro—The New Platforms Major Projects

---

Box 4.5   Platforms: A Base from Which to Operate

Many businesses now look to platforms as a way to think about strategic thrusts in product development. The original notion of a platform was very much **product-based**. For example, the PDMA handbook defines a platform product as "design and components that are shared by a set of products in a product family. From this platform, numerous derivatives can be designed." Thus Chrysler's engine-transmission from its K-car was a platform that spawned other vehicles, including the famous Chrysler minivan.

The notion of platforms has since been broadened to include **technological capabilities**. For example, ExxonMobil's Metallocene platform is simply a catalyst that has yielded an entirely new generation of polymers. Thus a platform is like an oil drilling platform in the ocean, which you invest heavily in. From this platform, you can drill many holes, relatively quickly and at low cost.

In new products, the platform establishes the capability, and this capability spawns many new product projects—much more quickly and cost-effectively than starting from scratch each time. Examples are a deposit software platform in a bank, from which many different end-user deposit products can be developed; or a printer head assembly from which multiple generations of printers are built.

The definition of platforms has also been broadened to include **marketing or branding concepts** as well as technological capabilities. For example, some consider 3M's **Post-It Notes**™ to be a marketing platform, which has created many individual products; while General Mills' **Old El Paso**™ products—a line of Tex-Mex ingredients and complete meals—is another example of a marketing platform.

---

into a product-technology roadmap as a tool to help management link business strategy, product plans, and technology development.[31]

Most often, the specification of projects on your product roadmap is left fairly general and high-level: for example, designations such as "a low-carb beer for the Atkins diet market" or "ceramic-coated tooling for the aerospace industry" or "low power petroleum blenders," as in Exhibit 4.11, are often the way these projects are shown on the product roadmap timeline. That is, *place-marks* for projects "yet to be defined" are the norm: The roadmap is meant to be directional and strategic, but not provide detailed product and project definitions. As each project progresses through the idea-to-launch process, however, increasingly the project and the product become specified and defined.

Developing Your Strategic Product Roadmap

The development of a product roadmap flows logically from your product innovation strategy. Delineating the major initiatives required as part of your product roadmap is a multifaceted task and includes the following:

- *Strategic assessment:* Sometimes the mere specification of a strategic arena as top priority leads logically to a list of those products and projects that are necessary to enter and be successful in that arena. For example, a major health products company identified "wound care" as a priority strategic arena (the company already sold a few products in this health-care sector, but was a minor player). However, once "wound care" was made top priority, the specific products one needed to be a force in this sector became evident, and the development programs to generate these products fell into a logical sequence in a product roadmap.
- *Portfolio review of existing products:* Here, one takes a hard look at the business's current product offerings, and decides which are tired and should be pruned, and which should be replaced. Forecasts of products' life cycles often reveal the need and timing for replacement products, or perhaps even a new platform. Additionally, gaps in the product line are identified. In this way, place-marks are inserted in your product roadmap for these required developments. Such an exercise is undertaken periodically in order to keep the product line fresh, current, and complete.
- *Competitive analysis:* Where are your products and product lines relative to your competitors'? Here you assess your competitors' current and probable future offerings, where they have advantage, and assess your gaps. This exercise often points to the need for new products either immediately or in the foreseeable future.
- *Technology trend assessment:* Here one forecasts technology and what new technologies, and hence new platform developments, will be required and their timing. For example, the advent of each new cell-phone technology signals a host of development projects within cell-phone manufacturing firms, and also within service providers.
- *Market trends assessment:* Again, this is a forecasting exercise, which looks at major market trends and shifts. In this exercise, often you are able to pinpoint specific initiatives that you must undertake in response to these evident trends; for example, in the food business, "the development of a line of nutriceutical 'good-for-you' foods."

Including Platform Developments in Your Roadmap

New and existing platforms are often defined in the strategic product roadmap. For example, having identified certain markets as strategic arenas, in order to win in these market arenas, certain new technology platforms may be envisioned—see Box 4.5.[32]

> *An example:* In the Chempro case, along with strategic buckets, a product roadmap is also developed (Exhibit 4.12). This roadmap outlines the major new product projects and platforms, and their timing, needed to successfully attack the designated strategic arenas.[33] For example, top priority is given to extension of the current platform—agitators and mixers—to both the chemical and petroleum industries. A new platform is envisioned as the next major initiative after extension possibilities are exhausted: Priority is thus given to the development of a family of high-efficiency surface aerators based on this new platform and targeted initially at the pulp and paper industry. Next, extending this new platform into chemical waste treatment is mapped out in the roadmap . . . and so on, as shown in the roadmap in Exhibit 4.11.

Notes for Senior Management

Strategic product roadmaps that lay out the major initiatives—major developments, products, and platforms—is also a powerful concept, and can be used with or without strategic buckets. Note that this roadmap should be strategic, with place-marks for major projects, some of which are yet to be defined. And it should be a timeline for the longer term (not just a list of products and projects for this year). I outlined different approaches for developing your strategic roadmap. And you might also consider taking the next step and develop the technology roadmap, outlining what technologies are needed and when in order to implement the product roadmap.

Putting Your Product Innovation Strategy to Work

We approach the end of the two chapters on product innovation strategy and strategic deployment of resources. Let's reflect on how your product innovation strategy together with strategic portfolio management should guide your business's development efforts.

Discovery: Searching for Product Ideas

Generating great new product ideas (which I label the "Discovery stage") and developing a product innovation and technology strategy overlap considerably—and so they should! Indeed, progressive companies build a heavy dose of strategy development into their Discovery stage: The search for major new product ideas begins with a strategic analysis of your marketplace (or your customer's industry) coupled with a core competencies assessment of your own business. The goal: looking for opportunities in the form of gaps, discontinuities, emerging arenas, new technologies, new platforms, and unarticulated needs.

Your product innovation strategy helps to shape the Discovery stage. For example, specifying your new product arenas (Exhibit 3.11) provides guidance to the idea search effort. Armed with a knowledge of the arenas the business wishes to target, those charged with seeking new product ideas now have a clear definition of where to search: The hunting grounds are defined. Moreover, it becomes feasible to implement formal search programs—seeking unmet customer needs and undertaking voice-of-the-customer research; initiating fundamental scientific research; implementing suggestion schemes, sales force programs, and creativity sessions; and all the other methods highlighted in Chapter 7—to generate new product ideas. The search for ideas is more efficient, generating product ideas that are consistent with the business's focus.

> *An example:* In Chempro's case, all personnel, from the president to sales trainees, gained a clear view of which new product arenas the company wished to concentrate on. First, the strategic exercise identified some "must-do" projects, which are outlined in the product roadmap (Exhibit 4.12). But the new insights also made it possible for good new product ideas in the designated arenas to pour in from everyone in the company.

More Effective Project Selection

The most critical criterion for selecting new product projects is whether the project is aligned with and supports your business's strategy. All too often the question is answered with blank stares and shrugs. A clear delineation of your business's new product arenas provides the criterion essential to answer the "strategic alignment" question. Either the new product proposal under consideration fits into one of the designated arenas, or it does not. And your strategic buckets guide project selection, and force limits on some types of projects. Finally, your strategic product roadmap, which defines place-marks for strategic projects, also provides directional guidance to the selection of specific development projects. The result is more effective and efficient project screening and investment decisions: Precious management time and resources are not wasted on new product proposals that may seem attractive on their own merits, but simply do not mesh with the long-term strategy or direction of the business.

Personnel and Resource Planning

Resources essential to new products—R&D, engineering, marketing, operations—cannot be acquired overnight. Without a definition of which arenas the business intends to target, planning for the acquisition of these resources is like asking a blindfolded person to throw darts.

> *An example:* For Chempro, aerators for the pulp and paper industry is defined as one top-priority arena. R&D management hired researchers in the field of biochemistry and waste treatment; the engineering department acquired new people in the field of aeration equipment design and aeration application engineering; and plans were made to add aeration experts to the sales force. Finally, several small exploratory technical and market research programs were initiated in aeration and bio-oxidation.

Notes for Senior Management

This brings to an end our discussion of developing a product innovation strategy. . . or maybe it's just the beginning for you and your business. You've seen the evidence—how important a product innovation strategy is, and what a strong positive impact such a strategy has on performance. And in this chapter and the previous one, I've laid out a pathway for developing such a strategy. Follow the flow and thought process in Exhibit 3.3. The pathway begins with your goals (Chapter 3) and ends with resource deployment decisions, namely, strategic buckets and strategic roadmaps (in this chapter).

If you're thinking that your business lacks such a clearly articulated innovation strategy, and that maybe now is the time to lay the groundwork for developing such a strategy, you're probably right on both counts. This is a task for the leadership team—the generals!

Notes

1. This chapter is based on a number of books and articles by the author and co-workers: R. G. Cooper, *Product Leadership: Creating and Launching Superior New Products.* Reading, MA: Perseus, 1998; R. G. Cooper, S. J. Edgett, & E. J. Kleinschmidt, *Portfolio Management for New Products,* 2nd ed. Reading, MA: Perseus, 2002; R. G. Cooper, *Winning at New Products: Accelerating the Process from Idea to Launch,* 3rd ed. Reading, MA: Perseus, 2001; R. G. Cooper, S. J. Edgett, &

E. J. Kleinschmidt, "Portfolio Management in New Product Development: Lessons from the Leaders—Part I," *Research-Technology Management*, September–October 1997, 16–28; Part II, November–December 1997, 43–57; R. G. Cooper, S. J. Edgett, & E. J. Kleinschmidt, "New Problems, New Solutions: Making Portfolio Management More Effective," *Research-Technology Management*, 43, 2, 2000, 18–33; and R. G. Cooper, S. J. Edgett, & E. J. Kleinschmidt, "Portfolio Management: Fundamental to New Product Success," in The *PDMA Toolbox for New Product development*, edited by P. Beliveau, A. Griffin, & S. Somermeyer. New York: Wiley, 2002, 331–364.

2. APQC benchmarking study: see note 29 in Chapter 1. Available as: *Best Practices in Product Development: What Distinguishes Top Performers* at www.prod-dev.com.

3. Parts of this section are taken from an article by the author and co-worker: R. G. Cooper & S. J. Edgett, "Overcoming the Crunch in Resources for New Product Development," *Research-Technology Management*, 46, 3, 2003, 48–58.

4. The conclusions regarding NPD resource problems and causes are based on several benchmarking studies cited previously: see note 29 in Chapter 1; also the two portfolio management studies cited: see note 13, below. An additional and rich source of information, particularly the anecdotal information and many quotations cited in this chapter, are the results of "problem detection sessions" held in over 100 businesses over the last three years (this methodology is based on *SG-Bencharker*™—see www.stage-gate.com).

5. APQC benchmarking study: see note 2.

6. APQC benchmarking study: see note 2.

7. APQC benchmarking study: see note 2.

8. Earlier benchmarking studies by Cooper and Kleinschmidt: see note 29 in Chapter 1.

9. R. G. Cooper, *Winning at New Products: Accelerating the Process from Idea to Launch*, 3rd ed. Reading, MA: Perseus, 2001. Chapter 2 provides a good overview of quality of execution in new product projects and insights into which activities are particularly weak. See also Chapter 6.

10. APQC benchmarking study: see note 2. See also Chapter 6 for detailed results on quality of execution.

11. Success/failure studies: see note 28 in Chapter 3.

12. See note 3.

13. The results of the study of portfolio management practices in industry are in R. G. Cooper, S. J. Edgett, & E. J. Kleinschmidt, "Portfolio Management in New Product Development: Lessons from the Leaders—Part I," *Research-Technology Management*, 40, 5, September–October 1997, 16–28; and R. G. Cooper, S. J. Edgett, & E. J. Kleinschmidt, "Portfolio Management in New Product Development: Lessons from the Leaders—Part II," *Research-Technology Management*, 40, 6, November–December 1997, 43–52; also R. G. Cooper, S. J. Edgett, & E. J. Kleinschmidt, "Best Practices for Managing R&D Portfolios," *Research-Technology Management*, 41, 4, July–August 1998, 20–33.

A second major benchmarking study of portfolio management practices, undertaken with the Industrial Research Institute, probes portfolio management practices and performance. Results are in R. G. Cooper, S. J. Edgett, & E. J. Kleinschmidt, "New Product Portfolio Management: Practices and Performance," *Journal of Product Innovation Management*, 16, 4, July 1999, 333–351; and R. G. Cooper, S. J. Edgett, & E. J. Kleinschmidt, "Portfolio Management for New Product Development: Results of an Industry Practices Study," *R&D Management*, 31, 4, October 2001, 361–380.

14. C. M. Crawford, "The Hidden Costs of Accelerated Product Development," *Journal of Product Innovation Management*, 9, 3, September 1992, 188–199.

15. The BCG model is described and assessed in B. Heldey, "Strategy and the Business Portfolio," *Long Range Planning*, 1977; and G. Day, *Analysis for Strategic Marketing Decisions*. St. Paul, MN: West, 1986.

16. A. Griffin & A. L. Page, "PDMA Success Measurement Project: Recommended Measures for Product Development Success and Failure," *Journal of Product Innovation Management*, 13, 6, November 1996, 478–496.

17. APQC benchmarking study: see note 2.

18. Earlier benchmarking studies by Cooper and Kleinschmidt: see note 8.

19. Box 4.2 is modified from R. G. Cooper, "The Invisible Success Factors in Product Innovation," *Journal of Product Innovation Management*, 16, 2, April 1999, 115–133.

20. As reported in R. G. Cooper, *Winning at New Products: Accelerating the Process from Idea to Launch*, 3rd ed. Reading, MA: Perseus, 2001, Chapter 2.

21. Box 4.3 is modified from R. G. Cooper, note 19.

22. Portfolio management is defined in R. G. Cooper, S. J. Edgett, & E. J. Kleinschmidt, "Portfolio Management in New Product Development: Lessons from the Leaders—Part I," *Research-Technology Management*, September–October 1997, 16–28; Part II, November–December 1997, 43–57.

23. P. Roussel, K. N. Saad, & T. J. Erickson, *Third Generation R&D, Managing the Link to Corporate Strategy*. Boston: Harvard Business School Press & Arthur D. Little, Inc., 1991.

24. Portfolio management practices and performance study: see note 13.

25. The results in this section are from the APQC benchmarking study: see note 2. Many of the examples cited are from this study as well.

26. Parts of this section are taken from an article by the author: R. G. Cooper, "Maximizing the Value of Your New Product Portfolio: Methods, Metrics and Scorecards," *Current Issues in Technology Management*. Hoboken, NJ: Stevens Institute of Technology (Stevens Alliance for Technology Management), 7, 1, Winter 2003, 1.

27. E. Roberts & C. Berry, "Entering New Businesses: Selecting Strategies for Success," *Sloan Management Review*, Spring 1983, 3–17.

28. A. Griffin & A. L. Page, see note 16.

29. R. G. Cooper, S. J. Edgett, & E. J. Kleinschmidt, *Portfolio Management for New Products*, 2nd ed. Reading, MA: Perseus, 2002.

30. Much of this section on roadmapping is taken from Lucent Technologies (Bell Labs). See R. E. Albright, "Roadmaps and Roadmapping: Linking Business Strategy and Technology Planning," in *Proceedings, Portfolio Management for New Product Development*, Institute for International Research and Product Development & Management Association, Ft. Lauderdale, FL, January 2001. See also M. H. Meyer & A. P. Lehnerd, *The Power of Platforms*. New York: The Free Press, 1997.

31. Source of technology roadmap definition: see note 29.

32. The PDMA definition of "platform" in the sidebar is found in the glossary of *The PDMA Handbook of New Product Development*, edited by M. D. Rosenau Jr. New York: Wiley, 1996.

33. See Meyer & Lehnerd, note 30.

5

Portfolio Management for New Products—Picking Winners and Investing in the Right Projects

> Take calculated risks. That is quite different from being rash.
> —George S. Patton, U.S. General

Focusing Resources on the Right Projects

There are two fundamental ways to win at new products:[1]

1. *Doing projects right*—ensuring that cross-functional teams are in place, that they do the upfront homework, build in voice-of-the-customer, strive for competitive advantage, are time-driven, and so on. Having a first-rate idea-to-launch process to guide how projects should unfold—the topic of Chapters 6 and 7—is one of the *four points of performance* in the *Innovation Diamond*.
2. *Doing the right projects.* As one executive put it: "Even a blind man can get rich in a goldmine, simply by swinging a pick-axe. You don't have to be a good miner—just be in the right mine!" Thus project selection, a key facet of portfolio management, becomes paramount to new product performance. And that's the topic of this chapter—picking the right new product and development projects to invest in.

New product resources are too valuable and scarce to waste on the wrong projects. But many new product projects are losers. Either they fail commercially in the marketplace, or they are cancelled prior to product launch: Only one in seven concepts actually becomes a commercial winner.[2]

Project selection—the ability to pick the right projects for investment—therefore becomes a critically important task for the leadership team of the business.[3]

Two Decision Levels in Portfolio Management

Recall from the previous chapter that strategic decisions and portfolio management can be treated as a hierarchical process, with two levels of decision making (see Exhibit 5.1):[4]

1. **Strategic portfolio decisions:** Strategic portfolio decisions answer the question: Where should your business spend its NPD resources (people and funds)? Establishing *strategic buckets* and defining *strategic product roadmaps* are effective tools that I proposed in Chapter 4.
2. **Tactical portfolio decisions:** Tactical portfolio decisions focus on projects, and address the questions: What specific new product and development projects should you do? What are their relative priorities? And what resources should be allocated to each? Such tactical decisions are shown at the bottom part of Exhibit 5.1, and are the main topic of this chapter.

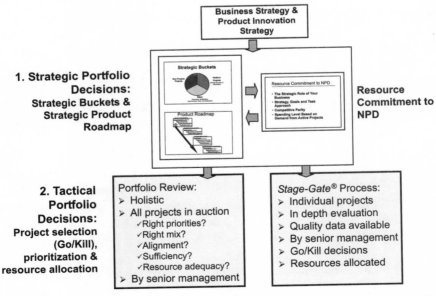

Exhibit 5.1 The Portfolio Management System and Its Elements—the Two Levels of Decision Making

To make effective tactical decisions, I recommend that you install two project selection processes, working in harmony as in Exhibit 5.1 (bottom):

1. Gates: Embedded within your idea-to-launch new product framework are Go/Kill decision-points called "gates" (bottom right of Exhibit 5.1). Gates provide an in-depth review of individual projects, and render Go/Kill, prioritization, and resource allocation decisions—hence gates must be part of your portfolio management system.

Many companies already have a gating process in place, and confuse that with a comprehensive portfolio management system. Doing the *right projects* is more than simply individual project selection at gate meetings; rather, it's about the *entire mix* of projects and new product or technology investments that your business makes:

- Project selection *deals only with the fingers*: Go/Kill decisions are made on individual projects, each judged individually and on its own merits.
- Portfolio management deals *with the fist*: It is holistic, and looks at the entire set of project investments together.

2. Portfolio review: The second decision process is the periodic *portfolio review* (bottom left of Exhibit 5.1). Senior management meets perhaps two to four times per year to review the portfolio of all projects. Here, senior management also makes Go/Kill and prioritization decisions, where *all projects* are considered on the table together, and all or some could be *up for auction*. Key issues and questions are:

- ✓ Are all projects strategically aligned (fit the business's strategy)?
- ✓ Do you have the right priorities among projects?
- ✓ Are there some projects on the active list that you should kill? Or perhaps accelerate?
- ✓ Is there the right balance of projects? the right mix?
- ✓ Are there enough resources to do all these projects?
- ✓ Do you have sufficiency—if you do these projects, will you achieve your stated business goals?

Both decision processes—gating and portfolio reviews—are needed. Note that the gates are project-specific and provide a thorough review of each project, in-depth and in real time. By contrast, the portfolio reviews are holistic: They look at all projects together, but in much less detail on each project. In some businesses, if the gates are working, not too many decisions or major corrective actions are even required at the portfolio review. Some companies indicate that they don't even look at individual projects at the portfolio review, but only consider projects in aggregate! But in other businesses, the majority of decisions are made at these quarterly or semi-annual portfolio reviews.

Notes for Senior Management

Establish a hierarchical approach to portfolio management, as in Exhibit 5.1. Recognize that there are strategic decisions (directional and high-level) and tactical decisions (project selection and prioritization). The strategic portfolio decisions were dealt with in the previous chapter; you should employ either strategic buckets or strategic product roadmaps (or both) in order to translate your strategy into operational decisions. But recognize that project decisions—Go/Kill, prioritization, and resource allocation—must still be made. Two decision processes complement each other here: your idea-to-launch *gating process*, which focuses on individual projects; and your *portfolio review* approach, which looks at the entire set of projects.

The Tools to Use for Effective Gates and Portfolio Reviews

Within these gates and portfolio reviews, a number of tools can be used to help you achieve your portfolio goals, namely, maximize your portfolio's value, achieve the right balance and mix or projects, and ensure portfolio sufficiency, yet not overload the development pipeline.

Maximizing the Value of Your Portfolio

The methods used to achieve this goal range from financial models to balanced scorecard models. Each has its strengths and weaknesses. The end result of each is a rank-ordered or prioritized list of "Go" and "Hold" projects, with the projects at the top of the list scoring highest in terms of achieving the desired objectives: The portfolio's value in terms of that objective is thus maximized. Here are the specific methods:

1. Rank your projects using their economic value, or net present value (NPV): The simplest approach is merely to calculate the NPV of each project on a spreadsheet. Most businesses already require the NPV and a financial spreadsheet as part of the project's business case, so the NPV number is already available.

The NPV, a proxy for the *economic value* of the project to the business, can be used in two ways:

- First, make Go/Kill decisions at gates based on NPV. Require that your project teams use the minimum acceptable financial return or hurdle rate (as a percent) for projects of this risk level as the discount rate when calculating their projects' NPVs. If the NPV is positive, then the project clears the hurdle rate. So NPV is a key input to Go/Kill decision at gates.

  Suggestion: Ask your finance department to develop a *standardized spreadsheet* for this calculation (so all project teams produce a consistently calculated NPV). Also, ask the finance department to develop a table of *risk-adjusted discount rates* for project teams to use for different risk levels of projects: low risk (a cost reduction) to high risk (genuine new product, first of its kind).

- Second, at portfolio reviews, rank all projects according to their NPVs. The Go projects are at the top of the list. Continue adding projects down the list until you run out of resources. You end up with a prioritized list of projects, which logically should maximize the NPV of your portfolio (example in Exhibit 5.2).

Project	PV (present value of future earnings)	Develop- ment Cost	Commer- cialization Cost	NPV (net present value)	Ranking Based on NPV	Decision
Alpha	30	3	5	22	4	Hold
Beta	64	5	2	57	2	Go
Gamma	9	2	1	6	5	Hold
Delta	3	1	0.5	1.5	6	Hold
Echo	50	5	3	42	3	Hold
Foxtrot	66	10	2	58	1	Go

All figures are $M.
Using this method, the top four projects are: Foxtrot, Beta, Echo and Alpha.
There is a resource limit of $15M Development budget, however.
Thus, only two projects are Go: Foxtrot and Beta (these two top-rated projects consume all the $15M). The value of the portfgolio is NPV = $115M from these two projects.

Exhibit 5.2   Using NPV to Rank and Prioritize Projects

Fine in theory . . . but there are some problems: The NPV method assumes that financial projections are accurate (they usually are not!); it assumes that only financial goals are important—for example, that strategic considerations are irrelevant; it ignores probabilities of success and risk (except by using risk-adjusted discount rates); and it fails to deal with constrained resources—the desire to maximize the value for a limited resource commitment, or getting the most bang for the limited buck. A final objection is more subtle: the fact that NPV assumes an all-or-nothing investment decision, whereas in new product projects, the decision process is an incremental one, more like buying a *series of options* on a project.[5]

This NPV method has a number of attractive features, however. First, it requires the project team to submit a financial assessment of the project: That means they must do some research, make some fact-based projections, and think through the commercial implications of the project. Second, a discounted cash flow method is used, which is the correct way to value investments (as opposed to the ROI or payback period). Finally, all monetary amounts are discounted to today (not just to launch date), thereby appropriately penalizing projects that are years away from launch.

2. Rank your projects using the productivity index based on the NPV: Here's an important modification to the NPV ranking approach in order to maximize the value of your portfolio, but recognizing that you have limited resources.[6] The problem is that some projects—for example, Foxtrot and Beta in Exhibit 5.2—are great projects and have huge NPVs, but they consume a lot of resources, thus making it impossible to do other less attractive but far more efficient projects. Other projects, although having lower NPVs, are quite efficient: They can be done using relatively few resources. How does one decide?

Simple: The goal is to maximize the bang for buck. And the way to do this is to take the ratio of what one is trying to maximize (in this case, the NPV) divided by the constraining resource (the R&D dollars required)—and voilà, the bang for buck.* You may choose to use R&D people, or work-months, or the total dollar cost remaining in the project (or even capital funds) as the constraining resource. This bang-for-buck ratio, or "productivity index," is shown in column 4 in Exhibit 5.3:

$$\text{Productivity Index} = \frac{\text{NPV of the project}}{\text{Total resources remaining to be spent on the project}}$$

*This decision rule of rank-order according to the ratio of what one is trying to maximize divided by the constraining resource seems to be an effective one. Simulations with a number of sets of projects show that this decision rule works very well, truly giving "maximum bang for buck"!

Project	NPV	Develop-ment Cost	Productivity Index=NPV/ Dev Cost	Sum of Dev Costs
Beta	57	5	11.4	5
Echo	42	5	8.4	10
Alpha	22	3	7.3	13 Limit reached
Foxtrot	58	10	5.8	23
Gamma	6	2	3.0	25
Delta	1.5	1	1.5	26

The Productivity Index is used to rank projects until out of resources. The horizontal line shows the limit: $15M Development Costs is reached.
Go projects are now Beta, Echo and Alpha. Foxtrot drops off the list. The value of the Portfolio is NPV = $121M from these three projects.

Exhibit 5.3 Ranking Projects According to the NPV-Based Productivity Index

Now it's time to re-sort the list of projects. But first the constraint: The R&D spending constraint is $15 million for new products in this business (and the projects add up to $26 million in Exhibit 5.3). To select the Go projects, simply reorder the project list, ranking projects according to the productivity index (this reordering is shown in Exhibit 5.3). Then go down the list until you run out of resources. Note that column 6 shows the cumulative resource expenditure. You run out of resources—hit the $15 million limit—after Project Alpha.

The point to note here is that introducing the notion of constrained resources, which every business has, dramatically changes the ranking of projects. Compare the ranked list in Exhibit 5.2 with that in Exhibit 5.3: Note that Foxtrot, the number one project in Exhibit 5.2, drops off the list entirely using the productivity index in Exhibit 5.3; the resulting portfolio contains more projects, and its overall economic value is higher.

This NPV-productivity-index method yields benefits in addition to those inherent in the straight NPV approach. By introducing the productivity index ratio, the method favors those projects that are almost completed (the denominator is small, hence the productivity index is high). And the method deals with resource constraints, yielding the best set of projects for a given budget or resource limit.

3. Introduce risk by using expected commercial value (ECV): This method seeks to maximize the commercial value of your portfolio, subject to certain budget constraints, but introduces the notion of *risks and probabilities*. The ECV method determines the probability-adjusted value of each project to the corporation, namely, its *expected commercial value*. The calculation of the ECV is based on a decision tree analysis and considers the future stream of earnings from the project, the probabilities of both commercial success and technical success, and both commercialization costs and development costs (see Exhibit 5.4 for the calculation and definition of terms). Because the method treats NPD investment decisions in a series of stages, the solution is a close proxy for *options pricing theory* or *real options*.

The ECV can be used at gate meetings as an input to the Go/Kill decision, much like the NPV, except risk and probabilities are built in. For portfolio reviews, in order to arrive at a prioritized list of projects, consider what resources are scarce or limiting, much like the NPV-productivity-index example above. Then, take the ratio of what you are trying to maximize—the ECV—divided by the constraining resource to yield another version of the productivity index. Projects are rank-ordered according to this new productivity index until the resource limit is reached: projects at the top of the list are Go, while those at the bottom (beyond the resource

A model of a two-stage investment decision process: First, invest $D in development, which may yield a technical success with probability P_t. Then invest $C in commercialization, which may result in a commercial success with probability P_{cs}. If successful, the project yields an income stream whose present value is $PV. More sophisticated versions of this model would entail more stages than the two shown here, and an araray of possible outcomes from each stage.

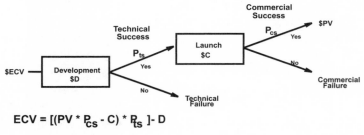

$$ECV = [(PV * P_{cs} - C) * P_{ts}] - D$$

ECV = Expected Commercial Value of the project

P_{ts} = Probability of Technical Success

P_{cs} = Probability of Commercial Success (given technical success)

D = Development Costs remaining in the project

C = Commercialization (Launch) Costs

PV = Net Present Value of project's future earnings (discounted to today)

Exhibit 5.4 Determination of Expected Commercial Value of a Product
Source: As reported in notes 13 and 29 in Chapter 4.

limit) are placed on Hold. The method thus ensures the greatest "bang for buck"; that is, the ECV is maximized for a given resources limit.

This ECV model has a number of attractive additional features: It includes probabilities and risk, which are inherent in any new product project; it recognizes that the Go/Kill decision process is an incremental one (the notion of purchasing options—a stage-wise decision process); and it deals with the issue of constrained resources, and attempts to maximize the value of the portfolio in light of this constraint.

4. Try a simulation financial model for major projects: Another way to introduce risk and probabilities is the use of a computer-based Monte Carlo simulation model, such as *At Risk*. Here's how these models are used: Instead of merely inputting a point estimate for each financial variable in your spreadsheet, such as Year 1 Sales, Year 2 Sales, and so on, one inputs three estimates for each variable: a best case, a worst case, and a likely case. A probability curve (much like a bell-shaped curve) is drawn through each set of estimates. So each financial estimate—sales, costs, investment, and so on—has a probability distribution.

The model begins by calculating multiple scenarios of possible financial outcomes, all based on your probability distributions. Tens of thousands of scenarios are quickly generated by the computer, each one yielding a financial outcome such as the NPV. The distribution of the NPVs generated in these thousands of scenarios becomes your profit distribution—an expected NPV as well as a probability distribution of NPVs.

You can use the NPV and its distribution to help make the Go/Kill decision at gates, much like in method 1 above; and then take the expected NPV and divide by the costs remaining in the project, and rank the projects according to this probability-adjusted NPV, much like in method 2 above.

These models, such as *At Risk*, are commercially available and relatively easy to use. But there are a few quirks or assumptions in the model that cause problems. For example, the model fails to deal with the options notion of a new product projects, and it permits the generation of all-but-impossible scenarios. Nonetheless, it's a solid method, and particularly appropriate for projects that involve large capital expenditures and where probability distributions of input variables are available.

5. Use a balanced scorecard approach: Scoring models or balanced scorecards are based on the premise that a more balanced approach to project selection is desirable—that not everything can be reduced to a single NPV or ECV metric. Thus a variety of criteria are used to rate the project. These criteria are based on research into what makes new product projects successful, and hence are proven proxies for success and profitability.

In a scorecard system, senior managers each rate the project on a number of criteria on 1–5 or 0–10 scales. Typical criteria include:

✓ strategic alignment
✓ product and competitive advantage
✓ market attractiveness
✓ ability to leverage core competencies
✓ technical feasibility
✓ reward versus risk

The scores from the various gatekeepers at the gate review are tallied and combined, and the project attractiveness score—the weighted or unweighted addition of the item ratings—is computed. This attractiveness score is the basis for making the Go/Kill decision at gates, and can also be used to develop a rank-ordered list of projects for portfolio reviews. A sample scoring model for well-defined new product projects is shown in Exhibit 5.5.

Scoring models generally are praised in spite of their limited popularity. Research into project selection methods reveals that scoring models produce a strategically aligned portfolio that reflects the business's spending priorities; they yield effective and efficient decisions, better than financial tools; and they result in a portfolio of high-value projects.[7]

Factor 1: Strategic Fit & Importance
• Alignment of project with our business's strategy
• Importance of project to the strategy
• Impact on the business

Factor 2: Product & Competitive Advantage
• Product delivers unique customer or user benefits
• Product offers customer/user excellent value for money
• Competitive rationale for project
• Positive customer/user feedback on product concept (concept test results)

Factor 3: Market Attractiveness
• Market size
• Market growth & future potential
• Margins earned by players in this market
• Competitiveness – how tough & intense competition is

Factor 4: Core Competencies Leverage
• Project leverages our core competencies & strengths in:
  - technology
  - production/operations
  - marketing
  - distribution/salesforce

Factor 5: Technical Feasibility
• Size of technical gap
• Familiarity of technology to our business
• Newness of technology (base to embryonic)
• Technical complexity
• Technical results to date (proof of concept?)

Factor 6: Financial Reward vs. Risk
• Size of financial opportunity
• Financial return (NPV, ECV)
• Productivity index
• Certainty of financial estimates
• Level of risk & ability to address risks

Projects are scored by the gatekeepers (senior management) at the gate meeting, using these six factors on a scorecard (0-10 scales). The scores are tallied, averaged across the evaluators, and displayed for discussion. The Project Attractiveness Score is the weighted or unweighted addition of the scores, taken out of 100. A score of 60/100 is usually required for a Go decision.

Exhibit 5.5 A Typical Balanced Scorecard for NP Project Selection

6. Evaluate radical innovations and disruptive technologies differently: Many companies seek a target proportion of breakthroughs, radical innovations, and disruptive technology projects within their development portfolios, perhaps 10 to 20% of the total. This is a laudable goal, as evidenced from the portfolio breakdown of top-performing businesses in Exhibit 4.9. These more venturesome projects should be included in the strategic buckets determination: For example, in Honeywell's "Mercedes Star" diagram (Exhibit 4.6), the category "platforms that will change the basis of competition" denotes spending destined for breakthrough platforms—radical innovations and significant technology projects; that is, the business deliberately sets aside a certain percentage of resources for more radical projects. Some businesses even include such radical innovations in their product or technology roadmaps.

Tactically, however, these same organizations often cannot cope with such projects once they enter their idea-to-launch framework. In Chapter 7, I recommend that you adopt a special version of *Stage-Gate®* to handle these radical projects: the *technology development process* (see Exhibit 7.7). And be sure to evaluate radical innovations or disruptive technology projects differently than traditional new product projects. One of the strengths of the strategic buckets approach is that different types of projects are separated into different categories, so that you do not compare apples and oranges, and that *different evaluation criteria are used for projects in different buckets.*

If you have established a bucket for "radical innovations" or "disruptive technology projects," then be sure to use different criteria for these types of projects—criteria that are more visionary and less financial, and recognize that such projects are less predicable and more loosely defined. Exhibit 5.6 shows a sample scorecard used for advanced technology and radical innovation projects[8]—a scorecard that is quite different from the one for normal new products in Exhibit 5.5.

Seeking the Right Balance of Projects

A major portfolio goal is a balanced portfolio: a balanced set of development projects in terms of a number of key parameters. The analogy is that of an investment fund, where the fund manager seeks balance in terms of high-risk versus blue chip stocks, and balance across industries and geographies, in order to arrive at an optimum investment portfolio.

Visual charts effectively display balance in new product project portfolios. These visual representations include portfolio maps or bubble diagrams (Exhibit 5.7)—an adaptation of the four-quadrant BCG (Star; Cash Cow; Dog; Wildcat) diagrams that have seen service since the 1970s as strategy models—as well as more traditional pie charts and histograms.

	Score = 0 (on 0-10 scale)	Score = 10 (on 0-10 scale)
1. Business Strategy Fit		
Congruence	Only peripheral fit with our business strategies	Strong fit with several key elements of strategy
Impact	Minimal impact; no noticeable harm if program dropped	Business unit future depends on this program
2. Strategic Leverage		
Propriety Position	Easily copied; no protection	Position protected (upstream & downstream) through a combination of patents, trade secrets, raw material access, etc.
Platform for Growth	Dead end; one-of-a-kind; one-off	Opens up many new product possibilities in new technical & commercial fields
Durability (technical & marketing)	No distinctive advantage; quickly leapfrogged	Long life cycle with opportunity for incremental improvements
Synergy with Other Operations within the Corporation	Limited to a single business unit	Could be applied widely across the corporation
3. Probability of Technical Success		
Technical Gap	Large gap between solution & current practice; must invent new science	Incremental improvement; easy to do
Program Complexity	Difficult to envision the solution; many hurdles along the way	Can see a solution; straightforward to do
Technology Skill Base	Technology new to company; almost no skills	Technology widely practiced within the company
Availability of People & Facilities	Must hire & build	People & facilities immediately available
4. Probability of Commercial Success		
Market Need	Extensive market development required; no apparent market need	Product immediately responsive to a customer need; a large market exists
Market Maturity	Declining markets	Rapid growth markets
Competitive Intensity	High; many tough competitors in this field	Low; few competitors; not strong
Commercial Applications Development Skills	New to company; must develop	Already in place
Commercial Assumptions	Low probability; very speculative	Highly predicable; high probability
Regulatory/Social/Political Impact	Negative	Positive impact on high profile issue
4. Reward		
Absolute Contribution to Profitability (5 year cumulative once commercial; ball-park estimates only)	Less then $10M	More than $250M
Payback Period (guestimate)	Greater than 10 years	Less than 3 years
Time to Commercial Start-up	Greater than 7 years	Less than 1 year

Exhibit 5.6 A Sample Scorecard for Advanced Technology Projects

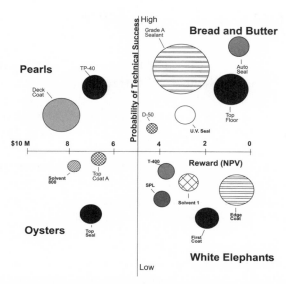

Projects are plotted as bubbles on this two-dimensional risk and reward grid. The bubble sizes denote the resources committed to each project.

Exhibit 5.7   The Popular Risk-Reward Bubble Diagram

A casual review of portfolio bubble diagrams will lead some readers to observe that "these new models are nothing more than the old strategy bubble diagrams of the 70s!" *Not so.* Recall that the BCG strategy model, and others like it (such as the McKinsey-GE model), plot *business units* on a "market attractiveness" versus "business position" grid. Note that the unit of analysis is the business unit—an existing business, whose performance, strengths, and weaknesses are all known. By contrast, today's new product portfolio bubble diagrams, while they may appear similar, plot individual new product projects—future businesses, or *what might be.* As for the dimensions of the grid, here too the "market attractiveness" versus "business position" dimensions used for existing business units may not be as appropriate for new product possibilities, so other dimensions or axes are extensively used.

What are some of the parameters that your business should plot on these portfolio diagrams in order to seek balance? Different pundits recommend various parameters and lists, and even suggest the best plots to use:

1. Risk-reward bubble diagrams: The most popular bubble diagram is the *risk-return chart* (see Exhibit 5.7). About 44% of businesses with a systematic portfolio management scheme in place use this bubble diagram or one like it.[9] Here, one axis is some measure of the *reward* to the company, the other is a *success probability*:

▶ One approach is to use a *qualitative estimate* of reward, ranging from "modest" to "excellent."[10] The argument here is that too heavy an emphasis on financial analysis can do serious damage, notably in the early stages of a project. The other axis is the probability of overall success (probability of *commercial* success times probability of *technical* success).

▶ In contrast, other firms rely on very quantitative and financial gauges of reward, namely, the probability-adjusted NPV of the project.[11] Here the probability of *technical* success is the vertical axis, as probability of commercial success has already been built into the NPV calculation.

A sample bubble diagram is shown in Exhibit 5.7 for a business unit of a major chemical company. Here the size of each bubble shows the annual resources committed to each project (in dollars per year; it could also be people or work-months allocated to the project).

The four quadrants of the portfolio model in Exhibit 5.7 are:

▶ *Pearls* (upper left quadrant): These are the potential star products—projects with a high likelihood of success, and which are also expected to yield a very high reward. Most businesses desire more of these. There are two such Pearl projects, and one of them has been allocated considerable resources (denoted by the sizes of the circles).

▶ *Oysters* (lower left): These are the *long-shot* projects—projects with a high expected payoff, but with low likelihoods of technical success. They are the projects where technical breakthroughs will pave the way for solid payoffs. There are three of these; none is receiving many resources.

▶ *Bread and Butter* (upper right): These are small, simple projects—high likelihood of success, but low reward. They include the many fixes, extensions, modifications, and updating of projects of which most companies have too many. More than 50% of spending is going to these Bread and Butter projects in Exhibit 5.7.

▶ *White Elephants* (lower right). These are the low-probability and low-reward projects. Every business has a few White Elephants—they inevitably are difficult to kill; but this company has far too many. One-third of the projects and about 25% of spending falls in the lower right White Elephant quadrant.

Given that this chemical business is in a speciality area and is a star business seeking rapid growth, a quick review of the portfolio map in Exhibit 5.7 reveals many problems. There are too many White Elephant projects (it's time to do some serious project pruning!); too much money spent on Bread and Butter, low-value projects; not enough Pearls; and heavily under-resourced Oysters.

One feature of this bubble diagram model is that it forces senior management to deal with the resource issue. Given finite resources, *the sum of the areas of the circles must be a constant*. That is, if you add one project to the diagram, you must subtract another; alternatively, you can shrink the size of several circles. The elegance here is that the model forces management to consider the resource implications of adding one more project to the list—that some other projects must pay the price!

Also shown in this bubble diagram is the product line that each project is associated with (via the shading or cross-hatching). A final breakdown is via color (timing) (not shown in my black-and-white map). Thus, this apparently simple risk-reward diagram shows a lot more than simply risk and profitability data: It also conveys resource allocation, timing, and spending breakdowns across product lines.

2. Bubble diagrams with axes derived from scoring models: A combination scoring model and bubble diagram approach can also be employed to visualize the risk profile of your portfolio. Here, the scoring model is used to make Go/Kill decisions on projects and also to rank-order projects on a prioritization list. In this example from Speciality Minerals, Inc., seven factors are considered in the firm's scoring model (see Exhibit 5.8). These *same factors* then provide the input data to construct the bubble diagram:

- ✓ The horizontal axis, labeled "value to the company," is comprised of the financial attractiveness and competitive advantage factors, added together in a weighed fashion.
- ✓ The vertical axis is "probability of success" and is made up of three factors: customer interest, technical feasibility, and fit with technical/manufacturing capabilities (again, a weighted addition).

The unique feature here is that this company's seven-factor scoring model does double duty: It is the basis for Go/Kill decisions at gate reviews. It also provides five of the factors (and data) to construct the two axes of the portfolio bubble diagram.

3. Bubble diagrams that capture newness-to-the-firm: Two key dimensions that senior managers should consider when mapping their development portfolio are:[12]

- ◗ market newness—how new or "step-out" the markets are for projects underway
- ◗ technology newness—how new the development and manufacturing technology is to the business.

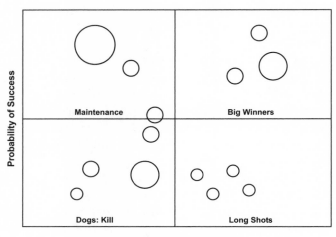

The two axes – Value and Probability – are computed from Scoring Model (Scorecard) results (0-10 scales)
The computation is:
   •Value = .67 (Profitability) + .33 (Competitive Advantage)
   •Probability of Success = .25 (Customer Interest) + .5 (Technical Feasibility) + .25 (Fit)

Exhibit 5.8   Risk-Reward Bubble Diagram Using Scored Axes

Source: Specialty Minerals Inc.; reported in *Portfolio Management for New Products,* note 1.

Both dimensions are proxies for risk and aggressiveness (Exhibit 5.9).

Here, development projects are plotted on these two axes in order to help management view the current portfolio, and whether it has the right balance and mix of step-out versus close-to-home projects. Again, circle sizes denote resources allocated to each project. This is the second most popular bubble diagram used for NPD portfolio management by industry.

4. Traditional charts to display resource breakdowns: There are numerous other parameters, dimensions, or variables across which one might wish to seek a balance of projects. As a result, there is an endless variety of histograms and pie charts that help to portray portfolio balance. Some examples:

Resource breakdown by project types is a vital concern. What is your spending on genuine new products versus product renewals (improvements and replacements), or product extensions, or product maintenance, or cost reductions and process improvements? And what should it be? Pie charts effectively capture the spending split across project types—actual versus desired splits (Exhibit 5.10). Pie charts that show the resource breakdown by project types are a particularly useful sanity check when your business has already established strategic buckets, as outlined in Chapter 4. Now you can compare the current resource split—the "what is"—to the target

Projects are shown as bubbles, whose size denotes resources being spent on each project.

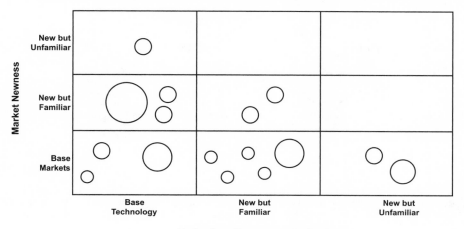

Exhibit 5.9 Familiarity Matrix Bubble Diagram—Resource Split Across Market and Technology Newness Categories

Source: Bayer Inc., as reported in *Portfolio Management for New Products,* note 1.

split—the "what should be"—as defined by your strategic buckets, as in Exhibit 5.10.

Markets, products, and technologies provide another set of dimensions across which managers seek balance. The question is: Do you have the appropriate split in R&D spending across your various product lines? Or across the markets or market segments in which you operate (see Exhibit 5.10)? Or across the technologies you possess? Pie charts are appropriate for capturing and displaying this type of data. And once, again, these pie charts close the loop on your strategic buckets exercise, revealing the "what is" versus the "what should be."

Timing is a key issue in the quest for balance. One does not wish to invest strictly in short-term projects, nor totally in long-term ones. Another timing goal is for a steady stream of new product launches spread out over the quarters—constant "new news," and no sudden logjam of product launches all in one quarter. A histogram captures the issue of timing and portrays the distribution of resources to specific projects according to quarters or years of launch.

Another timing issue is *cash flow*. Here the desire is to balance one's projects in such a way that cash inflows are reasonably balanced with cash outflows in the business. Some companies produce a timing histogram that portrays the total cash flow per year from all projects in the portfolio over the next three to five years.

Breakdown by Project Types   **Breakdown by Market Sector**

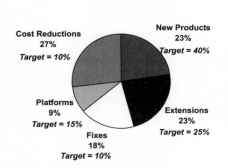

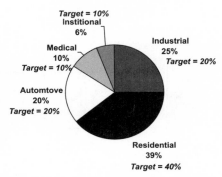

A Strategic Buckets exercise yields target splits, shown in italics (see Chapter 4). The pie chart slices show expenditure breakdowns to date. Note that Market Sector splits (right pie) are almost "on target", but Project Types (left pie) are too heaviliy weighted towards Cost Reductions & Fixes.

Exhibit 5.10   Pie Charts Showing Actual Versus Targeted Resource Allocation in the Portfolio

Ensuring Portfolio Sufficiency Versus Your Overall NPD Goals

Here the concept is quite simple, although the calculations are a little too complex to go into much detail here. The question is: When you consider the new product projects you plan to do, will their expected results satisfy your business goals?

> *An example:* Suppose you had set a goal for the next year (2006) of "18% of sales will come from new products, launched within the previous three years" (refer to Exhibit 5.11, top, left). Your total sales that year are forecast to be $200 million, so sales from new products must equal $36 million in 2006.
>
> What will be the source of these sales? Since the goal was for products "launched in last three years," you can count back two years: sales from products launched in 2005 and 2004. These products have already been launched and are on the market, so forecasts for the next year (2006) should be fairly reliable: $20 million.
>
> Now consider all projects currently in your development pipeline that will yield sales in 2006. Estimate their 2006 sales and apply a probability factor, because these sales estimates of future products are always optimistic (see Exhibit 5.11, bottom, left)! These sales from "projects in the pipe" are estimated to be $12 million.
>
> The vertical bar chart in Exhibit 5.11 shows the gap: $4 million, or about 11% short. That is, this business's current development portfolio

Information:

Projected Company Sales [Year 2006]	$200 M
NP goals: % of Sales, 3 yrs	18%
Goals translated into dollars (for 2006)	$36 M
2006 projected sales, products already launched	$20 M
2006 Sales from projects in the pipe	$12 M
Total Sales Expected	$32 M
Gap	$4 M

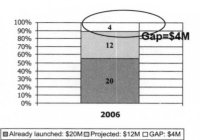

Projects in the Pipeline ($000)

Project	Projected Sales: 2006	Probability	Adjusted Sales: 2006
Alpha	$4,200	80%	$3,360
Beta	3,000	70%	2,100
Gamma	2,500	80%	2,000
Delta	1,780	50%	890
Epsilon	1,300	50%	650
Other: Small	3,000	75%	3,000
Total			**$12,000**

Exhibit 5.11   Sufficiency Test of the Portfolio—One Year Ahead

is deemed *insufficient*: The portfolio will not meet the business's goals. Given this early alert, management can take timely steps to either improve the portfolio or perhaps rethink their 2006 goals.

Balancing the Number of Projects with the Resources Available

Don't overload the development pipeline! Inherent in many of the project selection tools outlined above are *resource constraints*. That is, management must try to achieve the goals of maximum value, strategic alignment, and the right balance, but always wary of the fact that if too many projects are approved for the limited resources, then *pipeline gridlock* is the result. Note that many of the tools outlined above do indeed deal with resource constraints. For example, the productivity index versions of NPV and ECV rank projects until out of resources, and bubble diagrams show resources allocated to projects as the bubble sizes. Nonetheless, some managements ignore the resource constraint, and begin to overload the NPD pipeline with too many projects.

The problem of too many projects and too few resources can be partly resolved by undertaking a final check in the form of a *resource capacity-versus-demand analysis*, introduced in the previous chapter.[13] When you compare the resources available in your business against the resources required to undertake the active projects in your development pipeline, you usually discover two things:

▶ First, you find a gap between resources available and resource demand. This gap means that projects will either take longer than anticipated, or project teams will cut corners and skip steps in order to meet their timelines.

▶ Second, you often find major gaps in specific departments, hence potential bottlenecks. Then senior management must decide how many of the "approved" projects can realistically be done, given the resource capacity analysis results. Often at portfolio reviews, senior management is forced to put a cap on active projects, and put some on hold.

Popularity and Effectiveness of Portfolio Methods

Which methods are the most popular? And which work the best? In practice, not surprisingly, the *financial methods* dominate portfolio management, according to our portfolio best practices study.[14] Financial methods include various profitability and return metrics, such as NPV, ECV, ROI, EVA, or payback period—metrics that are used to rate, rank-order, and ultimately select projects. A total of 77.3% of businesses use such a financial approach in portfolio management (see Exhibit 5.12). For 40.4% of businesses, this is the *dominant method*.

Other methods are also quite popular:

▶ *Strategic approaches:* Letting the strategy dictate the portfolio is a popular approach, and includes strategic buckets, product roadmapping, and other strategically driven methods. A total of 64.8% of businesses use a strategic approach; for 26.6% of businesses, this is the dominant method.

▶ *Bubble diagrams or portfolio maps:* 40.6% of businesses use portfolio maps, but only 8.3% use this as their dominant method. The most popular map is the risk-versus-reward map in Exhibit 5.7, but many variants of bubble diagrams are used.

▶ *Scoring or scorecard models:* Scaled ratings are obtained by using scorecards at gates, and are added to yield a project attractiveness score. These models are used by 37.9% of businesses; in 18.3%, this is the dominant decision method.

▶ *Checklists:* Projects are evaluated on a set of Yes/No questions. Each project must achieve either all Yes answers, or a certain number of Yes

---

Notes for Senior Management

You've seen a number of methods to rate, rank, and balance projects in your development portfolio. By now, you're probably a bit overwhelmed—but no one said portfolio management is easy!

Some tips:

▸ Use one of the financial models—NPV or ECV—to help make gate Go/Kill decisions; but also use the *productivity index* calculated from the NPV or ECV for ranking projects at portfolio reviews.

▸ In conjunction, use a balanced scorecard at the gate meetings (Exhibit 5.5 provides an outline of a first-rate scorecard). And if you are doing quite different types of projects, consider *different scorecards* for these different project types—the scorecard in Exhibit 5.5 for normal new products; Exhibit 5.6 for radical innovations and technology developments; and so on.

▸ Select and use one bubble diagram, either the popular risk-reward diagram in Exhibit 5.7, or the newness diagram in Exhibit 5.9. Both capture the risk profile of your portfolio.

▸ Show the balance by using perhaps two or three pie charts. Break down your resources by project types, geographies, and business areas (business areas can be markets, industry sectors, product lines, or anything that's relevant to you, the leadership team of the business). And compare these pie chart splits—the "what is"—with your strategic buckets—the "what should be."

▸ Make sure someone has done the sufficiency calculation as well as the resource capacity analysis, and presents these results at your portfolio review for debate and discussion.

---

answers to proceed. The number of Yes's is used to make Go/Kill and/or prioritization (ranking) decisions. Only 17.5% of businesses use checklists; and in only 2.7% is this the dominant method.

Popularity does not necessarily equate to effectiveness, however. When the performance of businesses' portfolios was rated on six metrics in our study, those businesses that relied heavily on financial tools as the dominant portfolio selection model *fared the worst*. Financial tools yield an unbalanced portfolio of lower-value projects and projects that lack strategic alignment. By contrast, strategic methods produce a strategically aligned and balanced portfolio. And scorecard models appear best for selecting high-value projects, and also yield a balanced portfolio. Finally,

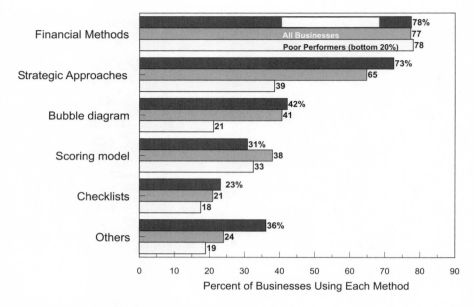

Exhibit 5.12 Popularity of Portfolio Methods

businesses using bubble diagrams obtain a balanced and strategically aligned portfolio.

It is ironic that the most rigorous techniques—the various financial tools—yield the worst results, not so much because the methods are flawed, but simply because reliable financial data are often missing at the very point in a project where the key project selection decisions are made. Often, reliable financial data—expected sales, pricing, margins, and costs—are difficult to estimate, in many cases because the project team simply has not done their homework. As one executive exclaimed, "We're trying to measure a soft banana with a micrometer," as he referred to his business's sophisticated financial model being applied to projects with very soft data. In other cases, it's a matter of an over-zealous project leader making highly optimistic projections in order to secure support for his or her project.

An Effective Portfolio Management System— How to Integrate These Tools

Now let's turn to how to operationalize and integrate the technical tools outlined above into an effective portfolio management system. The purpose of the system: to make the tactical decisions, namely, Go/Kill decisions on specific projects, project prioritization decisions, and resource allocation decisions to projects (bottom part of Exhibit 5.1).

Notes for Senior Management

A number of tools have been described that help you select projects and visualize your portfolio. The choice of which portfolio tools to use may not be that critical. Indeed, the best performers use an average of 2.4 tools each, as no one tool can do it all. In short, several tools used in conjunction is probably the best route.

Data reliability is also an issue. All these methods are only as good as the data on which they are based. Securing more reliable data should be one goal, and indeed is a key outcome of an effective idea-to-launch process, outlined in Chapter 7.

Now, read on to see how the various technical tools are employed at gate meetings and portfolio reviews to help the leadership team make better Go/Kill and prioritization decisions.

Portfolio Reviews for Project Selection

Portfolio reviews are one mechanism for selecting and prioritizing projects (bottom left, Exhibit 5.1). Portfolio reviews occur periodically (typically quarterly or semi-annually), and can last several days. The portfolio reviewers are usually the leadership team of the business—senior management—who "own" the resources needed for the projects.

Format of a portfolio review: The crucial portfolio review session is typically structured like this:

- All projects beyond a certain point in your idea-to-launch process are "on the table" or "in the auction." (Define at which point in your process there is enough information on that project for it to be ranked at a portfolio review, usually Gate 2 or 3 in Exhibit 7.3. Very early projects are typically not discussed at the portfolio review.)
- The portfolio reviewers first identify the "must-do" projects: the untouchables. These are projects that are either well along and still good projects, or are strategic imperatives. These projects along with their resources are removed from the auction; they and their resources are "protected."

One reason for "protecting projects" is that projects that are well along yet still meet the Go criteria *should be moved forward*. Yes, better and more exciting projects may enter the pipeline, and there's always the temptation to halt the mature project and redirect resources to the new ones—new projects always seem to look better. But taken to an extreme, no project would ever be completed!

▶ Then, management votes on and identifies "won't do's," which are killed outright. In many companies, a quick gate meeting is arranged: The project teams from those projects in trouble are asked to make a quick presentation and update, and a Go/Kill decision is made. A best practice philosophy here is that *no project should ever be killed without the project team in the room,* so that the team can update management and you can ensure that the Go/Kill decision is a transparent one.

An example: In portfolio reviews at one business unit of a major firm, executive summaries of all projects are displayed on the walls of the meeting room on large cards. The leadership team meeting begins, and each project is then discussed and debated. Then each executive is given a handful of green sticky dots; they use these to "vote" on the projects that they wish to protect, sticking them on the project cards displayed on the walls. Then red sticky dots are handed out: Any project that receives two red dots is flagged as "in trouble," and the project team is invited in for a quick review and decision: an instant gate meeting. This red-dot, green-dot method is very visual; it promotes animated discussion and interaction among leadership team members; and it achieves good decisions in an efficient manner.

▶ Next, the projects in the middle are evaluated. There are different methods here:
  • Many firms use the same criteria (both the scorecard and financial metrics) that they use at gate meetings:
    – In some cases, the data and results from the most recent gate meeting are also employed at portfolio reviews; that is, management simply uses the scorecard rating results and the financial estimates (for example, the productivity index) available from each project's most recent gate meeting to rank-order the projects.
    – Other managements request an update of all data on projects, and also re-score the projects on the scorecard right at the portfolio review. One can employ a shorter list of criteria, however, than the list found in the typical gate scorecard.
  • Forced ranking on criteria is also used. Here management ranks the projects *against one another*—1 to N—on each criterion (where N is the number of projects). Again, a handful of major criteria are used, such as those used by Kodak at its portfolio review:[15]

✓ strategic fit
✓ product leadership (product advantage)
✓ probability of technical success
✓ market attractiveness (growth, margins)
✓ value to the company (profitability based on NPV)

All of these methods yield a list of projects, rank-ordered according to objective criteria. Then the resources required to do each project are displayed—the "resource loadings," as EXFO Engineering calls them. Projects are then ranked until one runs out of resources. This ranked list is the first cut or *tentative portfolio.*

Following this, check for portfolio balance and strategic alignment. The proposed portfolio is displayed using some of the bubble diagrams, prioritized lists, and pie charts described earlier in this chapter (see the example in Exhibit 5.13). The purpose here is to visualize the balance of the proposed portfolio and also to check for strategic alignment. If the tentative portfolio is poorly balanced or not strategically aligned, projects are removed from the list and other projects are bumped up. The process is repeated until balance and alignment are achieved. Note that excellent software now exists to display a variety of views of the portfolio and with different scenarios (see, for example, *SG-Tracker*™[16]).

Strategic buckets and portfolio reviews: If you employ strategic buckets—for example, buckets for project types—first sort the projects into different buckets. Then do separate ranking exercises—one ranking exercise per bucket—as in Exhibit 4.8. You should use different ranking criteria and methods for the different buckets. For example, using Mercedes Star buckets diagram in Exhibit 4.6:

- For projects in the "new products" bucket, use a scorecard model (Exhibit 5.5) together with the ECV-productivity index.
- For platform and technology developments, use the advanced technology scorecard (more visionary, less financial) in Exhibit 5.6.
- For the "Other Projects" bucket, which comprise extensions, fixes, and cost reductions, use a simple cost/benefit ratio or payback period to rank projects.

Gates for Project Selection

Gates are the second mechanism for project selection and prioritization (see bottom right of Exhibit 5.1). Gates are meetings between the project team and senior management designed to assess the quality of the project,

Prioritized Scored List of Active and On Hold Projects

Project	Rank (Priority Level)	Total Project Score	Portfolio Balance Factor	Adjusted Total Project Score
Soya-44	1	80	1.10	88
Encapsulated	2	82	1.00	82
Legume N-2	3	70	1.10	77
Spread-Ease	4	75	1.00	75
Charcoal-Base	5	80	0.90	72
Projects on Hold				
N2-Fix	1	80	1.00	80**
Slow-Release	2	70	1.10	77*
Multi-Purpose	3	75	.90	68
etc..	etc..			

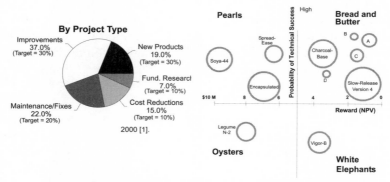

At end of ranking, display the portfolio, checking for balance and alignment

Exhibit 5.13 A Typical Portfolio Display during a Portfolio Review

Source: Research-Technology Management 2000, note 1.

make the Go/Kill and prioritization decisions, and approve the needed resources for the next stage (see Box 5.1). Gates are a key facet of the idea-to-launch process, the topic of Chapter 7, and will be outlined in more detail there. But for now, here are a few notes on gates:

- Gates are defined throughout the idea-to-launch process. Typically there are about five gates for a major project, from the "Idea Screen" through to the "Go-to-Launch" decision-point.
- Gates focus on one project at a time (by contrast, portfolio reviews consider the entire set of projects). Gates tend to provide a much more in-depth assessment of the individual project.

▶ Gates have defined decision makers: the gatekeepers (see Box 5.1).
▶ Effective gates utilize the various tools seen in this chapter to sharpen the decision making.

Box 5.1   Some Gate Definitions

Gates
These are project review and decision meetings—the vital Go/Kill decision-points in the *Stage-Gate*™ idea-to-launch framework. At gates, projects are evaluated by management; projects are approved and prioritized, and resources are allocated to projects; poor projects are killed before additional resources are wasted.

Gatekeepers
Gatekeepers are a management team of decision makers and resource owners responsible for facilitating the rapid commercialization of selected projects.

Gatekeeping
Gatekeeping is the management practices, behaviors, procedures, and rules of engagement that govern decision making at the gates. These practices are designed to enable project teams to move good projects forward rapidly and effectively through to launch. Note that the emphasis here is on enabling and facilitating projects—not just on judging and critiquing.

I recommend the use of the balanced scorecard approach (the scoring model as shown in Exhibit 5.5 or 5.6) to make the Go/Kill and prioritization decisions at gates, simply because it yields more effective and efficient decisions than the other methods. One or more of the financial models outlined earlier (for example, NPV or ECV) can be built into the scorecard, as shown in Exhibit 5.5.

More on how gates should be structured for most effective decision making in Chapter 7.

What about gating the strategic projects? Note that even projects that are elected for strategic reasons and projects for which there are place-marks in the product roadmap *must go through the project selection and gating process*. Too many projects that are deemed "strategic" simply sail through gate meetings, rubberstamped without scrutiny, and end up being disasters. Just because a project might appear to be "strategic" or "part of your roadmap" does not necessarily mean that you automatically do it. On the surface, conceptually and strategically, it's a great project; but a more detailed look may reveal serious flaws: technical, financial, or marketing. Thus it's important to scrutinize each and every project via a robust project selection and gating process.

Notes for Senior Management

New product portfolio management has become a vital concern, particularly among leading firms. And benchmarking results show that a portfolio management system has major payoffs (Exhibit 5.1). So make a commitment to install a *systematic portfolio management scheme.*

A hierarchical approach to portfolio management has been outlined in this and the previous chapter. It begins with your product innovation strategy, then moves to strategic portfolio decisions, and finally to tactical or project selection decisions.

Be sure to go beyond just the strategic facet of portfolio management in Exhibit 5.1, and establish an effective project selection and prioritization method. This should consist of (bottom of Exhibit 5.1):

- periodic portfolio reviews, whereby senior management scrutinizes the entire list of projects, seeking the right priorities among projects, the right balance and mix, and strategic alignment
- effective Go/Kill gates as part of your idea-to-launch framework, complete with defined gate criteria, an agreed-to selection/prioritization method, and gatekeepers delineated for each gate (see Chapter 7)

Regardless of the portfolio approach and tools you elect, do move ahead: Map out a method and implement it! Our research shows clearly that those businesses that feature a systematic portfolio management process, regardless of the specific approach, outperform the rest.

Notes

1. This chapter is based on a number of books and articles by the author and co-workers: see note 1 in Chapter 4.

2. A. L. Griffin, *Drivers of NPD Success: The 1997 PDMA Report.* Chicago: Product Development & Management Association, 1997.

3. Paragraph based on R. G. Cooper, "The NewProd System: The Industry Experience," *Journal of Product Innovation Management* 9, 1992, 113–127. *NewProd®* has been renamed *SG-Selector™*: see www.stage-gate.com.

4. Parts of this section are taken from an article by the author: R. G. Cooper, "Maximizing the Value of Your New Product Portfolio: Methods, Metrics and Scorecards," *Current Issues in Technology Management*. Hoboken, NJ: Stevens Institute of Technology (Stevens Alliance for Technology Management), 7, 1, Winter 2003, 1.

5. T. Faulkner, "Applying 'Options Thinking' to R&D Valuation," *Research-Technology Management*, May–June 1995, 50–57.

6. See note 4.

7. R. G. Cooper, S. J. Edgett, & E. J. Kleinschmidt, *R&D Portfolio Management Best Practices Study*. Washington, DC: Industrial Research Institute (IRI), 1997; and R. G. Cooper, S. J. Edgett, & E. J. Kleinschmidt, "Best Practices for Managing R&D Portfolios," *Research-Technology Management*, 41, 4, July–August 1998, 20–33.

8. Celanese Corporation (formerly Hoechst Chemical), as in *Portfolio Management for New Products*, note 1.

9. Portfolio management practices and performance study: see note 13 in Chapter 4.

10. Bubble diagrams with "value" measured *qualitatively* are recommended in P. Roussel, K. N. Saad, & T. J. Erickson, *Third Generation R&D, Managing the Link to Corporate Strategy*. Boston: Harvard Business School Press & Arthur D. Little, Inc., 1991.

11. P. Evans, "Streamlining Formal Portfolio Management," *Scrip Magazine*, February 1996; and D. Matheson, J. E. Matheson, & M. M. Menke, "Making Excellent R&D Decisions," *Research-Technology Management*, November–December 1994, 21–24.

12. Based on Roberts and Berry's newness matrix: see note 37 in Chapter 3.

13. R. G. Cooper, "The Invisible Success Factors in Product Innovation," *Journal of Product Innovation Management*, 16, 2, April 1999, 115–133.

14. Portfolio practices and performance study: see note 13 in Chapter 4.

15. E. Patton, "The Strategic Investment Process: Driving Corporate Vision through Portfolio Creation," in *Proceedings: Product Portfolio Management: Balancing Resources with Opportunity*. Boston: The Management Roundtable, 1999.

16. *SG-Tracker*™, a portfolio management software package, displays alternate views and scenarios of your portfolio of development projects. Available from Stage-Gate Inc. at www.stage-gate.com. Such software proves invaluable in gate meetings and portfolio reviews, so that senior management can visualize their portfolio—its balance and composition—and also the impacts of adding new projects.

6

Building Best Practices into Your Idea-to-Launch Framework

Winning isn't everything . . . it's the only thing.
—Vince Lombardi, U.S. football coach

Where's Your Idea-to-Launch Framework?

Picture a North American football team without a game plan. The coach gathers his players in the pre-game locker room, and urges them to "go out there and play hard . . . play to win." Wonderful words of encouragement, but without a playbook or game plan, there's likely to be chaos on that football field!

What is a playbook? It simply outlines how to move the ball from one end of the football field down to the goal line. The playbook defines the various plays and how to execute them; it specifies accountability, showing what each player is expected to do on that team for each play. Best practices are built into the playbook: which maneuvers and moves it takes to carry out each play in the best possible way in order to win.

Let's carry this analogy to new products. Instead of defined plays, such as the "quarterback sneak," there are stages: the Scoping stage, the Development stage, the Launch stage. There are typically five or six stages from one end of the field to the goal line, or from idea through to launch. And instead of huddles on the field, there are gates that precede each stage. Gates are where management meets with the team, and decides whether to move forward or not, and the best way to move forward.

A new product process, or idea-to-launch framework, is simply a "playbook" or "game plan" to guide new product projects from beginning to end. In this chapter, we look at eight best practices that top-performing businesses have built into their framework or playbook (see Box 6.1). The following chapter provides the details of what a best-in-class idea-to-launch framework looks like—a generic view of such a process.

Box 6.1   Best Practices in the Idea-to-Launch Framework

1. Put in place a best-in-class idea-to-launch framework to drive new products to market, quickly and efficiently. And make sure that both senior management and project teams understand, embrace, and stick to this process.
2. Emphasize quality of execution of key tasks from idea to launch: no short-cutting and no corner-cutting. Eighteen key activities are listed that are pivotal to NPD success.
3. Seek competitive advantage through superior new products: differentiated products that offer the customer or user unique benefits and provide the user better value for money.
4. Ensure that the voice-of-customer is built in throughout the entire NPD playbook. This means the whole project team interfacing directly with customers or users, listening to their problems, and understanding unmet needs and desires.
5. Demand sharp, early product definition—the target market, product concept and positioning, the value proposition, and the features and specs—before any project enters the Development stage. And make sure this definition is fact-based and signed off on by the entire project team.
6. Insist on solid upfront homework by the project team before the project is released to the Development stage. And make sure your idea-to-launch framework (item 1 above) incorporates a good dose of upfront or front-end homework, both technical and marketing.
7. Build tough gates or Go/Kill decision-points into your idea-to-launch framework. And make sure that some projects really do get killed!
8. Put metrics in place, both to measure the results of individual new product projects and also to gauge how well the business is faring overall at product innovation.

A World-Class Idea-to-Launch Framework

An idea-to-launch framework, or *Stage-Gate®* process, properly designed and implemented, is a much-heralded key to NPD success.[1] By "new product framework," we mean more than just a flowchart with arrows and boxes; the term includes all process elements: the stages, stage activities, gates, deliverables, gate criteria, roles, and responsibilities that constitute a well-defined new product process.

For more than a decade, managements have been urged to design and implement such a new product framework, and they appear to have heeded the experts. Indeed, having a well-defined new product process is the *strongest best practice* observed in our APQC benchmarking study[2] and detailed outlines of five benchmark companies' processes are available.[3]

> *Some examples*
> ExxonMobil Chemicals:
> "This process, a company-wide stage-and-gate framework, has become institutionalized and is ingrained in the language and culture of the company."
>
> Kraft Foods:
> "Kraft emphasizes the front-end, pre-development activities. These upfront activities typically involve extensive use of both external and internal consumer data."
>
> Bausch & Lomb:
> "B&L's new product development process is easy to follow, and built on internal and external successes and best practices. The NPD team has built a process with stages and gates that is practical, but not restrictive."
>
> EXFO Engineering:
> "EXFO believes its product development, or stage-and-gate process, to be its second best practice. EXFO implemented a stage-and-gate process when the organization became ISO certified in 1994."
>
> Air Products & Chemicals:
> Best Practice: "An integrated work process for technology innovation involves integration along two axes: business and technology."

The results from these and other firms have been impressive. For example, the director of NPD at Bausch & Lomb, when asked about the impact their process has had, said, "A contact lens project would typically have taken three years before our PDMP [product development management process] was implemented. Today we are looking at 18 months to two years. The payback is real."

The Elements of an Idea-to-Launch Framework

So what do NPD playbooks found in top-performing businesses look like? First, the framework is a *clearly defined* idea-to-launch new product process—one that is well mapped out.[4] By contrast, many companies have processes that are surprisingly complex and hard-to-understand, and resemble an electrical wiring diagram rather than an easy-to-follow playbook. Next, the process is *visible and well-documented* in order to provide genuine guidance to project teams and leaders. There are *clearly designated stages*—for example, Ideation, Scoping, Building Business Case, Development, Test, and Launch. And *activities are defined* for each stage: what happens within each stage (including guidelines on the "how-to's").

The idea-to-launch framework in top performers is an *enabling process* for project teams, helping them get their projects onto management's radar screens, secure the needed resources, and drive their projects to market. It is also an *adaptable and scalable* process: It is flexible, and can be adapted to the needs, size, and risk of each project. And the process is *really used*, and is not something that is circumvented or viewed as "to be avoided."

Gates are a strong facet of most top-performing businesses' NPD frameworks: *defined Go/Kill decision-points* where senior management meets with the project team to decide whether the project is a Go and is resourced for the next stage. There are also *visible Go/Kill criteria* at gates—the criteria that projects will be judged on to make Go/Kill and prioritization decisions—in the form of a gate scorecard, as seen in the previous chapter. *Deliverables are defined* for each gate: a menu of what the project team is expected to deliver to each gate meeting, usually in the form of templates. And *gatekeepers are designated* for each gate: the people who make the Go/Kill decisions at gates.

Finally, there is a *process manager in place*—full- or part-time—to shepherd the NPD framework, ensuring that it works. Duties include coaching project teams, facilitating gate meetings, ensuring project deliverables are ready and distributed to gatekeepers, training, and keeping metrics.

The process is broken: That's the ideal, and indeed best performers in our APQC benchmarking study have most or all of these elements in place. But in many businesses that claim to have a new product process, it is broken: The process is plagued by errors, lacks consistency, and suffers from poor quality of execution. Often the process is bureaucratic and cumbersome, gets in the way, and is painfully slow. Some processes fail to build in best practices (in spite of the fact that most managers profess to understand what the best practices are): For example, there are no real Go/Kill decision-points with visible criteria; or there is little emphasis on pre-Development homework, building in the voice-of-customer, and focusing on superior products. And in some firms, it's an engineering or technical process, not a business process, and so the marketing and manufacturing folks don't buy in.

Perhaps the worst sin is a lack of discipline: The idea-to-launch process is not practiced well. For example, project teams circumvent the process or pay lip-service to it; key activities are done in haste in the interest of "moving projects along"; and senior management really does not commit to the process—they don't adhere to their roles as gatekeepers and mentors.

The point is that there are huge differences between the best and the worst businesses in how they went about designing and implementing their idea-to-launch frameworks. Most firms claim to have a new product process; but a minority have it right, and really live their process!

Notes for Senior Management

Merely having a new product process does not separate the best from worst performers. But possessing a first-rate idea-to-launch framework is a common denominator of virtually every top-performing business we studied. So, if your business lacks a solid NPD playbook or framework, or it's only a high-level or unspecific process, it's time to install a best-in-class process, complete with the ingredients or elements outlined above and found in top-performing businesses. More on what this process looks like in the following chapter.

Now read on, for the rest of this chapter outlines seven more best practices that top performers build into their idea-to-launch frameworks. Do you? If not, you are missing some of the key performance drivers.

Build in Quality of Execution from Idea Through to Launch

"The devil is in the details"—*execution* is the key driver of success. This is one overriding conclusion of virtually every study of new product performance, including our APQC benchmarking study. Indeed, new product success is very much within the hands of the men and women who lead and work on their project. Certain key activities—how well they are executed, and whether they are done at all—are strongly tied to success.

Just how well are NPD projects executed? And which actions or activities are most pivotal to success? I identify 18 commonly cited activities that should be built into NPD projects and into your idea-to-launch framework (these activities are defined in Boxes 6.2 and 6.3). And Exhibit 6.1 shows the quality-of-execution results for these 18 activities.[5]

Note the two provocative findings from these exhibits. First, see how poorly the average business executes the majority of these idea-to-to-launch activities in a typical new product project. With performance like this, it's surprising that any product gets to market! Second, witness how much better the top performers execute new product projects. Indeed,

---

Box 6.2   Vital Front-End Activities to Build into Your Idea-to-Launch Framework

1. Idea generation—ideation or coming up with new product ideas. Many companies have systematic, proactive, and aggressive idea generation, capture, and handling systems.
2. Initial screening—the first decision to move ahead on a new product project. Often this idea screen is handled by a mid-management group, and relies on simple scorecard criteria for making the Go/Kill decision.
3. Preliminary market assessment—the first but cursory assessment of the market. This often includes accessing available information sources and conducting some very limited market research.
4. Preliminary technical assessment—the first technical assessment of the project, identifying potential technical risks, probable solutions, and technical issues.
5. Preliminary operations (or manufacturing) assessment—an initial assessment of the manufacturing or operations process before Development begins, including process design, source of supply, operating costs, and equipment requirements.
6. Detailed market study, market research, or voice-of-customer studies—market research, involving a reasonable sample of customers/users to determine their problems, needs, wants and preferences (as an input to the product's design).
7. Concept testing—to determine the customer/user reaction to the proposed new product (validating the product concept with the user/customer) and gauging purchase intent.
8. Value assessment—determining the value of the product to the business (for example, economic, strategic, and customer retention value).
9. Business/financial analysis—a financial or business analysis leading to a Go/Kill decision prior to the Development phase. This often includes a strategic assessment, along with a spreadsheet analysis (NPV, IRR, sensitivity analysis).

---

almost all of the 18 activities shown in Exhibit 6.1 strongly distinguish the best- from the worst-performing businesses.[6]

There is a quality crisis in product innovation, according to these benchmarking results in Exhibit 6.1. No, not product quality problems, but serious weaknesses in the way that projects are carried out: Look down the list of activities in these two exhibits, particularly at the middle or black bars (the average business). There are only four activities out of 20 that are proficiently executed in at least 50% of the businesses. This means that 16 out of 20 activities—80% of tasks—are substandard and poorly executed in more than half the businesses.

Imagine that you are a football coach and keep a record of how well each play is carried out by your team over a number of football games. In the first play, they did well 19% of the time (but dropped the ball 81% of the time); in the second play, the team executed well 15% of the time (but they missed the pass 85% of the time); in the third play, they fumbled the ball 74% of the time; and so on down the field. These are the *exact results* that Exhibit 6.1 shows for this product innovation game!

Box 6.3 Vital Back-End Activities
from the Development Stage Onward

10. Product development—the actual design and development resulting in a prototype or sample product.
11. In-house product testing in the lab or in-house under controlled conditions (lab, in-house, or alpha testing).
12. Customer test of product under real-life conditions with customers and/or in the field (field trials, preference tests, beta tests, in-use tests, etc.).
13. Test market or trial sell to a limited or test set of customers to test the marketing plan for full launch.
14. Trial production—transfer to the plant (or to operations) and trial production/operations to test the production/operations facilities—trial, limited, pilot, or batch production/operations.
15. Pre-launch business analysis—a financial or business analysis following the Development phase, but prior to full-scale or commercial market launch.
16. Production or operations start-up—the start-up of full-scale or commercial production or operations.
17. Market launch—the launch or market roll-out of the product on a full-scale and/or commercial basis—an identifiable set of marketing, promotion, and selling activities.
18. Post-launch review—the review and evaluation of the project some months after launch; assessment of results achieved versus targets; lessons learned; formal termination of the project.

When was the last time that you, as an executive, accepted results like these and thought this was good performance? It isn't. These are poor quality ratings; but they are typical, and may very well be true of your business too. In short, our studies reveal that key activities don't happen as they should, when they should, or as well as they should; success and profitability suffer as a result.

Key activities poorly executed: What we also witness is that the *most important activities* in the NPD process—those that separate the best and

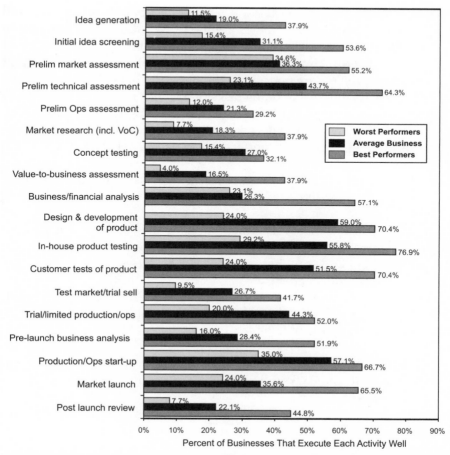

Legend:
- **Worst Performers**
- **Average Business**
- **Best Performers**

Activity	Worst Performers	Average Business	Best Performers
Idea generation	11.5%	19.0%	37.9%
Initial idea screening	15.4%	31.1%	53.6%
Prelim market assessment	34.6%	36.3%	55.2%
Prelim technical assessment	23.1%	43.7%	64.3%
Prelim Ops assessment	12.0%	21.3%	29.2%
Market research (incl. VoC)	7.7%	18.3%	37.9%
Concept testing	15.4%	27.0%	32.1%
Value-to-business assessment	4.0%	16.5%	37.9%
Business/financial analysis	23.1%	26.3%	57.1%
Design & development of product	24.0%	59.0%	70.4%
In-house product testing	29.2%	55.8%	76.9%
Customer tests of product	24.0%	51.5%	70.4%
Test market/trial sell	9.5%	26.7%	41.7%
Trial/limited production/ops	20.0%	44.3%	52.0%
Pre-launch business analysis	16.0%	28.4%	51.9%
Production/Ops start-up	35.0%	57.1%	66.7%
Market launch	24.0%	35.6%	65.5%
Post launch review	7.7%	22.1%	44.8%

Percent of Businesses That Execute Each Activity Well

19% of businesses do an excellent job on idea generation. This is a key but weak activity—note that 37.9% of best performers (and only 11.5% of poor perfromance) handle idea generation proficiently.

Exhibit 6.1   Quality of Execution of Key Activities—Impact on Performance

the worst performers—are also those activities which on average *are executed most poorly!* This is solid evidence of the quality-of-execution crisis in NPD, and that too many businesses are under-emphasizing critical activities.

There's more! Note *where the major deficiencies are* in Exhibit 6.1—the business and marketing activities are far weaker than the technical ones. For example:

- Of the eight exceptionally weak activities in Exhibit 6.1, *half are marketing-* or customer-related!

- By contrast, the technical work on projects appears much stronger. The three best-rated activities are the technical development of the product, in-house product testing, and production start-up.
- Additionally, quality-of-execution ratings for all six marketing activities in Exhibit 6.1 are poor (less than one-third of businesses on average execute the six marketing tasks proficiently).
- By contrast, the mean quality-of-execution rating for the six technical and operations activities is respectable (almost half of businesses execute well here)—not perfect, but much better than the parallel marketing tasks.
- The business tasks (screening, business analysis, post-launch review) are also rated badly.

So, in spite of the fact that NPD is often thought of as a technical, engineering, or scientific endeavor, in fact it's the *business and marketing activities* that are the killers: Clearly there are major deficiencies on one side of the field in the new product arena.

Another insight is that *the front end of the project* is more poorly executed than the back end. Compare the ratings of the front-end versus back-end activities—the two parts of Exhibit 6.1:

- Only 26.6% of businesses on average execute the front-end tasks well.
- By contrast, the back-end activities are executed well in 42.3% of businesses.
- And all three of the top-rated activities occur in the back end of projects, while five of the eight worst-executed tasks occur in the front end.

More time, attention, and care must be devoted to the front end of NPD projects.

As a leadership team, focus on the game-making plays! Put your emphasis on those facets of the new idea-to-launch process that are the weakest and also have the greatest leverage to yield results. The eight activities with the *greatest impact on performance* are (in descending order of impact):

1. **Conducting a post-launch review (PLR)**: Review and evaluate the project some months after launch: This PLR is a very weak area overall, with only 22.1% of businesses conducting a solid and formal post-launch review. Top performers are six times as likely to undertake this PLR proficiently when compared to poor performers: They review results achieved versus targets and hold the project team

accountable; they learn from their mistakes and strive to do the next project better; and they formally terminate the project. Worst performers do not. This is a *standout best practice!*

2. **Value assessment:** Best performers are *nine times more likely* to undertake a solid assessment of the value of the product to the business (when compared to worst performers). But this is a particularly weak area overall, with only 16.5% of businesses on average executing well here.

3. **Test market or trial sell to a limited set of customers:** Again, this is a deficient area, with only 26.7% of businesses handling the test market or trial sell well. But best performers are four times more likely to undertake a test market or trial sell of the product to confirm commercial acceptance prior to full market launch.

Notes for Senior Management

The message is clear: The best way to make your new product efforts more profitable is to strive for significant improvements in the way your idea-to-launch process unfolds. Senior management must get back to basics in NPD, and *emphasize quality of execution*—doing it right the first time. Management and project teams must develop a more disciplined approach to product innovation: The way to save time and money is *not* to cut corners, execute in a hurried and sloppy fashion, or cut out steps. This is false economy: It results in more time and effort spent later in the project, and it leads to a higher failure rate.

Many of the root causes of poor quality of execution include a lack of resources, too many projects, and not enough time or resources to do a quality job. These too are areas where senior management can take corrective action. Note also that a disciplined adherence to an idea-to-launch framework *should yield* better quality of execution, since best practices, quality-of-execution standards, and prescribed deliverables are laid out in such world-class NPD processes. Many businesses claim to have such processes in place, but are not executing them in the prescribed fashion: Theory and practice are miles apart when it comes to businesses' NPD process and actual execution of projects!

You, the leadership team of the business, are the gatekeepers at the key check-points or gates in the process, and hence you are in effect the *quality controllers* of the process. This is an important role for senior people: challenging project teams, and spotting and halting projects that feature poor-quality work.

4. **Concept testing** (to determine the customer/user reaction to the proposed new product and to gauge purchase intent before Development begins): This is a weak area overall. But 32.1% of best performers undertake proficient concept testing (versus only 15.4% of poor performers).
5. **Idea generation:** Top performers are three times as likely to do an excellent job at idea generation as poorer businesses. Overall, idea generation is a deficient area.
6. **Customer tests of the product under real-life conditions:** This is a fairly strong activity overall, with 51.5% of businesses doing this well. Best performers excel (70.4% are proficient here), while worst performers fare more poorly.
7. **Detailed market study, market research, or voice-of-the-customer study:** Best performers are five times more likely to build a solid market study or voice-of-the-customer research into their projects versus worst performers. This is another key best practice—more on this later in the chapter.
8. **Pre-launch business analysis:** Best performers also excel here, with 51.9% of these businesses undertaking a proficient pre-launch analysis (versus only 16.0% of worst performers).

Seek Competitive Advantage Through Differentiated, Superior New Products

The one vital success ingredient, and which many firms fail to address directly, is the *product itself.* One of the top success factors we uncovered is delivering a *differentiated product* with *unique customer benefits* and *superior value for the user.* This one factor separates winners from losers more often than any other single factor! For example, our project studies show that such superior products have five times the success rate, over four times the market share, and four times the profitability as products lacking this ingredient.[7] Just how pivotal a unique, superior product is can be seen in Exhibit 6.2. Note how top performers appear to have figured it out—they deliver new products that possess unique and important benefits for the user, are of better value for the customer, are superior to competing products in terms of meeting user needs, and have superior product quality.[8]

This result should come as no surprise to product innovators. Apparently it isn't obvious to everyone, however: A number of studies point out that "tired products" and "me too" offerings are the rule rather than the exception in many firms' new product efforts. The three most common project scenarios that lead to poor performance are:

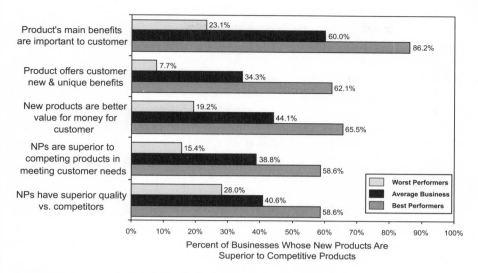

Exhibit 6.2 New Product Superiority—Impact on Performance

- copycat projects that yield boring, undifferentiated products with no new benefits for the customer. Often these projects are the result of an overly rushed effort to get something out to market quickly.
- extensions, modifications, and minor improvements that are easy to do, often needed urgently, and necessary to keep the product line fresh. But these "low hanging fruit projects" won't deliver the high profits and major impact desired by senior management.
- technology-driven projects, where the business's technical community decides what the customer wants. The engineer, scientist, or designer then builds a monument to himself or herself—a great technological achievement—and wonders why thousands of customers stay away.

A missing ingredient: Surprisingly, very few businesses can point to specific facets of their new product methodology that emphasize this one vital success ingredient. Often "product superiority" or "sustainable competitive advantage gained via the product" is noticeably absent as a project selection or prioritization criterion; rarely are steps deliberately built into the process that encourage the design and delivery of such superior products. It's almost as though the process architects—the people that designed the idea-to-launch playbook—were content to design a process destined to yield mediocre products!

ʼrse, the preoccupation with cycle time reduction and the ten-
ʼor simple, inexpensive projects actually penalize projects that
ʟead to product superiority. Management is in such a rush to get the product to market that they sacrifice product superiority. In so doing, they sacrifice profits as well.

The challenge is to ensure that the five elements of product superiority
are built into your new product projects (these elements are listed in
Exhibit 6.2). In short, the list of the five ingredients of product superiority
should be embedded in your idea-to-launch framework; they become personal objectives of your project teams; and they also become goals of
senior management in challenging and providing guidance to teams:

**1. Focus on new products that offer customers/users main benefits
that are important to them:** This is the most prevalent element of competitive advantage, with 52.4% of businesses claiming that their products do
indeed deliver important benefits to customers (Exhibit 6.2). It is also a
strong discriminator between best and worst performers, with 86.2% of best
performers, and only 23.1% of worst performers launching new products
with important benefits. Too often, however, companies get it wrong: They
assume that interesting product features and functionality are the same as
customer benefits, when in fact they may be of little value to the customer.

> *An example:* A major pump manufacturer designed and developed a
> "smart" large industrial pump. The pump was equipped with multiple
> sensors that could sense upstream and downstream pressure, and
> adjust the speed of the pump for optimal performance. One reputed
> benefit was longer pump life and less maintenance due to the opti-
> mized performance. However, when weighed against the huge extra
> initial price of the pump, the reliability and maintenance feature was
> not much of a benefit at all. The company sold one pump!
>
> Subsequent voice-of-customer research by the company revealed
> that a significant benefit that might be realized was reduced power
> cost. By operating the pump at just the right speed—a single sensor
> could determine the pressure in the pipe, and motor controls would
> adjust the speed of the pump's motor—power consumption could be
> significantly reduced. Thus, the pump was redesigned and greatly
> simplified so as to yield a "efficient smart pump," and has since done
> very well in the marketplace.

**2. Develop new products that provide new and unique benefits to
customers or users** (not found in competitive products): Businesses perform moderately here on average, with 34.3% of businesses claiming

strengths in terms of new/unique benefits in their products. Best performers excel here.

> *An example:* One unusual case of delivering "unique benefits" is found in a smaller firm, Bio-Pro in Florida.[9] The company has had a winner with a urine cleaner for the professional market. In the late 1990s, the company began researching different strains of bacteria and enzymes that could be used in the poultry industry to reduce odors and reduce skin irritation suffered by chickens standing in their own litter. But the resulting product proved too expensive for the poultry industry.
>
> Then, in 2000, one of the business's employees complained that her 12-year-old dog was having trouble making it through the night without urinating on her expensive rugs. The CEO suggested she try the recently developed product for poultry in her home, and it worked like a charm—she reported that the stains and odor were gone! Management realized the potential, and relaunched it as a professional product targeted at hotels, restaurants, airports, and bars. The product delivered a unique benefit not available from any other product on the market, and has become a winner for Bio-Pro.

3. Seek new products that deliver better value for money to the customer—a superior value proposition: Best performers again score well here, with 65.5% of top performers delivering better value-for-money new products; by contrast, only 19.2% of poor performers get this right.

> *An example:* Here's a best practice we observed in the form of a mandatory gate deliverable: The project team must provide the gatekeepers (senior management) with *demonstrated confirmation from potential customers* that the product will deliver true value to them. The team is free to choose the most appropriate approach to demonstrate this value. This requirement has resulted in much more robust product definitions, as these definitions are now fact-based and verified by the target user.

4. Your new products must be superior to competitors' products in terms of meeting customer needs: The majority (58.6%) of best performers do indeed develop superior products, but most businesses miss the mark: Only 35.2% of all businesses overall develop superior products.

An important point here is that "product superiority" is defined from the customer's or user's standpoint, not in the eyes of the R&D or design departments. More than unique features and functionality are required to make a product superior. Remember: Features are those things that cost you, the supplier, money. By contrast, benefits are what customers pay money for! Often the two—features and benefits—are not the same. So in defining "unique benefits," think of the product as a "bundle of benefits" for the user/customer and a benefit as something the user/customer views as having value to him or her.

5. Offer products with superior quality versus competitive products (however the customer measures quality): The majority of top performers (58.6%) do offer new products with superior product quality; poor performers are particularly deficient here, with only 28% offering superior quality. Emphasize *superior product quality* in your new product programs.

Notes for Senior Management

Product superiority—delivering new products with unique customer benefits, a superior value proposition (better value for money), with important customer benefits, better quality, and meeting customer needs better—is one of the top best practices in NPD:

- First, emphasize product advantage and superiority in your idea-to-launch framework. For example, these items listed above and in Exhibit 6.2 should become part of your scorecard criteria at Go/Kill decision-points (note, for example, that product superiority is a key scoring item in the recommended scorecard in Exhibit 5.5). Next, the ingredients of product superiority (Exhibit 6.2) should be key topics of discussion at project reviews, and senior management must challenge project teams when they fail to deliver a product definition that scores well on these items.
- Second, arriving at unique, superior value products is not easy. Occasionally it's the result of inspiration or a technological breakthrough—an "aha." But most often it comes from tough work, including some of the activities and tasks that I highlight later in this chapter: undertaking excellent voice-of-customer research to truly identify needs, problems, benefits sought, and functionality desired; and executing the upfront homework activities superbly. This work does not guarantee product superiority, but it provides a solid foundation. More on these practices below.

And when defining "product quality," make sure that you define it from the standpoint of the customer or user: what he or she sees as "quality."

Build in the Voice-of-Customer

Successful businesses, and teams that drive winning new product projects, pay special attention to the voice-of-customer. Countless studies have cited the need for better market information as one key to NPD success.[10] And voice-of-customer research is often proposed as a mandatory step in the development of a new product.

New product projects that feature high-quality marketing actions—preliminary and detailed market studies, customer tests, field trials and test markets, as well as launch—are blessed with more than double the success rate and 70% higher market shares than those projects with poor marketing actions.[11] Further, a strong market orientation increases success rates by 38.6 percentage points and is strongly correlated with new product performance. In our APQC benchmarking study, a process that emphasizes the customer and marketplace via market studies, market research, concept tests, competitive analysis and customer field trials is significantly correlated with the profitability and success of the business's total new product efforts (see Exhibit 6.3).[12]

> *An example:* Transitions Optical, a joint venture between PPG Industries of Pittsburgh, Pennsylvania, and Essilor International, Paris, France, has had stunning success in the eye-glasses market with its *Transitions III* plastic lenses that adjust to sunlight in prescription eyeglasses. Extensive market research revealed that consumers were unhappy with the traditional product—*Photo Gray Extra* from Corning. This 20-year-old technology was perceived as heavy, for older people, and "worn by farmers." But the concept of variable-tint eye-glasses—whose tinting changes to accommodate bright sunlight or darker rooms—was appealing. Market research was undertaken in numerous countries to *identify customers' needs* in this lucrative market. The research showed that consumers were looking for lightweight, modern, variable-tint eye-wear, whose tinting changed quickly. At the same time, the lens had to be really clear when worn indoors. PPG, a world leader in the production of glass and coatings, was capable of developing the photochromic technology, and Essilor possessed the distribution network. But would the proposed product be a winner? To find out, numerous *concept tests* were undertaken with the proposed product—shopping mall interviews and focus groups of consumers—to confirm customer liking and purchase intent, not only in the United States, but in France, Germany, and the United Kingdom. When *Transitions III* was launched, it proved to be *right on* for the market, and very quickly achieved the leading market share.

A major reason for failure: A failure to adopt a strong market orientation in product innovation, an unwillingness to undertake the needed market assessments, and leaving the customer out of product development spell disaster. It's like a broken record: Poor market research; inadequate market analysis; weak market studies, test markets, and market launch; and inadequate resources devoted to marketing activities are common

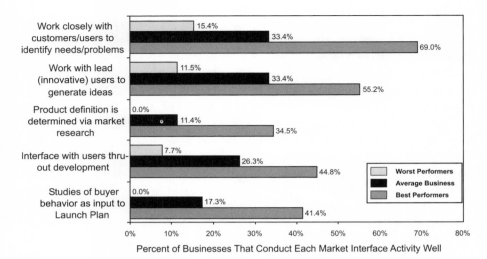

Exhibit 6.3 Voice-of-the-Customer and Market Inputs—Impact on Performance

weaknesses found in virtually every study of why new products fail, including our own.

Sadly, a market orientation and customer focus is noticeably lacking in many businesses' new product projects. The marketing actions are among the most weakly executed in the entire new product process: Witness the mediocre scores accorded marketing actions (Exhibit 6.1). And other investigations reveal that relatively few resources and little money are spent on the marketing actions, particularly those that occur in the early stages of a project.[13]

> *An example:* In one major chemical company, a new product benchmarking analysis of all of its business units revealed a common deficiency: inadequate marketing input to new product projects. A meeting of business unit general managers very quickly identified the reason why: a lack of marketing people. For every 60 scientists, it was estimated *there was only one marketing person,* and often this one person had not been formally trained as a marketer. A resource audit, which looked at typical projects and required tasks, revealed that for this company, the ideal ratio was about *one marketer for every four scientists*—not the 60:1 current ratio! Management is now acting on a commitment to dramatically increase the number of marketing professionals.

The message is clear: Spare no effort in building the customer or user into your new product process. This means right from the beginning of the process, namely, *ideation*: Seventy-five percent of all successful new products see the idea come from the marketplace. And a focus on the customer must prevail throughout your idea-to-launch framework, right through to launch.

Five key marketing best practices identified in our APQC benchmarking study include (see Exhibit 6.3):[14]

1. Identify customers' or users' real or unarticulated needs and problems. This requires voice-of-customer research, and should be a key input to ideation and to product design. Only 33.4% of businesses, however, work closely with customers here. This is *a most important activity*, and we rate the identification of customers' real needs via voice-of-customer research as a strong best practice, with 69% of best performers embracing this method—far more so than the other four approaches in Exhibit 6.3.

2. Work with highly innovative users or customers. This is yet another tool employed by voice-of-customer pundits. The argument here is that if one works with *average customers*, one gets *average ideas*; but innovative customers or users are likely to be the source of much more innovative ideas.[15] This is a relatively weak practice, with only 33.4% of businesses indicating strengths here. Again, this is a critical practice: The majority of best performers use this approach, and it helps to discriminate between the best and worst performers.

3. Insist on market research as a tool to help define the product—its requirements, features, functionality, and high-level specs. Again we witness deficiencies here, with a small minority of businesses (11.4%) claiming that their product definitions are truly based on market research of the customer or user (Exhibit 6.3). Best performers, however, generally do employ such market research to define the product, and this activity separates the best from the worst performers in a strong way.

> *An example:* The pizza brand team at Kraft Foods identified a consumer need for high-quality frozen pizza, closer to restaurant quality. They noted the big gap between the frozen pizza available at the supermarket for $4 and what one could buy at a delivery or take-out pizza shop for $12. Kraft undertook numerous consumer-based quantitative and qualitative tests and identified that the main source of consumer dissatisfaction with frozen pizza was its dry, cardboard-like crust.
>
> Development was initiated in 1995. Improving the crust became the primary challenge for the technical team. Considerable research had been done over the years on the crust, so the technology team was well positioned to develop a higher-quality dough. The team also took advantage of new technologies developed for formula, process, and package, as well as industry research on pre-proofed frozen dough.

The result was *rising crust pizza*—a thin crust that rose when in the oven to yield a thicker, less dense, and tastier crust. Consumers loved it in taste tests!

Seven years later, *DiGiorno*™ is the number one self-rising pizza brand sold nationally in the United States. This innovation, based on solid market research to help define the product, refuted the myth that people wouldn't pay a significant premium for a frozen pizza.[16]

Box 6.4   Good Market Studies to Build into Your New Product Framework

These should be a key part of your idea-to-launch framework:

- Make sure that your voice-of-customer research focuses on customer needs and problems—on benefits sought and desired product functionality. If your voice-of-customer research comes back with just a list of desired product features and specifications, you've missed the point!
- As part of your voice-of-customer research, try to better understand the customer's or user's values and desires, their satisfiers and benefits sought, what their problems are, and how they view quality. In this way, you're in a better position to design a product that yields higher customer satisfaction, fewer customer complaints, and better customer perception of quality.
- Undertake a competitive analysis. Most businesses do this, and the methodologies are well understood, but it remains a best practice.
- Build in concept testing of the proposed new product before Development begins. Use models, CAD drawings, very early prototypes (as does Kraft), protocepts, or even virtual prototypes to gauge customer interest, liking, preference and purchase intent.
- Try to incorporate some price sensitivity analysis into your idea-to-launch framework. This is a very weak area, even for best performers, and many businesses struggle here. As part of your voice-of-customer research, try to gain insights into the value of the product: its economic impact on the user (you might even include a formal value-in-use analysis, thus quantifying the product's economic value to the user).

The point is that the customer or user must be *an input into product design,* and not just an after-the-fact check that the design is satisfactory. Investigations to determine users' needs, wants, and preferences and voice-of-customer research provide insights that are invaluable guides to the design team before they charge into the design of the new product.[17] Similarly, probing competitive product strategies, and their product strengths and weaknesses, provides additional and vital design input (see Box 6.4).

Too often, market research, when done at all, is misused in the new product process. It tends to be done as an afterthought—after the product design has been decided and to verify market acceptance. If the results of the market study are negative, most often they are conveniently ignored and the project is pushed ahead regardless. The mistake is clear: Market research must be used as an input to the design decisions, and not solely as an after-the-fact check. Note that studies done earlier in the project have much more impact than those done later![18]

Even in the case of technology-push new products (where the product emanates from the lab or technology department, perhaps the result of a technological breakthrough or a technology platform project), there still should be considerable marketing input as the technology is shaped into a final product design. That is, following the technical discovery, but before full-fledged development gets underway, there is ample opportunity to research and interact with the customer to determine needs and wants, to shape the final product the way the customer wants it, and to gauge likely product acceptance.

4. **Make the customer or user an integral part of your Development process**, with each iteration of the product being tested with the customer as the product is being developed. This is also a strong activity in terms of separating the best from worst performers: Top performers are five times

---

Notes for Senior Management

What many voice-of-customer advocates have been arguing for years is true: Voice-of-customer research and market inputs are vital to a successful NPD effort. Not only is this one of the strongest factors to separate best and worst performers, it's also an area where major deficiencies exist. Seeking market inputs and building voice-of-customer into your idea-to-launch framework must become an area of top priority if stellar results are the goal.

Note that voice-of-customer really means that: The project team must go out and *listen* to what the customer or user says. This *does not mean* the voice of the product manager or voice of the salesperson. While individuals within your own organization may be very knowledgeable about the customer, they do not speak for him or her. Thus, insist that *the entire project team*—not just the marketing/sales folks—undertake a customer visitation program as part of the project. They must go out and *touch real customers* and users, before the Development stage gets underway. Best performers do!

more likely to employ this practice. But only 23.8% of businesses report that the project team constantly interfaces with key users of a new product during the entire Development stage to validate product acceptance.

Seeking customer inputs and testing concepts or designs with the customer is very much an interactive or "back and forth" process. During the Development phase of the project, and after the market research is done, *constant and continuing customer contact* remains essential. "Spiral development" or a series of "build-and-test" iterations is the proposed scheme: Keep bringing the customer into the process to view facets of the product as the prototype or final product takes shape, via multiple iterations of rapid prototypes and tests. For example, develop rapid prototypes, working models, or facsimiles of the product as early as possible to show to the customer in order to seek feedback regarding market acceptance and needed design changes. Don't wait until the very end of the Development stage—the field trials or user tests—to unveil the product to the customer. There could be some very unpleasant surprises!

5. **Use market studies and studies of buyer behavior to help plan the market launch**. Such studies are noticeable for their absence, with only 17.3% of businesses conducting such market studies, the second weakest area in the list of five in Exhibit 6.3 This is a very strong best practice, and a key discriminator between the best and worst performers. These studies should focus on buyer behavior: Who is the buyer and who are the key purchase influencers; how do they go about purchasing the product (for example, where do they get their product information); and what are their choice criteria when it comes to selecting a brand or supplier?

Insist on Sharp, Early Product Definition Before Development Begins

A failure to *define the product* before Development begins—its target market; the concept, benefits, and positioning; and its requirements, features, and specs—is a major cause of both new product failure and serious delays in time-to-market.[19] In spite of the fact that early and stable product definition is consistently cited as a key to success, businesses continue to perform poorly here. Our APQC benchmarking study reveals that about 70% of businesses do a mediocre or poor job of product definition (Exhibit 6.4).

Research finds a strong and direct link between sharp, early, stable product definition and success. Our recent benchmarking study shows clearly that sharp, early product definition is significantly connected to performance: Simply stated, best performers undertake a thorough product definition before Development begins; poor performers do not![20] In a similar vein, the project studies demonstrate a very strong impact of product

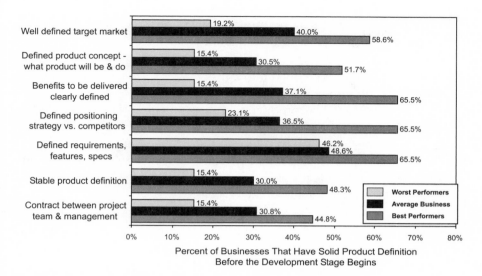

Exhibit 6.4 Sharp, Early Product Definition—Impact on Performance

definition on performance: Early and stable product definition enhances project success rates by 59.2 percentage points; such well-defined projects have 3.7 times the success rate and 1.6 times the market share as those which lack definition; and product definition is significantly and strongly correlated with performance.[21]

While a minority of firms do get sharp, early product definition in place, in most businesses, this product definition needs to be sharpened. Here are some of the elements of product definition that best performers get right (see Exhibit 6.4):[22]

1. The target market defined—at which segment the product will be targeted. From market segmentation, all else flows! Thus, an important element of product definition is to specify the target market or intended user for the new product.
2. The product concept defined—a simple statement of what the product will be and do, conceptually. Ideally it is written in the words of the customer or user: how she or he would describe the product to colleagues. Surprisingly, this is a very weak area, with only 30.5% of businesses undertaking concept definition well.
3. The benefits to be delivered to the customer—how the product will benefit the customer or user, translated into the value proposition: why they will buy it.
4. The positioning strategy defined—how the product will be positioned in the eyes of customers/users versus competitive products.

5. The product's features, requirements, and specifications defined—
the technical side of the product definition.

These elements can be fashioned into a first-rate *product definition template*, which is then built into your idea-to-launch framework.

Some more caveats: This product definition must be based on facts, the result of solid upfront homework and a strong early customer involvement; it should be signed off by all project team members to demonstrate total alignment of all relevant functions; and then it should be signed off by you, the leadership team of the business, to demonstrate buy-in and functional alignment at the top of the business.

Overcoming major time-wasters: Two of the greatest time-wasters in NPD are *unstable product specs* and *project scope creep*. Unstable specs is a serious deficiency, with only 30% of businesses maintaining product definition stability through the Development stage (Exhibit 6.4). The scenario is this: The project team thinks they have a good idea of customer requirements, so they skip through the homework phase, define the product on paper, and rush into Development. Much later in the game—perhaps after the final prototype has been developed, and during the field trials—the team discovers a number of new features or performance requirements that *suddenly must be built into the product*.

Worse yet, the entire scope of the project may have shifted. It began as a single-application product, but now is suddenly a multimarket product. And so the project team must back-track; the product and project are redefined; and more months are added to development. It's like trying to score a goal in soccer, but someone keeps moving the goalposts.

Note that top performers seek and gain *stable product specifications* before entering the Development stage—this is a key to success. And using a *teaming contract* between the project team and management to define the product, the project, and expectations before the Development stage is considered a better practice by some businesses in an attempt to bring stability and rigor to the product and project definition.

> *Some examples:* The concept of a *teaming contract* is one that is gaining increasing popularity. 3M relies on a "team charter" to obtain agreement between project team members and their executives, while Bausch & Lomb uses a "project strategic decision package." Once signed, any subsequent changes must be approved by all team members and management who signed the original agreement. This contract, coupled with the essential signatures, prevents unnecessary scope creep in the project.

Success and speed: Projects that have such sharp, early fact-based definition prior to Development are both more successful and speed to market faster. Here's why:

- Building a definition step into the new product process forces more attention to the upfront or pre-development activities. If the home-work hasn't been done, then arriving at a sharp definition that all parties will agree to is next to impossible.
- The definition serves as a communication tool and guide. All-party agreement or buy-in means that each functional area involved in the project has a clear and consistent definition of what the product and project are and is committed to it. There is functional alignment and consistent priorities across functions.
- This definition also provides a clear set of objectives for the Develop-ment stage of the project and the development team members. With clear product objectives, development typically proceeds more effi-ciently and quickly: no moving goalposts and no fuzzy targets!

Notes for Senior Management

Management in best practice companies demand and get sharp, early product definition prior to the commencement of the Development stage. This definition includes some or all of the seven elements listed in Exhibit 6.4. Use these elements as a guide for a product definition template.

When designing or overhauling your idea-to-launch framework, build a *product definition step* or *check-point* into the process before Develop-ment begins. Make product definition a *mandatory deliverable* as part of the project team's business case. Moreover, this product definition must be fact-based and signed off by all members of the project team. And consider the use of a teaming contract, which includes the product defi-nition, between senior management and team. Make it a rule: No project enters Development without this product definition in place!

Make Sure the Upfront Pre-Development Homework Is Done

The front end of the NPD process is the most problematic phase of new product projects.[23] It's here where the new product idea is fleshed out into a clear product definition; where the magnitude of the opportunity is assessed and the business case constructed; and the action plan for the project is mapped out. All these activities are supposed to occur before serious development work begins—at least, that's the theory! But in practice this homework phase is much weaker: As Exhibit 6.5 reveals, only 44.8% of businesses place a strong emphasis on upfront homework, which means that 55% do not: The homework is handled in a weak or mediocre fashion. But most important, solid upfront homework is clearly a best practice: 62.1% of best performers place considerable emphasis on this homework phase, while only 38.5% of worst performers do.

Too many new product projects move from the idea stage right into Development with little or no assessment or upfront homework. Why? Because *senior management allows it to happen*; and because senior management has not mandated or embraced a new product framework which demands that solid upfront homework be done! Homework includes those many activities that occur before Development begins: initial screening; market, user, and competitive studies; technical and manufacturing appraisals; and financial analysis.

The results of a "ready, fire, aim" approach are usually disastrous. In our project studies, inadequate upfront homework is a major reason for new product failure.[24] A failure to spend time and money on the upfront steps, and moving directly from an idea into a full-fledged development effort, are familiar themes in new product misfires.

By contrast, more homework prior to the initiation of product design and development is consistently found to be a key factor in success. Our research shows that the quality of execution of the pre-development

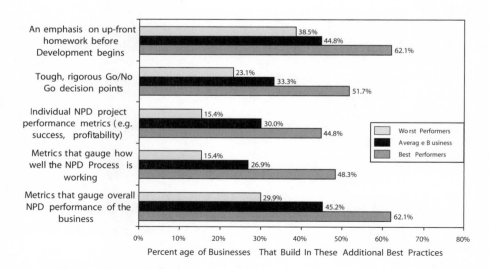

Exhibit 6.5   Impact of Other Best Practices Built into the Idea-to-Launch Framework

steps—initial screening, preliminary market and technical studies, market research, and business analysis—is closely tied to the a business's NPD performance (see Exhibit 6.1). There's more: Solid upfront homework drives up new product success rates by 43.2 percentage points and is strongly correlated with performance; and projects that boast solid upfront homework achieve 2.4 times the success rate and 2.2 times the market share as those with poor homework.[25]

> *A solution:* A common problem that plagues the upfront homework phase is there is no one with the time to do the front-end activities of early-stage projects. Air Products & Chemicals recognizes how important these front-end activities are. The company thus allocates 20 to 30 hours of budgeted time to concept development per project; moreover, this person is dedicated to only one concept at a time. This allocation ensures that the early-stage project receives the necessary focus, and that the required front-end activities receive attention and effort.

The emphasis that the Japanese devote to the planning stage of the new product process is described by Havelock and Elder: Japanese developers make a clear distinction between the "planning" and the "implementation" phases of a new technology initiative. The objective of planning is complete understanding of the problem and the related technology before a Go decision is made. It is reported to be an unrushed process that might look agonizingly drawn out to Western eyes.[26]

Key homework questions: The pre-development, upfront homework activities are important because they qualify and define the project. They answer key success questions such as:

- Is the project an economically attractive one? Will the product sell at sufficient volumes and margins to justify investment in development and commercialization?
- Who exactly is the target customer? And how should the product be positioned?
- What exactly should the product be to make it a winner? What features, attributes, and performance characteristics should be built into it to yield a product that will delight the customer?
- Can the product be developed and at the right cost? What is the likely technical solution and what are the technical risks here? And how will it be produced and delivered, with what risks, and at what costs?

Take the time to save time: Some managers seem skeptical about the need for this vital homework because they're in too big a hurry: "More homework means longer development times to market!" is their excuse. This is a valid concern, but the facts reveal that homework pays for itself not only via higher success rates, but also through reduced development times. The result is faster to market:[27]

- First, all the evidence points to a much higher likelihood of product failure if the homework is omitted. So the choice is yours: *fast failures* or thoughtful successes!
- Second, solid homework results in better product definition, which in turn speeds up the development process. When projects are poorly defined as they enter the Development phase (vague targets and moving goalposts), it is often the result of weak upfront homework.
- Third, rarely does a product concept remain the same from beginning to end of the project. Given this inevitable product design evolution, the time to make the majority of these design changes is not as the product is moving out of Development and into production. More homework upfront anticipates these changes and encourages them to occur earlier in the process rather than later, when they are more costly.

Notes for Senior Management

Take a hard look at your new product idea-to-launch framework. If homework is typically lacking (it often is!), then you have no one to blame but yourselves. *Homework doesn't get done because senior management does not demand it!* I find that either senior management has failed to establish guidelines or expectations to ensure that the right homework is done, or management fails to enforce the discipline of the process.

The solution: When you overhaul your idea-to-launch framework, be sure to build a detailed homework stage (or two) into your process—a homework phase that results in a business case based on fact rather than speculation. These initial screening, analyses, and definitional stages are critical to success. As a member of your business's leadership team, resist the temptation to allow projects to skip over these vital upfront stages, and don't approve an ill-defined and poorly investigated project moving into the Development stage. Insist that solid upfront homework be undertaken.

Build In Tough and Demanding Go/Kill Gates

Senior management must learn to *drown some puppies!* Indeed, having tough Go/Kill decision-points in the idea-to-launch framework—where some projects really do get killed—is strongly connected to businesses' NPD performance, with 2.5 times as many best performers incorporating tough gates into their new product playbooks as poor performers (Exhibit 6.5). Building rigorous Go/Kill decision-points into your idea-to-launch framework in the form of tough gates is a clear best practice.

The problem is that most businesses have *too many projects*, and often the *wrong projects* in their development pipelines: a lack of focus. Exhibit 4.4 revealed how weak the portfolio of projects generally is. In short, the gating system is broken! Many new product projects are either. . .

- ⬧ unfit for commercialization: They are simply bad concepts—a weak market, no fit with the company, or no competitive advantage; or
- ⬧ low-value projects: These projects deliver only marginal value to the business.

One cause of this lack of focus is that there is *no kill mechanism* in place: There are no demanding Go/Kill decision-points in the idea-to-launch framework. This is indeed a very weak ingredient of new product processes, with only one-third of businesses featuring such rigorous Go/Kill decision-points (Exhibit 6.5). Some businesses *claim to have Go/Kill gates* in their new product processes; but a closer inspection reveals that these are often merely "project review points" or "milestone reviews" with no tough decisions made. As one executive declared: "We never kill projects . . . we just *wound* them!" The fact is that most of the critical Go/Kill decision-points—from initial screening through to pre-commercialization business analysis—are plagued by serious weaknesses: decisions not made, little or no real prioritization, poor information inputs, no criteria for decisions, and inconsistent or capricious decision making.[28]

A parallel cause is *management's inability to say no*. Once projects gain momentum, it becomes increasingly difficult to stop them—to really drown some puppies. Some projects move far into Development without serious scrutiny, and thus they get a life of their own. And so the process is more like a *tunnel* than a *funnel*. One senior technical leader confessed that his projects become like "express trains, slowing down at the stations but never with the intention of stopping until they reach their final destination, the market-place."[29]

This lack of tough Go/Kill decision-points means too many projects for the limited resources available; resources squandered on the wrong projects;

and too many late kills or product failures at launch. Another result of weak Go/Kill decision-points is that many marginal projects are approved, while the truly deserving projects are starved.

The solution: When you design your new product idea-to-launch framework, be sure to build in robust and rigorous Go/Kill gates. Use some of the decision-making tools I outlined in Chapter 5 at your gates. And finally, incorporate some of the ingredients of a best-in-class idea-to-launch framework described earlier in this chapter, namely:

- clearly defined Go/Kill decision-points or gates
- visible Go/Kill criteria at gates
- deliverables defined for each gate
- gatekeepers designated for each gate

These practices and tools aren't just theory. They've been incorporated into best performers' idea-to-launch frameworks, and they work!

Put NPD Performance Metrics in Place

You cannot manage what you don't measure! How can you even begin to improve your business's NPD results unless you measure them to begin with? Top-performing businesses keep score in the product innovation war, according to our APQC benchmarking study; and I rate *establishing NPD performance metrics as a critical best practice.* So, if you seek improved new product results, then a key step is to put performance metrics in place.

Setting up NPD performance metrics is one of the vital best practices designed to ensure that your idea-to-launch framework delivers results. These performance metrics are important for four reasons:

1. *Performance metrics mean senior management focuses on and pays attention to NPD.* Bonuses and personal objectives based on NPD results changes senior management's behavior and emphasis. For example, management performance bonuses based on a metric such as "percentage of sales from NPs" cause management to become more long-term oriented (as opposed to just emphasizing quarter-to-quarter results).
2. *Performance metrics are a useful diagnostic tool*—an alert for something wrong. For example, a slip rate* greater than 30% signals schedule

---

*Slip rate is an on-time performance metric, defined in Chapter 2.

and time-to-market problems, and points to the need for corrective action to remove the time-wasters.

3. *Performance metrics help to establish project team accountability.* Some metrics gauge project performance results versus promises by the project team. This is a key best practice, so build a post-launch review into every project.

4. *Performance metrics help senior management keep score over time.* They gauge whether your NP results are getting better or worse year-to-year, and hence may signal needed action: course changes or corrections, or perhaps even dramatic moves.

Three types of metrics are employed to gauge NPD results:

1. Metrics for NPD projects: "Was that project a success? No one knows!" exclaimed a frustrated senior marketing person. He is not alone: Most firms don't keep score when it comes to tracking results from new product projects. The use of metrics to gauge how well individual projects perform—project success, profitability, NPV, and the like—is a major weakness, with only 30% of businesses having such metrics in place. More best performers do (44.8%), while only 15.4% of the worst measure project results (Exhibit 6.5).

Some examples from top performers:

- "People are mobilized by what is measured" claims the VP of R&D at EXFO Engineering. Within its NPD process, EXFO measures time to volume, project cost, earned value, and ROI. It also examines the *dynamic time-to-market*, which is a comparison of the projected schedule to the actual time at project reviews held every two weeks.
- ExxonMobil Chemical conducts two post-launch reviews on completed new product projects. The first is one to three months after launch and includes comparisons of the project *cost and time targets* versus actual performance. The second occurs three to 12 months later and captures early commercial results, such as market receptivity and manufacturing and technology performance.
- Procter & Gamble measures new product performance against "critical successes factors." These success factors, such as "Year 1 Sales" and "realized NPV," are established fairly early in the project and are used to make Go/Kill decisions throughout the project; but they are also measured after launch to gauge how well the project fared.

Most companies use multiple project performance metrics to gauge whether a particular new product project is successful (4.97 different metrics per business, on average). Exhibit 6.6 provides a list of the most popular

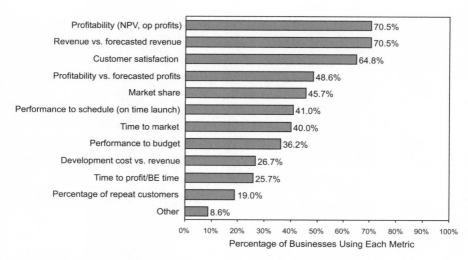

Exhibit 6.6 Metrics Used to Gauge Individual Project Performance

project metrics, which provides insights into which measures to use in your business.

2. Metrics on how well the NPD process is working: These metrics focus on whether the NPD process is working well—whether projects are following the process, effective gates are being held, and the like. EXFO's *dynamic time to market* cited above is an example. These metrics are also a major weakness in many businesses' NPD processes, with 34.6% of businesses scoring poorly here, and only 26.9% using such metrics effectively. Again, best performers tend to have such metrics in place, three times as likely as worst performers.

> *An example:* Air Products conducts a quarterly review of the performance of their new product process. The metrics employed gauge whether projects are on track, are doing well, and are on schedule.
>
> *Another example:* Dow Corning uses its "red-green" chart as a visual metric to spot projects in trouble, or gates and stages in trouble (Exhibit 6.7). Here the various gates in their *Stage-Gate®* process are shown across the top of the grid, while the projects are listed down the side. Inside each box is the expected date for the gate meeting: when the project should have reached that review point. The actual date—when it really arrived—is also shown. When a project is "on time," color the box green; when it is late, color the box red.
>
> Reading across the rows, one can spot projects that are clearly in trouble: missing key gate review dates. Reading down the columns shows the gates that are missed, suggesting that the previous stage is very much in trouble. For example, in the grid in Exhibit 6.7, Projects B

	Gate 2	Gate 3	Gate 4	Gate 5	PLR
Project A	Aug 1/02 Sept 1/02	Dec 1/02 Feb 1/03	Sept 1/03 Sept 1/03	Dec 1/03	--
Project B	Jul 1/02 Sept 1/02	Aug 1/02 Nov 1/02	Dec 1/02 Feb 1/03	Mar 1/03 Jun 1/03	Jun 1/04
Project C	Feb 1/02 Apr 1/02	Jun 1/02 Aug 1/02	Dec 1/03 Feb 1/03	June 1/03 Jul 1/03	Jul 1/04
Project D	Jun 1/02 Jun 1/02	Jul 1/902 Nov 1/02	Feb 1/03 Mar 1/03	Jul 1/03 Aug 1/03	Aug 1/04
Project E	Sept 1/02 Sept 1/02	Nov 1/02 Dec 1/02	Aug 1/03 Sept 1/03	Dec 1/03	--
Project F	Nov 1/02 Dec 1/02	Mar 1/03 May 1/03	Dec 1/03	--	--

In use, the light shaded cells are green; the dark shaded cells are red (not shown in this black-and-white diagram). Color a cell red when the actual and scheduled arrival date at a gate is more than one month apart (project is one month late). Color a cell green if the project is on-time at the gate. Reading across the rows, one can easily spot projects in trouble. And reading down the columns, one can see stages and gates that are problematic.

Exhibit 6.7   Red-Green Chart Showing Time Slippage at Gates

and C are clearly off course; while Stage 2, the Feasibility stage, appears to be the most problematic stage in the process.

3. Metrics to gauge the business's overall NPD performance: The majority of top-performing businesses (62%) keep score in the product innovation war: They measure and report *overall new product results for the business* (see Exhibit 6.5). By contrast, only 30% of poor-performing businesses measure overall performance results. Note that keeping score is a moderately weak area, with less than half (45.2%) of the businesses actually measuring how well they perform at NPD. Most businesses use multiple metrics to gauge how well their total NPD effort performs: the average business employs 2.85 different overall-performance metrics (the most popular metrics are shown in Exhibit 6.8).[30]

In all cases, a time frame is defined: new products launched over the last two, three, or five years. Often the definition of "what is a new product" proves problematic, but in better practice firms, this has been precisely defined to enable the use of the metrics in Exhibit 6.8.

Before you jump to selecting one of these metrics for your business, some words of warning: Although the measures in Exhibit 6.8 are popular, be aware that they are *not necessarily the right or only metrics* to gauge

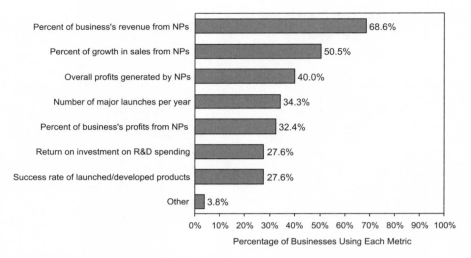

Exhibit 6.8 Metrics Used to Gauge Performance of Business's Total NPD Effort

performance. As one astute and experienced CTO in a major mechanical equipment manufacturer noted:

> Percentage of sales is a "good news, bad news" metric. One of our business units has a very high percentage of sales from new products. But this is due to a *combination of negative factors*: high and costly product obsolesce in their market; new products that did not perform—either technically or financially—and needed to be fixed and/or replaced; and over-reaction to every single customer request. The result is a lot of undesirable "churn" in the product line, which is very costly to the business. So a high percentage of sales by new products is not always a good thing.

The point is that not even the most popular NPD business metrics are perfect. And relying on a single metric, as in this example, may induce poor performance. Instead, I recommend the use of at least *several business metrics* to gauge NPD performance, taken from the list outlined in Exhibit 6.8 and also from the experiences of best performers:

- ‣ percentage of your business's *revenue* or *profits* derived from new products (or the percentage of your business's *sales or profit growth* coming from new products)
- ‣ overall annual profits generated by your new products ($000)
- ‣ realized value (actual project NPVs as a percent of forecasted NPVs, summed across all projects)
- ‣ success rate: percent of projects meeting first-year sales (or profits) targets

- the slip rate (or some other measure of on-time performance), averaged across all launches
- percentage of late kills

Note that many of these business metrics are simply the aggregation of individual project measures (item 1 above), but reported in a different way.

Notes for Senior Management

When implementing or overhauling your idea-to-launch framework, don't forget to emulate the best performers:

- Build in tough Go/Kill decision-points or gates, where bad projects really do get killed, complete with visible criteria, defined deliverables, and designated gatekeepers. Use the project selection tools outlined in Chapter 5 at your gates.
- And don't forget to put metrics in place to gauge:
  - how successful or profitable your projects are (as part of a post-launch review),
  - how well your NPD process is working
  - how well your business is doing at product innovation

You'll find that you need at least several metrics per category, as no one metric seems to do the whole job. Indeed, over-emphasis on a single metric may actually encourage or reward the wrong type of management behavior (witness the dilemma with the "percentage of sales" metric).

Both practices—tough Go/Kill gates and performance metrics—are typically weak areas, yet strongly separate the best from worst performers.

Toward an Effective Idea-to-Launch Framework

In this chapter, you've seen the need for a playbook, game plan, or idea-to-launch framework. And you've also gained some insights into some of the best practices that top performers build into their new product playbooks. So read on, because in the next chapter, we'll look at a real idea-to-launch framework—one that is based on what the best firms have in place, and the kind of framework that you might want to install in your own business.

Notes

1. *Stage-Gate®* processes, or idea-to-launch frameworks, are identified as an NPD best practice in M. M. Menke, "Essentials of R&D Strategic Excellence," *Research-Technology Management*, 40, 5, September–October 1997, 42–47; A. Griffin, *Drivers of NPD Success: The 1997 PDMA Report.* Chicago: Product Development & Management Association, 1997; and R. G. Cooper, *Winning at New Products: Accelerating the Process from Idea to Launch*, 3rd ed. Reading, MA: Perseus, 2001.

2. Many of the research findings and conclusions cited in this chapter are taken from our APQC benchmarking study; see note 29 in Chapter 1; also R. G. Cooper, S. J. Edgett, & E. J. Kleinschmidt, "Benchmarking Best Practices in NPD: Part III—The NPD Process & Decisive Idea-to-Launch Practices," *Research-Technology Management*, 47, 6, November–December 2004.

3. Source of quotations is our APQC benchmarking study, see note 2. Case studies of each of these five companies, complete with outlines of their new product idea-to-launch frameworks, are available in the appendix of the full APQC benchmarking report. Available as: *Best Practices in Product Development: What Distinguishes Top Performers* at www.prod-dev.com.

4. APQC benchmarking study: see note 2.

5. These idea-to-launch activities are defined in more detail in R. G. Cooper, *Winning at New Products: Accelerating the Process from Idea to Launch*, 3rd ed. Reading, MA: Perseus, 2001.

6. The research results on quality-of-execution are from our APQC benchmarking study: see note 2.

7. *NewProd®* projects studies: see note 30 in Chapter 1.

8. APQC benchmarking study: see note 2.

9. "Urine-Off Cleaner: Success by Accident," *Sarasota Herald Tribune,* January 10, 2004, D-1.

10. See Cooper, note 1; C. A. Di Benedetto, "Identifying the Key Success Factors in New Product Launch," *Journal of Product Innovation Management*, 16, 6, November 1999, 530–544; S. Mishra, D. Kim, & D. H. Lee, "Factors Affecting New Product Success: Cross Country Comparisons," *Journal of Product Innovation Management*, 13, 6, November 1996, 530–550; M. M. Montoya-Weiss & R. J. Calantone, "Determinants of New Product Performance: A Review and Meta Analysis," *Journal of Product Innovation Management*, 11, 5, November 1994, 397–417; and X. M. Song & M. E. Parry, "What Separates Japanese New Product Winners from Losers," *Journal of Product Innovation Management*, 13, 5, September 1996, 422–439.

11. *NewProd®* projects studies: see note 7.

12. APQC benchmarking study: see note 2.

13. Earlier benchmarking studies: see note 29 in Chapter 1.

14. APQC benchmarking study: see note 2.

15. See E. A. Von Hippel, S., Thomke, & M. Sonnack, "Creating Breakthroughs at 3M," *Harvard Business Review*, September–October 1999, 47–57.

16. Kraft Foods case study found in the APQC benchmarking study: see notes 2 and 3.

17. For voice-of-customer methods, see P. Lindstedt, & J. Burenius, *The Value Model: How to Master Product Development and Create Unrivalled Customer Value.* Sweden: NIMBA AB, 2003, www.nimba.com.

18. In-company private address by Prof. Abbie Griffin, former editor of the *Journal of Product Innovation Management*.

19. *NewProd®* projects studies: see note 7; also R. G. Cooper, "Developing New Products on Time, in Time," *Research-Technology Management*, 38, 5, September–October 1995, 49–57.

20. APQC benchmarking study: see note 2.

21. *NewProd®* projects studies: see note 7.

22. APQC benchmarking study: see note 2.

23. See R. G. Cooper, *Winning at New Products: Accelerating the Process from Idea to Launch*, 3rd ed. Reading, MA: Perseus, 2001; X. M. Song & M. E. Parry, note 10; S. Thomke, & T. Fujimoto, "The Effect of 'Front-Loading' Problem Solving on Product Development Performance," *Journal of Product Innovation Management*, 17, 2, March 2000, 128–142; and R. G. Cooper & E. J. Kleinschmidt, "An Investigation into the New Product Process: Steps, Deficiencies and Impact," *Journal of Product Innovation Management*, 3, 2, 1986, 71–85.

24. *NewProd®* projects studies: see note 7.

25. *NewProd®* projects studies: see note 7.

26. Havelock & Elder as cited in E. M. Rogers, "The R&D/Marketing Interface in the Technological Innovation Process," in M. M. Saghafi & A. K. Gupta, eds., *Managing the R&D Interface for Process Success: The Telecommunications Focus,* Vol. I, *Advances in Telecommunications Management.* Greenwich, CT: JAI, 1990.

27. R. G. Cooper, note 5; and R. G. Cooper, "Developing New Products on Time, in Time," *Research-Technology Management,* 38, 5, September–October 1995, 49–57.

28. These weaknesses were identified in our APQC benchmarking study: see note 2; also in a study of portfolio management and project selection practices, undertaken by the author and colleagues, Drs. Scott Edgett and Elko Kleinschmidt; see the two-part article series: R. G. Cooper, S. J. Edgett, & E. J. Kleinschmidt, "Portfolio Management in New Product Development: Lessons from the Leaders," *Research-Technology Management,* 40, 5, September–October 1997, and 40, 6, November–December 1997.

29. Taken from an internal Procter & Gamble report on new products.

30. APQC benchmarking study: see note 2.

7

A World-Class *Stage-Gate®* Idea-to-Launch Framework for Your Business

*A process is a methodology that is developed to replace the old ways
and to guide corporate activity year after year. It is not a special guest.
It is not temporary. It is not to be tolerated for a while and then abandoned.*
—**Thomas H. Berry,** *Managing the Total Quality Transformation*[1]

The *Stage-Gate®* Framework

An idea-to-launch framework for product innovation is one solution to what ails so many businesses' new product efforts.[2] Such a framework is also one of the *four points of performance* in the *Innovation Diamond* (see Exhibit 7.1). Facing increased pressure to reduce the cycle time, yet improve their new product success rates, companies implement *Stage-Gate®* methods to manage, direct, and control their product-innovation initiatives. That is, they have developed a systematic process—a playbook, game plan, or template—for moving a new product project through the various stages and steps from idea to launch. But most important, they have built into their framework the many *critical success factors* and *industry best practices* highlighted in Chapter 6 in order to heighten the effectiveness of their idea-to-launch framework.

Almost every top-performing company has implemented a stage-and-gate framework to drive their new product projects through to commercialization, according to our APQC benchmarking study, and a solid idea-to-launch process is the strongest best practice observed among the sample of businesses.[3] The PDMA's best practices study concurs: "nearly 60% of the firms surveyed use some form of *Stage-Gate®* process. Over half of the firms which have adopted *Stage-Gate®* processes have moved from

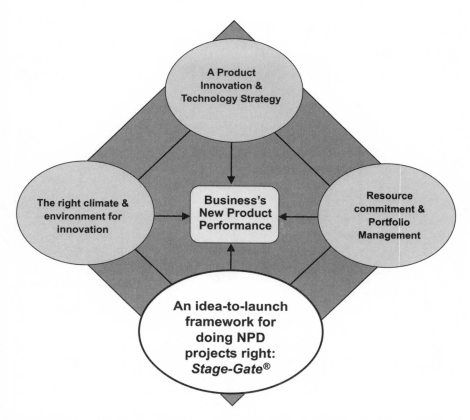

Exhibit 7.1 A Solid Idea-to-Launch Framework to Drive New Products to Market Is One of the *Four Points of Performance* in the *Innovation Diamond*

a basic process to more sophisticated versions with formal process owner-ship and facilitation (18.5% of the total) or third generation processes with more flexible gates and stage structures."[4]

Stage-Gate® methods work! According to the same PDMA best practices study cited above, "the Best [companies] are more likely to use some type of formal NPD process than the Rest. They are more likely to have moved from simpler *Stage-Gate*® processes to more sophisticated facilitated or third generation processes."[5] And our APQC benchmarking study found that many of the practices that businesses had embedded within their idea-to-launch process have a very strong positive impact on perfor-mance—they separate the best performers from the rest.

The challenge in this chapter is this: Given the best practices gleaned from new product success-and-failure investigations and the benchmarking studies (previous chapter), how can you translate these into an operational and effective new product methodology? For example, how do you build in quality of execution, or a strong market orientation, or better pre-development homework? And what is your role as a member of the leadership team to ensure that such a *Stage-Gate®* process is implemented in your business, and really does get practiced?

Notes for Senior Management

Do you have a systematic idea-to-launch framework for NPD in your business? Many leading companies do, and the results seem to be worth the effort. So, by this point, you're probably thinking that you should either . . .

▶ move to install an idea-to-launch framework, such as *Stage-Gate®*, in your business, and make sure it works; or if you already have a process. . .
▶ have your current process audited, and begin an overhaul of your current idea-to-launch method.

But before you proceed, here are some points to ponder—some of the goals that such a process must achieve. Does yours?

The Ten Goals of a Best-in-Class Idea-to-Launch Framework

Here is what you should try to build into an effective idea-to-launch framework for your business—essentially an integration and summary from previous chapters of what we know drives new product success.

Goal 1: Exemplary Quality of Execution—Second to None

The argument that the proponents of total quality management make goes something like this: "The definition of quality is precise: It means meeting all the requirements all the time.[6] It is based on the principle that all work is a process. It focuses on improving business processes to eliminate errors." The concept is perfectly logical and essentially simple. Most smart things are. And the same logic can be applied to new product development.

Product innovation is a process. It begins with an idea and culminates in a successful product launch. But processes aren't new to the business environment. There are many examples of well-run processes in business, such as manufacturing processes, information processes, and so on.

A quality-of-execution crisis exists, however, in the product innovation process. There is a need for a more *systematic and quality approach* to the way firms conceive, develop, and launch new products. The way to deal with the quality problem is to visualize product innovation as a process, and to apply *process management* and *quality management techniques* to this process. Note that any process in business can be managed, and managed with a view to quality. Get the details of your process right, and the result will be a high-quality output.

Quality of execution is the goal of the new product process. More specifically, the ideal process should:

1. *Focus on completeness:* Ensure that the key activities that are central to the success of a new product project are indeed carried out—no gaps, no omissions, a "complete" process.
2. *Focus on quality:* Ensure that the execution of these activities is first-rate; that is, treat innovation as a process, emphasize DIRTFooT (doing it right the first time), and build in quality controls and checks.
3. *Focus on the important:* Devote attention and resources to the pivotal and particularly weak steps in the new product process, notably the upfront and market-oriented activities.

Stage-Gate® builds into the innovation process *high quality of execution* in much the same way that quality programs that have been successfully implemented on the factory floor. How?

- by establishing quality control check-points—the gates—where the quality of projects, quality of work, and integrity of data are challenged by senior management.
- by designating the leadership team as the main gatekeepers in the business: You are the quality controllers!
- by using clear and consistent metrics at gates—the Go/Kill criteria—so that projects are judged objectively and effectively.
- by defining expectations: which activities, tasks, methods, and best practices should be built into the stages of the process to deliver a winning product.
- by specifying visible deliverables to gates, along with action standards: what the project team is expected to deliver to each gate review.
- by having an effective resource allocation method at gates, to ensure that resources—people, time, and money—are available to enable the project team to do a quality job.

The ultimate goal here is doing the *right projects*. . . and *doing them right!*

Goal 2: Sharper Focus, Better Project Prioritization

Most businesses' new product efforts suffer from a lack of focus: too many projects, and not enough resources. Adequate resources is a principal driver of businesses' new product performance, but a lack of resources plagues too many development efforts. Sometimes this lack is simply that: Management hasn't devoted the needed people and money to the company's new product effort. But often, this resource problem stems from trying to do *too many projects* with a limited set of resources—that is, from a *lack of focus*, the result of inadequate project evaluations. The root cause of this lack of focus is management's failure to set priorities and make tough Go/Kill decisions. In short, the gates are weak.

The need is for a *new product funnel*, rather than *tunnel*. A *new product funnel* builds in tough Go/Kill decision-points in the form of gates; the poor projects are weeded out; scarce resources are directed toward the truly deserving projects; and more focus is the result (Exhibit 7.2). These gates are the bail-out points where you ask, "Are you still in the game?" They are the *quality control check-points* in your new product process, and check the quality, merit, and progress of the project.

Goal 3: A Strong Market Orientation with Voice-of-Customer Inputs

If positive new product performance is the goal, then a market orientation—executing the key marketing activities in a quality fashion—must be built into the new product process as a matter of routine rather than by exception. Marketing inputs must play a decisive role from beginning to end of the project. The following nine actions are *integral and vital plays* in the new product game plan:

- preliminary market assessment
- voice-of-customer research to determine users' unmet needs and wants
- competitive analysis
- value-in-use analysis
- concept testing
- customer reaction and feedback during Development
- user tests, preference tests, and field trials
- test market or trial sell
- market launch based on a solid market launch plan

How do you ensure that your business's new product process is decidedly market-oriented?

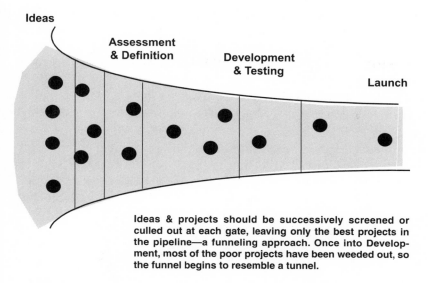

Ideas

Assessment & Definition

Development & Testing

Launch

Ideas & projects should be successively screened or culled out at each gate, leaving only the best projects in the pipeline—a funneling approach. Once into Development, most of the poor projects have been weeded out, so the funnel begins to resemble a tunnel.

Exhibit 7.2   A Funnel Leading to a Tunnel Weeds Out Poor Projects Early

▶ First, the key marketing tasks should be *designed into your new product process*. In many businesses' new product processes, they are not! If you already have a new product process, read through it, and see how many of the nine vital marketing actions have been left out.

▶ Second, the leadership team—the gatekeepers—must mandate that such marketing actions be undertaken in projects. When they're not, stop the project! The problem is that, in the short term, marketing actions are treated as *discretionary* or "optional." By contrast, technical activities, such as the physical development of the product, undertaking a trial production run, or doing lab tests to meet regulatory requirements, are normally not discretionary. Remember: Marketing actions listed above make the difference between winning and losing!

▶ Finally, make the marketing resources available to project teams. Recall from Chapter 4 how much more marketing and sales resources and people were available to NPD project team in top-performing businesses.

Goal 4: Better Upfront Homework and Sharp, Early and Stable Product Definition

New product success or failure is largely decided in the first few plays of the game—in those crucial steps and tasks that precede the actual development of the product. The upfront homework defines the product and builds the business case for development. The ideal new product process ensures that these early stages are carried out and that the product is fully defined before the project is allowed to become a full-fledged development project.

The need for solid upfront homework parallels the case for a stronger market orientation (Goal 3). Once again the onus is on you, the leadership team, to be the enablers. Your task is to ensure that your new product process does indeed include solid homework and stable, fact-based product definition. For example, build in a product definition check-point in your process. And be prepared to halt projects if the homework and product definition aren't in place. Finally, you must make available the resources required to do the upfront work.

Goal 5: A Fast-Paced Game Plan via Parallel Processing

New product teams face a dilemma. On the one hand, they are urged by senior management to compress the cycle time—to shorten the elapsed time from idea to launch. On the other hand, they are urged to improve the effectiveness of product development: cut down the failure rate . . . do it right! This desire to "do it right" suggests a more thorough, longer process.

Parallel processing is one solution to the need for a complete and quality process; it also meets the time pressures of today's fast-paced business world. Traditionally, new product projects have been managed via a *series approach*: one task strung out after another, in sequence. The analogy is that of a relay race, with each department running with the project for its 100 meter lap. Phrases such as "hand off" or "passing the project on," and even "dropping the ball" or "throwing it over the wall," are common in this relay race approach to new products.

In marked contrast to the relay race or sequential approach, with parallel processing many activities are undertaken *concurrently* rather than in series. The appropriate analogy is that of a rugby match rather than a relay race.[7] A team (not a single runner) appears on the field. A scrum or huddle ensues, after which the ball emerges. Players run down the field in parallel with much interaction, constantly passing the ball laterally. After 25 meters or so, the players converge for another scrum, huddle, or gate review, followed by another stage of activities.

With parallel processing, the game is far more intense than a relay race and more work gets done in an elapsed time period: three or four activities are done simultaneously and by different members on the project team. There is less chance of an activity or task being overlooked or handled poorly because of lack of time: The activity is done in parallel, not in series, and hence does not extend the total elapsed project time. Moreover, the activities are designed to feed each other—the metaphor of the ball being passed back and forth across the field. And finally, the entire new product process becomes cross-functional and multidisciplinary: The whole team—marketing, R&D, engineering, sales, manufacturing—is on the field together, participates actively in each play, and takes part in every gate review or scrum.

Goal 6: A True Cross-Functional Team Approach

The new product process is cross-functional: It requires the input and active participation of players from many different functions in the organization. The multifunctional nature of innovation coupled with the desire for parallel processing means that a *cross-functional team approach* is mandatory. Essential ingredients are:

- a cross-functional team with committed team players from the different functional areas
- a defined team captain or leader, accountable for the entire project
- a leader with formal authority (co-opting authority from the functional heads)
- a fluid team structure, with new members joining or dropped as work requirements demand
- a small core group of responsible, committed and accountable team players from beginning to end

We'll look much more closely about how to organize for effective cross-functional teams in Chapter 8, but for now, let's just adopt the principle of cross-functional teams as part of your idea-to-launch process.

Goal 7: Products with Competitive Advantage— Differentiated Products, Unique Benefits, Superior Value for the Customer

Don't forget to build in product superiority at every opportunity. This is one key to new product success, yet all too often, when redesigning their new product processes, firms fall into the trap of repeating current, often faulty, practices: There's no attempt to seek truly superior products. And so the results are predicable: more hohum, tired products. Here's how to drive the quest for product advantage:

- Ensure that at least some of the criteria at every gate focus on product superiority. Questions such as "Does the product have at least one element of competitive advantage?", "Does it offer the user new or different benefits?", and "Is it excellent value for money for the user?" become vital questions to rate and rank would-be projects.

‣ Require that certain key actions designed to deliver product superiority be included in each stage of the process. Some of these have been mentioned above (Goals 3 and 4) and include customer-focused ideation; voice-of-customer research to identify unmet needs; competitive product analysis; concept and protocept tests, preference tests, and trial sells; and constant iterations with customers during Development via rapid-prototypes-and-tests.

‣ Demand that project teams deliver evidence of product superiority to Go/Kill reviews. And make product superiority an important deliverable and issue at such meetings.

Goal 8: Fast-Paced with Non-Value-Added Items Removed

Your new product framework must be built for speed. This means eliminating all the time-wasters and work that add no value in your current new product process. Go through your process end to end and look at every required procedure, every form to be filled out, or any paperwork that must completed. There's probaly a lot of unnecessary work that really does not add any value to anyone. If it does not add value, get rid of it! And look at every committee that must sit and review projects or facets of projects. Again, if they're not really needed, get rid of them!

Goal 9: A Dynamic, Flexible, and Scalable Process

Your idea-to-launch framework must be flexible and dynamic, responsive to changing conditions and varying circumstances of projects. It cannot be a rigid, lockstep process. Some maneuvers that smart companies have built into their processes in the interest of flexibility and speed are:

- Ask the project team to map out the *best path forward* for their project, using the standard process as a guide—not every stage activity or gate deliverable is mandatory.
- Permit combining gates and collapsing stages, or even going back to a previous gate or stage.
- Move long lead-time items forward (for example, instead of awaiting a specific gate approval to order production equipment, certain long-lead-time items can be ordered in advance, as long as the risk is recognized).
- Allow overlapping stages—a project team can begin the next stage before the entrance gate even occurs (although taking this practice too far can lead to chaos).

- Use "self-managed gates," where the project team makes th
gate or Go/Kill decisions (no need to wait around for senior management to call a meeting).
- Allow fuzzy gates or conditional gates, where projects can be moved
ahead conditional on certain future events or future information.[8]

Additionally, recognize that not all development projects are the same
size and risk. Lower-risk projects do not need all the activities and stages
that higher-risk ones do. Leading firms have adopted different versions of
Stage-Gate® frameworks—for example, a three-stage, three-gate process,
or *Stage-Gate® Express* for small projects, such as extensions, modifications, and improvements. More on these scaled-down versions of *Stage-
Gate®* later in this chapter.

Goal 10: Performance Metrics in Place

Your idea-to-launch framework must feature solid performance metrics, so that senior management can assess how well NPD and the process
is working, and, most important, so that you can hold project teams
accountable for results. Chapter 6 revealed that putting metrics in place is
indeed a best practice with a strong positive impact, and showed the popularity of metrics that businesses employ.

How does one establish NPD performance metrics? At the business
level, it's fairly straightforward: Use various measures of NPD profitability and sales, available from your accounting and finance department (see
Chapter 6 and Exhibit 6.8). But measuring the performance of individual
projects is a bit more tricky, so here's a suggestion. At the "Go-to-Development" decision-point (Gate 3 in Exhibit 7.3), the project team typically presents a *business case*. Embedded within this business case are financial and
time forecasts. Examples are: sales for Year 1, 2, 3; the projected NPV of the
project; the expected launch date; and so on. These become the critical
metrics against which the project and project team should be measured as
the project unfolds:

- Use these metrics to judge the attractiveness of the project at successive gates, for example, at the "Go-to-Test" and "Go-to-Launch"
gates. If the project falls short of these pre-established hurdles, then
blow the whistle. . . something is wrong!
- Most important, use these same metrics to gauge the *ultimate success* of
the project after launch. Build in a post-launch review point 12 to 18
months after launch, where the project's results are assessed versus
those results promised back when the project was approved. In this
way, you have an objective way of assessing the "success of the project."

- Finally, hold the project team accountable for these results. If the team promised certain results—Year 1 sales, NPV, a specific launch date—at Gate 3, then measure these and compare results achieved versus results promised. This accountability session takes place at the post-launch review. In this way, project teams are forced to provide more realistic estimates in their business cases, and the project team members remain on the project and are accountable for the final result until the post-launch review is held.

Notes for Senior Management

You've just seen the 10 goals of a well-crafted idea-to-launch framework. Recall from the previous chapter that merely having a formal, documented process leads to *no improvement in performance*. Rather, it's the *nature* and *quality* of that process, along with how well it is implemented, that makes all the difference. Lots of businesses have new product processes, but many of them are simply badly designed! So step 1 is to focus on designing a best-in-class process.

If you've decided either to develop a new product process or to overhaul your existing one, you've probably set up a task force to do so. Make sure that your task force understands clearly these 10 goals. *Make these goals part of their mandate!* If they just go through the motions and merely document your current practice, you haven't gained a thing. Impress upon them that whatever else they do, they must design a process that truly delivers on these 10 goals.

The Structure of the *Stage-Gate*® Idea-to-Launch Framework

These 10 key goals have been fashioned into an effective new product process, or *Stage-Gate*® model. I don't expect that senior management should know all the details and intricacies of *Stage-Gate*®, but it is important that you know enough to decide whether your own process measures up, and where the gaps are. And if you do decide to lead here—to sponsor the design and implementation of a new product process in your business—then you should know a little about the concept and operations of a *Stage-Gate*® approach. Finally, since you are the gatekeepers, the expectation is that you have a good understanding of your own process, gate deliverables, criteria, and the like. So get set for a quick introduction to *Stage-Gate*®.

The *Stage-Gate*® new product approach is a conceptual and operational model for moving a new product project from idea to launch.[9] It is a blueprint for managing the new product process to improve effectiveness and efficiency. *Stage-Gate®* methods break down the innovation process into a predetermined set of stages, each stage consisting of a set of pre-scribed, cross-functional, and parallel activities (Exhibit 7.3). The entrance to each stage is a gate: These gates control the process and serve as the quality control and Go/Kill check-points. This stage-and-gate format leads to the name *"Stage-Gate"* process.*

The *Stage-Gate®* method is based on the experiences, suggestions, and observations of a large number of managers and firms and on my own and others' research in the field. Indeed, my observations of what hap-pened in over 60 case histories laid the foundations for the approach.[10] Since this *Stage-Gate®* method first appeared in print, it has been implemented in whole or in part in hundreds of leading firms worldwide, many of which have provided an excellent "laboratory setting" to further refine and improve the process.[11] For example, stage-gaters have periodic benchmarking sessions among themselves, where they compare notes and learn from each other, and I am often asked to attend these sessions. And standard off-the-shelf versions of *Stage-Gate®* also exist—a "stage-gate-in-a-box"—which can be quickly adapted and implemented in your business (for example, *SG-Navigator*™[12]).

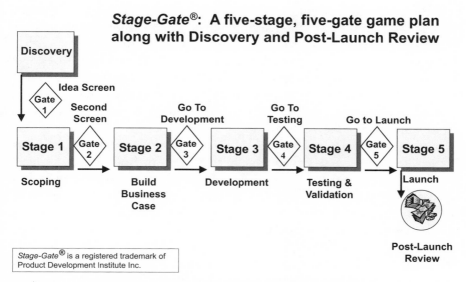

Stage-Gate®: A five-stage, five-gate game plan along with Discovery and Post-Launch Review

Stage-Gate® is a registered trademark of Product Development Institute Inc.

Exhibit 7.3 An Overview of the *Stage Gate®* Idea-to-Launch Framework

*Many other names are used besides *Stage-Gate*, including PDP (Product Delivery Process), PIP (Product Innovation Process), NPP (New Product Process), Phase-Gate, Gating System, and Product Launch System.

The Stages

Stages are where the action occurs. They are analogous to the plays in a North American football game. The players on the project team undertake key tasks in order to gather information needed to advance the project to the next gate or decision-point.

The stages are defined by the activities within them, and there is usually a *fairly standard* or *prescribed list of actions* for each stage. Specifying the activities within a stage amounts to answering the questions:

- What does management need to know at the end of this stage in order to make an informed decision to move forward?
- Therefore, what actions are required in order to get this information?

For example, in Stage 2, Build the Business Case, a number of key actions may be required to deliver a solid business case—actions such as under-taking voice-of-customer research, doing a competitive analysis, defining the product, and doing a source-of-supply assessment. These required or prescribed actions are mapped out within each stage of the *Stage-Gate®* framework.

Stages include best practices. It's not enough to map out a process that contains only your current practices—there's no improvement. So go back to Chapter 6 and also to the list of goals outlined earlier in this chapter, and make sure that these actions are built into each stage.

Stages are also cross-functional: There is no R&D or Marketing stage. Rather, each stage consists of a set of parallel activities undertaken by *people from different functional areas* within the firm, working together as a team and led by a project team leader. And these actions within each stage occur rapidly and in parallel—a rugby approach.

In order to manage risk via a *Stage-Gate®* method, the parallel activities in each stage must be designed to gather vital information—technical, market, financial, operations—in order to drive down *both* the *technical* and *business risks* of the project. Each stage costs more than the preceding one, so that the game plan is based on incremental commitments. As uncertainties decrease, expenditures are allowed to mount: Risk is managed.

From idea to launch—an overview: The general flow of the typical *Stage-Gate®* model is shown pictorially in Exhibit 7.3. Here the key stages are:

0. **Discovery:** pre-work designed to discover opportunities and to generate new product ideas.

1. **Scoping:** a quick, preliminary investigation of the project. This stage provides inexpensive information—based largely on desk research—to enable the field of projects to be narrowed before Stage 2.
2. **Build the Business Case:** a much more detailed investigation involving primary research—both market and technical—leading to a *business case.* This is where the bulk of the vital homework is done and most of the market studies are carried out. These result in a business case that includes the product definition, the project justification, and a project plan.
3. **Development:** the actual detailed design and development of the new product, along with some product testing work. The deliverable at the end of Stage 3 is an "alpha-tested" or "lab-tested product." Full production and market launch plans are also developed in this potentially lengthy stage.
4. **Testing and Validation:** tests or trials in the marketplace, lab, and plant to verify and validate the proposed new product, and its marketing and production/operations—field trials or beta tests; test market or trial sell; and operations trials.
5. **Launch:** commercialization—beginning of full operations or production, marketing, and selling. Here the market launch, production/operations, distribution, quality assurance, and post-launch monitoring plans are executed.

At first glance, this overview portrays the stages as relatively simple steps in a logical process. But don't be fooled: What you see above is only a high-level view of a generic process—the concept of the process. In a real company process, drilling down into the details of each stage reveals a much more sophisticated and complex set of activities. Here you'll find a detailed list of activities within a stage, the how-to's of each activity, best practices that the project team ought to consider, and even the required deliverables from each activity in that stage (for example, in the format of templates). In short, the drill-down provides a *detailed and operational playbook* for the project team—everything they need to know and do in order to complete that stage of the process and project successfully.

The Gates

Preceding each stage is an entry gate or a Go/Kill decision-point. The gates are the scrums or huddles on the rugby or football field. They are the points during the game where the team converges and where all new information is brought together. Effective gates are central to the success of a fast-paced, new product process:

- Gates serve as quality control check-points: Is this project being executed in a quality fashion?
- Gates also serve as Go/Kill and prioritization decision-points: Gates provide the funnels, where mediocre projects are culled out at each successive gate.
- Finally, gates are where the action plan for the next stage is decided, along with resource commitments.

Gate meetings are usually staffed by senior managers from different functions—the gatekeepers—who own the resources required by the project leader and team for the next stage. More on who the gatekeepers are later in this chapter.

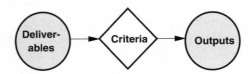

Gate format: Gates have a common format:

1. A set of required *deliverables*: What the project leader and team must bring to the gate decision-point (for example, the results of a set of completed activities). These deliverables are visible, are based on a standard menu for each gate, and are decided at the output of the previous gate. Management's expectations for project teams are thus made very clear.
2. *Criteria* against which the project is judged in order to make the Go/Kill and prioritization decisions (for example, the scorecards and financial criteria outlined in Chapter 5).
3. Defined *outputs*: for example, a decision (*Go/Kill/Hold/Recycle*), an approved action plan for the next stage (complete with people required, money and person-days committed, and an agreed time-line), and a list of deliverables and date for the next gate.

Types of gate criteria: Each gate has its own list of criteria for use by the gatekeepers. There are three types of gate criteria:

▶ *Readiness-Check:* These are Yes/No questions that check whether the key tasks have been completed, and that all deliverables are in place for that gate . . . in effect, a quality check. A No can signal a recycle to the previous stage: The project is not ready to move on. Checklists are the usual format for these readiness items.

Example:	Yes	No
Is the product definition complete?	☐	☐
Fact-based? Signed off by project team?	☐	☐

- *Must-Meet:* These are Yes/No or "knock-out" questions that include the minimum criteria that a project must meet in order to move forward. A single No signals a Kill decision. Again, checklists are the usual format for must-meet items.

Examples:	Yes	No
Is the project within our business's mandate?	☐	☐
Does the project meet our policies on values and ethics?	☐	☐
Is the project technically feasible (better than 50%)?	☐	☐

- *Should-Meet:* These are highly desirable project characteristics (so a No on one question won't kill the project). They are used to distinguish between superb projects and the minimally acceptable ones. These should-meet items are typically in a scorecard format (recall the scoring model and balanced scorecards in Exhibits 5.5 and 5.6).

Notes for Senior Management

Do you know where your development projects are? One of the first payoffs of implementing a *Stage-Gate®* framework is being able to locate projects within one of the five stages in the process. That is, you can map out your portfolio of projects, placing projects in each of the five stages. Often there are surprises: Projects thought to be in the final or launch stage are suddenly discovered to be missing key actions that ought to have been done in earlier stages. And so it's not clear where the project is!

If you currently have a new product process, take a critical look at it. Answer the following questions:

- ▶ Are your stages clearly defined? Are recommended activities and best practices outlined for each stage?
- ▶ Are your projects clearly located within stages (you can identify at which stage each of your projects are in)?
- ▶ Are gates or Go/Kill decision-points clearly defined, complete with a standard menu of deliverables, visible criteria for making the Go/Kill and prioritization decisions, and defined outputs of the gate?

If not, maybe your idea-to-launch framework is a little fuzzy and lacks substance. Perhaps it's time to make this scheme more concrete, visible, and actionable.

And the resulting project attractiveness score is used to make Go/Kill decisions and to help prioritize projects at gates.

Using the gate criteria: Gate criteria are designed to be used by you, the leadership team, at the gate meeting. After the project is presented and debated, the criteria are discussed one by one. The readiness-check and must-meet questions should be displayed on a video projector and debated openly by the gatekeepers. A single consensus No is enough to kill or recycle the project.

The should-meet questions are best handled on a physical scorecard. These criteria are scored by the gatekeepers independently of each other (paper and pen; or even computer-assisted scoring). Scores are tallied and displayed (again on a video projector) and the differences debated. A consensus Go/Kill and prioritization decision is reached. The Appendix outlines a best-in-class procedure for running an effective gate meeting—use it as a model!

A Walk-Through the *Stage-Gate*® Framework—Idea to Launch

Now for a bird's-eye look at the *Stage-Gate*® framework—what's involved at each stage and gate. Let's just have a quick walk-through of the model, which you can follow stage-by-stage in Exhibit 7.3.

Discovery Stage

Ideas are the feedstock or trigger to the process, and they make or break the process. Don't expect a superb new product process to overcome a shortage of good new product ideas. The need for great ideas coupled with a high attrition rate of ideas means that the idea generation stage is pivotal: You need great ideas and lots of them!

Many companies consider ideation so important that they handle this as a formal stage in the process, which I call Discovery. They build in a *defined, proactive idea generation and capture system.* Activities in the Discovery stage include undertaking fundamental but directed technical research; seeking new technological possibilities; working with lead or innovative users[13] or undertaking product value analysis with customers;[14] utilizing voice-of-customer research to capture unarticulated needs and customer problems;[15] competitive analysis and reverse brainstorming of competitive products; installing an idea suggestion scheme to stimulate ideas from your own employees; and using your strategic planning exercise to uncover disruptions, gaps, and opportunities in the marketplace.

Since Discovery is such a vital stage, *set up an idea capture and h system*, complete with IT support, as in Exhibit 7.4 . Here . . .

- Identify and access multiple source of new product ideas, and open up channels to these sources. Idea submissions from employees should be easy to prepare and submit via e-mail—a simple one-page idea-submission form.
- Designate a focal person—the Innovations Champion—to capture the ideas and to get a decision on each idea.
- Establish an idea screening group—the Gate 1 gatekeepers—to meet monthly to review ideas. Timely decisions are important. Make sure this Gate 1 group uses a consistent set of visible criteria, so that decisions are fair and timely feedback is provided to the submitter (with reasons why his or her idea was rejected or accepted).
- Go ideas move to Stage 1, so empower the Gate 1 gatekeepers to be able to allocate limited resources and people at the gate meeting. And consider some token awards or recognition to successful idea submitters, whose ideas progress past Gate 1.
- Establish an idea vault for Kill and Hold ideas (IT makes it possible for this vault to be public, so that others in your business can augment ideas in the vault).

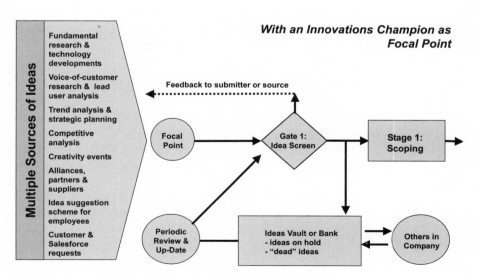

Exhibit 7.4   Set Up an Idea Capture and Handling System

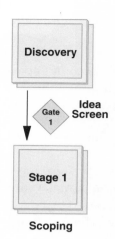

Discovery

Gate 1 — Idea Screen

Stage 1

Scoping

Gate 1: Idea Screen

Idea screening is the first decision to commit resources to the project: The project is born at this point. If the decision is Go, the project moves into the scoping or preliminary investigation stage. Thus, Gate 1 signals a preliminary but tentative commitment to the project: a flickering green light.

Gate 1 is a "gentle screen" and amounts to subjecting the project to a handful of key must-meet and should-meet criteria. Financial criteria are typically not part of this first screen, since relatively little reliable financial data are available here. A *checklist* for the must-meet criteria and a *scorecard* or scoring model (point count rating scales) for the should-meet criteria is used to help focus the discussion and rank projects in this early screen.

Stage 1: Scoping

This first and inexpensive homework stage has the objective of determining the project's technical and marketplace merits. Stage 1 is a quick scoping of the project, involving desk research or detective work; little or no primary research is done here. Stage 1 is often done in less than one calendar month's elapsed time, and five to 10 person-days' work effort.

A *preliminary market assessment is* one facet of Stage 1 and involves a variety of relatively inexpensive activities: an Internet search, a library search, contacts with key users, distributors, and salespeople, focus groups, and even a quick concept test with a handful of potential users. The purpose is to determine market size, market potential, and likely market acceptance, and also to begin to shape the product concept.

Concurrently a *preliminary technical assessment is* carried out, involving a quick and preliminary in-house appraisal of the proposed product. The purpose is to assess development and manufacturing routes (or source of supply), technical and manufacturing/operations feasibility, possible times and costs to execute, and technical, legal, and regulatory risks and roadblocks.

Stage 1 thus provides for the gathering of both market and technical information—at a low cost and in a short time—to enable a cursory and first-pass financial and business analysis as input to Gate 2. Because of the limited effort, and depending on the size of the project, very often Stage 1 can be handled by a team of just several people, usually from marketing and from a technical group.

An example: OMNOVA Solutions (formerly GenCorp) of Akron, Ohio, had the good fortune of stumbling across a new technology via fundamental research, which has become the platform for a number of new product projects. The new technology enables traditional polymers to have an extremely slippery surface, yet unlike other slippery materials, the resulting polymer retains its usual positive physical properties (for example, abrasion resistance and toughness).

The first product to be launched was vinyl wall-covering with a difference: It's a relatively low-cost, dry-erase whiteboard. Imagine having walls in meeting rooms or children's rooms that everyone can write on!

Before embarking on extensive development work for this project, a preliminary assessment or scoping was undertaken. The company was already in the wall-covering business, so ample in-house data on markets, sizes, and trends were available. Additionally, the project leader sought and found published data—trade publications, reports, and the like—on the existing whiteboard market. Informal chats with some distributors revealed the pricing structure. Technical work was relatively limited at Stage 1, as fundamental research had already uncovered the technical possibility. Nonetheless, a core group of scientists met with manufacturing people to discuss technical and manufacturing feasibility. (Note how early manufacturing was involved in the project.) Finally, a first-cut financial analysis was developed—based largely on guesstimates—but this sanity check revealed a huge opportunity.

MemErase™ was eventually developed, and successfully launched in 2000. It was an immediate success, and is still growing. The company has already launched colored and patterned versions, including its latest metallic colors, and extensions and new products based on the technology are still coming down OMNOVA's *Stage-Gate*® pipeline!

The general manager of the wallcovering division states that "*MemErase*™ has been a truly innovative coating technology platform . . . and has received incredible market acceptance. The Project Planning and Innovation Process [*StageGate*®] played a key role during the project development stages to achieve the commercial success that we enjoy today."

Gate 2: Second Screen

The project next proceeds to a second and somewhat more rigorous screen at Gate 2. This gate is essentially a repeat of Gate 1: The project is reevaluated in the light of the new information obtained in Stage 1. If the decision is Go at this point, the project moves into a heavier spending stage.

At Gate 2, the project is subjected to a set of readiness-check questions, along with a set of must-meet and should-meet criteria similar to those used at Gate 1. Here additional should-meet criteria may be considered,

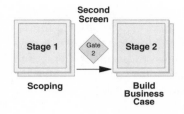

Second Screen

Stage 1 — Gate 2 — Stage 2

Scoping — Build Business Case

dealing with sales force and customer reaction to the proposed product, potential legal, technical, and regulatory "killer variables," the result of new data gathered during Stage 1. Again, a checklist and a scoring model facilitate this gate decision. The financial return is assessed at Gate 2, but only by a quick and simple financial calculation (for example, the payback period).

Stage 2: Build the Business Case

The business case is constructed in Stage 2. This stage is a detailed investigation stage, which clearly defines the product and verifies the attractiveness of the project prior to heavy spending. It is also the *critical homework* stage, the one found to be so often weakly handled.

Stage 2 sees *market research studies* (voice-of-customer) undertaken to determine the customer's needs, wants, and preferences—that is, to help define a superior and differentiated new product.

> *An example:* Fluke Corporation of Seattle is well noted for its innovative products in the field of hand-held electrical measurement instruments. A strategic decision to diversify into new markets led to the creation of the Phoenix team—a project team whose mandate was to deliver a superior product or two in a market outside of the firm's normal scope, namely, in the chemical industry.
>
> Facing a totally new market, the project team had no one in the company to turn to. So they began their voyage of discovery with some pre-work, namely, project planning, synectics (innovative team process training), and a review of the trade literature (magazines). The first team visit was to a chemical industry trade show in Chicago, followed by a few field visits to nearby chemical plants. The plant field visits were not based on sophisticated market research methodology—it was simply spending an afternoon in the control room, chatting with and observing the ultimate customer, the plant instrument engineers. The project leader calls this "fly on the wall research"; others might call it "anthropological research" or "ethnographic research."
>
> After some 25 site visits, the project team acquired a good understanding of the instrument engineer's problems and needs. One fact that was observed was the amount of equipment the engineers needed

---

*"Camping out" is the term that Hewlett-Packard uses to describe this immersion or ethnographic research, whereby the project team or designers spend much time with customers, really learning about the customers' operation, needs, problems, and so on.

to carry out to the plant merely to calibrate common instruments, such as pressure or temperature gauges. Every gauge and brand, it seemed, needed a different calibration instrument. Second, observation revealed that after the engineer had calibrated the gauge, he then spent quite a bit of time taking readings and recording these on a clipboard. After calibrating a number of gauges, the engineer returned to the control room, and then typed into a computer all the hand-recorded readings from the field . . . a time-consuming process.

You've probably guessed what the Phoenix team's new product became:

- a universal calibration instrument—could calibrate any gauge in the plant (this was made possible via the use of software rather than hardware in the hand-held instrument)
- an instrument that recorded the readings in the field—the user simply keyed in readings, which went into the instrument's memory; and upon returning to the control room, downloaded these directly into a computer

The Documenting Process Calibrator product line went on to become a great success, another testimony to really understanding customer needs and to designing a superior product in response to these needs.

Competitive analysis is also a part of this stage. Another market activity is concept testing: A representation of the proposed new product is presented to potential customers, their reactions are gauged, and the likely customer acceptance of the new product is determined.

A detailed *technical appraisal* at Stage 2 focuses on the technical feasibility of the project. That is, customer needs and a "wish list" are translated into a technically and economically feasible solution. This translation might even involve some preliminary design or laboratory work, but it should not be construed as a full-fledged development project. A manufacturing (or operations) appraisal is often a part of building the business case, where issues of manufacturability, source of supply, costs to manufacture, and investment required are investigated. If appropriate, detailed legal, patent, and regulatory assessment work is undertaken in order to remove risks and to map out the required actions.

Finally, a detailed *business and financial analysis* is conducted as part of the justification facet of the business case. The financial analysis typically involves an NPV or ECV calculation (described in Chapter 5), complete with sensitivity analysis to look at possible downside risks.

The result of Stage 2 is a *business case* for the project: the *product definition*—a key to success—is agreed to; and a thorough *project justification* and *detailed project plan* are developed.

Stage 2 involves considerably more effort than Stage 1, and requires input from a variety of sources. Stage 2 is best handled by a team consisting of cross-functional members: the core group of the eventual project team.

Gate 3: Go to Development

This is the final gate prior to the Development stage, the last point at which the project can be killed before entering heavy spending. Once past Gate 3, financial commitments are substantial. In effect, Gate 3 means "go to a heavy spend." Gate 3 also yields a "sign off' on the product and project definition. Because of the substantial resource commitments here, Gate 3 is usually staffed by the leadership team of the business.

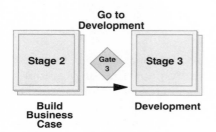

Gate 3 evaluation involves a review of each of the activities in Stage 2, checking that the activities were undertaken, the quality of execution was sound, and the results were positive. Next, Gate 3 subjects the project once again to the set of readiness-check, must-meet, and should-meet criteria similar to those used at Gate 2. Finally, because a heavy spending commitment is the result of a Go decision at Gate 3, the results of the financial analysis are an important part of this screen. Exhibit 5.5 shows a scorecard to use at Gate 3.

If the decision is Go, Gate 3 sees commitment to the product definition and agreement on the project plan that charts the path forward: The development plan and the preliminary operations and market launch plans are reviewed and approved at this gate. The full project team—an empowered, cross-functional team headed by a leader with authority—is designated.

Stage 3: Development

Stage 3 witnesses the implementation of the development plan and the physical development of the product. Lab tests, in-house tests, or alpha tests ensure that the product meets requirements under controlled conditions. And the production, operations, or source-of-supply process is mapped out. For lengthy projects, numerous milestones and periodic project reviews are built into the development plan. These are not gates per se: Go/Kill decisions are not made here; rather these milestone checkpoints provide for project control and management. Extensive in-house testing, alpha tests, or lab testing usually occur in this stage as well. The "deliverable" at the end of Stage 3 is a lab-tested or alpha prototype of the product.

The emphasis in Stage 3 is on technical work. But marketing and operations activities also proceed in parallel. For example, market-analysis and customer-feedback work continue concurrently with the technical development, with constant customer opinion sought on the product as it takes shape during development. These activities are back-and-forth or iterative, with each development result—for example, rapid prototype, working model, and first prototype—taken to the customer for assessment and feedback: *spiral development*. Meanwhile, detailed test plans, market launch plans, and production or operations plans, including production facilities requirements, are developed. An updated financial analysis is prepared, while regulatory, legal, and patent issues are resolved.

Gate 4: Go to Testing

This post-Development gate is a check on the progress and the continued attractiveness of the product and project. Development work is reviewed and checked, ensuring that the work has been completed in a quality fashion and that the developed product is indeed consistent with the original definition specified at Gate 3.

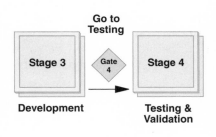

This gate also revisits the economic question via a revised financial analysis based on new and more accurate data. The test or validation plans for the next stage are approved for immediate implementation, and the detailed market launch and operations plans are reviewed for probable future execution.

Stage 4: Testing and Validation

This stage tests and validates the entire viability of the project: the product itself, the production process, customer acceptance, and the economics of the project. It also begins extensive external validation of the product and project. A number of activities are undertaken at Stage 4:

▶ *In-house product tests:* extended lab tests or alpha tests to check on product quality and product performance under controlled or lab conditions

▶ *User, preference, or field trials of the product:* to verify that the product functions under actual use conditions, and also to gauge potential customers' reactions to the product—to establish purchase intent

▶ *Trial, limited, or pilot production/operations:* to test, debug, and prove the production or operations process, and to determine more precise production costs and throughputs

▶ *Pre-test market, test market, or trial sell:* to gauge customer reaction, measure the effectiveness of the launch plan, and determine expected market share and revenues

▶ *Revised business and financial analysis:* to check on the continued business and economic viability of the project, based on new and more accurate revenue and cost data.

Sometimes Stage 4 yields negative results, and it's back to Stage 3.

> *An example:* All was proceeding well for the OMNOVA dry-erase wall covering. A successful trial production run in Stage 4 yielded sufficient semi-commercial product to permit customer trials in several test office buildings. The product had been extensively tested in the lab on all known performance metrics—temperature, humidity, and scuff resistance. But one small factor was overlooked, as it often is. Some customers used a certain brand of dry-erase markers with a unique solvent. The result: When left on the whiteboard for several days, writing from this one brand of marker proved difficult to erase. And so "ghosts" appeared. This *ghosting problem* was never identified until real customers started using the product. But OMNOVA's project team was alert, and acted on the field trial results: The project iterated for some time within Stage 4; the problem was rectified; and now the commercial product meets all customer requirements.

Gate 5: Go to Launch

This final gate opens the door to full commercialization: market launch and full production or operations start up. It is the final point at which the project can still be killed. This gate focuses on the quality of the activities in

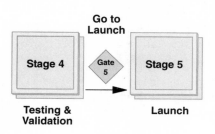

the Testing and Validation stage and their results. Criteria for passing the gate focus largely on the expected financial return, the project's readiness for launch, and the appropriateness of the launch and operations start-up plans. The operations and market launch plans are reviewed and approved for implementation in Stage 5.

Stage 5: Launch

This final stage involves implementation of both the market launch plan and the production or operations plan. Production equipment is acquired, installed, and commissioned (although sometimes this is done earlier in Stage 4, as part of the Stage 4 production trials); the logistics pipeline is filled; and selling begins. And barring any unforeseen events, it should be clear sailing for the new product . . . another new product winner!

Post-Launch Review

Two post-launch reviews are typical. The first, an interim review, occurs about two to four months after launch, when initial launch results are available. Here a post-audit is done while the details of the project are still fresh in team members' minds. This post-audit assesses the project's strengths and weaknesses, identifies what your business can learn from this project, and provides key learnings on how to do the next project even better. Additionally, interim commercial results—initial sales and production costs, for example—are reviewed, and needed course corrections are made.

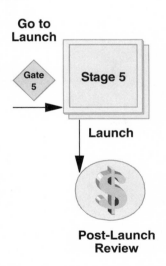

The final review is held once the project is "stable" and commercial results are known: 12 to 18 months into market. Here the project team is disbanded, and the product becomes a "regular product" in the firm's product line. This is also the point where the project's and product's performances are reviewed: the latest data on revenues, costs, expenditures, profits, and timing are compared to projections made at Gates 3 and 5 to gauge performance. Project team accountability is a central issue here: Did the team deliver the results they promised or forecast? This review marks the end of the project. Note that the project team and leader remain responsible for the success of the project through this post-launch period, right up to the point of the post-launch review.

Who Are the Gatekeepers?

Who are the people that staff these critical gates—the gatekeepers who make the Go/Kill and resource allocation decisions and that are essential

Notes for Senior Management

You've seen an overview of what a best-in-class idea-to-launch framework looks like. Now take this 10-item quiz on your own idea-to-launch process:

Questions   Answers

1. Does my idea-to-launch framework or process emphasize upfront homework before serious development begins? Is it the right homework? And is it constantly done for every major project?   Yes ☐ No ☐

2. Is a strong market orientation a feature of my process: solid market information; good voice-of-customer research; products designed with market and customer input?   Yes ☐ No ☐

3. Is there a product definition step built into the process before Development begins? Is the product definition sharp, fact-based, and stable?   Yes ☐ No ☐

4. Is there an emphasis on providing a unique superior product—one that is differentiated, superior to competitors' in meeting customers' needs, and better value-for-money? And have we built activities and criteria into the process that delivers such superior products?   Yes ☐ No ☐

5. Does my process achieve focus via tough Go/Kill decision-points or gates that weed out poor projects and allocate resources to the deserving projects? And are there visible criteria—in scorecard format—at these gates?   Yes ☐ No ☐

6. Is my framework cross-functional—projects done by defined and empowered cross-functional teams? accountable teams? teams with a defined leader?   Yes ☐ No ☐

7. Does my framework feature parallel processing—a rugby approach with activities from different functions undertaken concurrently, rather than sequentially—in order to speed up projects?   Yes ☐ No ☐

8. Is there a strong emphasis on quality of execution throughout the process? Are tasks within projects done well? Am I satisfied with quality of execution?   Yes ☐ No ☐

9. Is my process flexible and scalable, designed for speed, but without loss of discipline? And have we removed all the unneeded bureaucracy and time-wasters?   Yes ☐ No ☐

10. Finally, have we installed performance metrics in our process? Do we keep score? Do we know how well our projects are doing?   Yes ☐ No ☐

Score yourself and your business's new idea-to-launch framework: one point for each "Yes" answer.

0–5 points: You have a seriously deficient idea-to-launch framework, and are probably under-performing considerably. Time for a total overhaul of the process (or maybe even a new framework altogether)!

6–8 points: Fair, but still some problems. Identify the weaknesses and fix your idea-to-launch framework.

9–10 points: Good! Fix the outstanding items and carry on.

to making the new product process work? Obviously the choice of the gatekeepers is specific to each business and its organizational structure. But here are some rules of thumb:

> ‣ The first rule is simple: The gatekeepers at any gate must have the *authority to approve the resources* required for the next stage. That is, they are the owners of the resources.
> ‣ To the extent that resources will be required from different functions, the gatekeepers must *represent different functional areas*: R&D, marketing, engineering, operations, and perhaps sales, purchasing, and quality assurance. There's not much sense having a gatekeeper group just from one functional area, such as marketing or R&D!
> ‣ The gatekeepers usually *change somewhat from gate to gate.* Typically Gate 1, the initial screen, is staffed by a small group, perhaps four or five people who need not be the most senior in the organization. Here, the spending level is quite low. By Gate 3, however, where financial and resource commitments are substantial, the gatekeepers typically include more senior managers, for example, the leadership team of the business.
> ‣ There should also be some *continuity of gatekeepers* from gate to gate. In short, the composition of the evaluation group should not change totally, requiring a total start-from-the-beginning justification of the project at each gate. For example, some members of the leadership team—the heads of marketing and R&D, for example—might be at Gate 2, with the full leadership team at Gate 3.

Critical projects, or projects with major strategic implications, often involve the senior gatekeepers at earlier gates, even at Gate 1 in some businesses. The argument voiced by senior people is: "we don't want any projects starting that may ultimately involve millions of dollars in expenditures without our early approval!" In other businesses, the leadership team is happy to review projects at Gate 3 and on, leaving the earlier gate decisions to a more junior group; but they do want to be informed of these early gate decisions!

Different magnitude projects also require different levels of gatekeeper groups in some businesses. That is, not all projects should go to the senior gatekeeping group or leadership team of the business:

> *An example:* Business Banking at the Royal Bank of Canada has two levels of gatekeepers from Gate 3 on:
> • a senior gatekeeping group for larger, riskier projects (total cost > $500,000)

- a middle-level gatekeeping group for lower-risk and/or smaller projects

A final issue is the need for the same gatekeeping groups across all projects. Two companies I have worked with both initially implemented their *Stage-Gate®* processes with *different gatekeeping groups* for *different projects*. At Kodak, each project had its own gatekeeping team, but no one gatekeeper group had an overview picture of all the projects; the result was that resource allocation across projects became impossible—much like having several air-traffic control towers at the same airport! At Telenor, the Norwegian telephone system, the situation was similar, with each project having its own gatekeeper group; the evaluation teams quickly turned into steering committees and "cheerleaders" so that no projects were ever killed! Both companies have since revised their gatekeeping methods, and have moved toward "standing gatekeeper groups" that objectively review all Gate 3, 4, and 5 projects.

Linking the Gates to Portfolio Management

Gates are an important component of an effective portfolio management system introduced in Chapter 5 (bottom right in Exhibit 5.1). Unlike quarterly or semi-annual portfolio reviews (outlined in Chapter 5), gates are a *real-time decision process*, with gates activated many times throughout the year—whenever needed for a project decision. Gates provide an *in-depth review* of projects, one project at a time—much more in depth per project than at portfolio reviews.

In order to build portfolio management into your idea-to-launch process, gates must now become *two-part decisions* (Exhibit 7.5). The first part or half of the gate is a Pass-versus-Kill decision, where individual projects are evaluated using the financial, checklist, and scoring model valuation tools described in Chapter 5.[16]

The second half of the gate meeting involves *prioritization* of the project under discussion versus all other projects (Exhibit 7.5). In practice, this means making a Go-versus-Hold decision, and if Go, allocating resources to the project. A rank-ordered list of projects is displayed to compare the relative attractiveness of the project under discussion to the other Active and On-Hold projects. Here, projects can be ranked on a financial criterion (for example, the productivity index based on the NPV or, better yet, based on the ECV, both outlined in Chapter 5) and also ranked on the project attractiveness score obtained from the balanced scorecard rating scheme.

Additionally, the impact of the proposed project on the total portfolio of projects is assessed. The questions are:

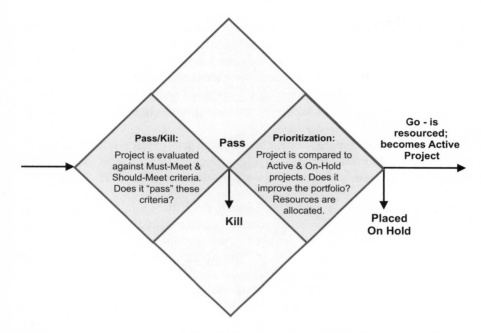

Exhibit 7.5   Gates Are a Two-Part Decision Process—Go/Kill Decisions and Then Prioritization Projects and Allocating Resources

Source: Research-Technology Management 2000, note 16.

▶ Does the new project under discussion improve the overall value of the portfolio?

▶ Does it improve the balance of projects (or detract from balance)?

▶ Does the project improve the portfolio's strategic alignment?

▶ Does the project impact negatively on other projects (for example, consume needed resources)?

The various portfolio charts we saw in Chapter 5 are helpful at gate meetings in order to address these questions, for example, the portfolio summary chart in Exhibit 5.13.

Project teams leave the gate meeting with a Go/Kill and prioritization decision and, most important, with committed resources—with a check in hand! But other projects are *not* discussed in depth *or* reprioritized at the gate; only the project in question is given a relative priority level versus the rest.

Stage-Gate® *Express* for Lower-Risk Projects

Stage-Gate® frameworks are scalable: different versions to handle different types of projects. The full-fledged *Stage-Gate*® model in Exhibit 7.3 is designed for larger, higher-risk projects with much at stake and many unknowns. But many projects are much smaller than this: They include modifications, extensions, improvements, simple sales requests, and single-customer projects. Forcing such smaller projects through the full five-stage model only creates frustration, unneeded work, and the impression of added bureaucracy—a sure way to cause people to circumvent an otherwise excellent framework.

When the project risk is low, consider using an abbreviated version of *Stage-Gate®*, namely, the three-stage *Stage-Gate® Express* framework (Exhibit 7.6).[17] Here's how the three-stage version works:

- Combine Stages 1 and 2 in Exhibit 7.3 into a single "homework" stage. The usual Stage 1 activities are then merged with Stage 2 tasks, but the work effort and level of detail are not as great as in the five-stage model (available information and experience reduce the time required to gather the required homework data).
- Combine Stage 3 (Development) with Stage 4 (Testing and Validation). The project team reviews the activities normally undertaken in Stages 3 and 4 and decides which are relevant to the smaller project and which should be omitted or abbreviated.
- Eliminate Gates 2 and 4 totally (often the project team conducts a "self-check" or "self-managed gate" prior to moving ahead).

The result is a *fast-track process* suitable to facilitate product development for low-risk projects.

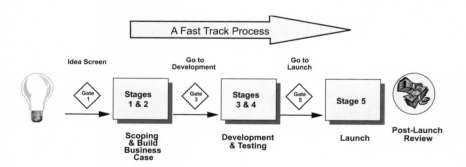

Stage-Gate ® Express is for lower risk, simpler projects: line extensions, product improvements, product modifications. A two-stage version can be used for single & simple customer requests.

Stage-Gate® is a registered trademark of Product Development Institute Inc.

Exhibit 7.6   *Stage-Gate® Express*—A Three-Stage Version for Lower-Risk Projects

An example: Mannington Flooring, a leading U.S. manufacturer of wood, carpet, and ceramic flooring, has three versions of *Stage-Gate®*. Major new product developments move through their full five-stage model, much like the model in Exhibit 7.3. Extensions, modifications, and improvements, while still significant projects, are much lower risk with fewer unknowns, and are handled in a three-stage version, which they call *Stage-Gate® Express*. Single-customer requests—a major client requesting a product, often a minor modification—are handled as a two-stage sales request project—these are fast-tracked due to their time urgency. Using this *triage system*, Mannington is able to effectively route its different size and type projects to the appropriate idea-to-launch model and speed new products to market.

Notes for Senior Management

Is your development process flexible and scalable—adjustable to suit the risk and size of different types of projects? If not, your people are probably trying to ram both large and small, simple and complex projects through the same model, and are ending up frustrated and with much make-work on their hands.

Define different types of projects according to size, complexity, and risk level. Then map out different processes or frameworks to suit each. Perhaps you should have a three-stage version for extensions, modifications, and improvements, and even a two-stage framework for sales and customer requests. *Note:* Although these processes might look much the same, their details—the stage activities, deliverables, criteria for Go, and even the gatekeepers—will be different.

What About Technology Development Projects?

Technology development or technology platform projects promise to open up new strategic opportunities to the business.[18] An obvious question is: Should your *Stage-Gate®* process be applied to these technology development projects? The answer is: Generally no . . . at least not as I've described *Stage-Gate®* in this chapter and in Exhibit 7.3. Here's why: If you try to force-fit a technology development or technology platform project through the traditional idea-to-launch process, you will surely create much frustration for the project team, obtain the wrong deliverables for such a project, and possibly do serious damage to the project. The point is that there is a poor fit between the traditional *Stage-Gate®* method (which is designed for fairly well-defined new product projects) and technology developments. Nonetheless, these are significant projects, and just because they're different and somewhat hard to define does not mean they merit no system at all—that you throw discipline out the window! A limited number of businesses that engage in such innovative developments have successfully employed a *Stage-Gate®* process to drive these special projects through to fruition—but it's a special type of *Stage-Gate®* methodology! ExxonMobil Chemical has even published a synopsis of its special *Stage-Gate®* process to handle their technology projects.[19]

First, here are some definitions to make sure we're all speaking about the same kinds of projects:

Technology development (TD) projects are those where the deliverable is new knowledge and a technological capability. I also call these "science projects" and "fundamental" or "basic research projects." This new capability or new knowledge may in turn spawn a number of specific new product projects (and thus may overlap with the notion of a platform project—a technology platform).

When the TD project begins, there may be no specific new product (or new manufacturing process) well defined. Rather, the scientist initiates some experiments with the hope of finding some technical possibilities and discoveries that might yield ideas for commercial products or processes. An example is Metallocene, a new catalyst developed by ExxonMobil Chemical, which spawned an entire new family of relatively inexpensive polyolefin polymers with engineering-plastics properties.

Disruptive technologies and radical innovations yield projects that are a special subcategory of technology developments—I introduced these in the Strategy chapter (Chapter 3). Recall that such developments have the potential to create both threats and opportunities to your business, and hence must be considered as part of your strategy development. But simply because these are "special projects"—special in the sense that their impact could be profound, their costs to implement high, and their futures often difficult to define—does not mean that they cannot be managed. The ExxonMobil example above certainly was a step-change development that yielded an entirely new category of plastics—a disruptive or radical innovation.

Technology development, disruptive technology, and radical innovation projects should be evaluated differently than standard new product projects, using a more visionary, less financial scorecard (a sample scorecard for advanced technology projects was provided in Exhibit 5.6).

Platform projects were previously defined in Chapter 4. Platforms build a capability componentry, an architecture or a marketing stage from which many new product projects may be launched. A platform project could be based on a new technology or a technology development (above), and is called a *technology platform project*.

The main difference between these and a typical new product project—for which *Stage-Gate®* in Exhibit 7.3 is designed—is that technology developments are often much broader, more loosely defined, and more difficult to predict at the outset than is the typical new product project. For example, in a technology development project designed to ultimately yield new products, it may take months of technical research before it's even clear what might be technically possible. So undertaking a market analysis in Stage 1 in Exhibit 7.3 and detailed market studies in Stage 2 makes little sense—the product hasn't even been defined or characterized! And the criteria for project selection are clearly different here than for a very tangible, well-defined new product project, as we saw in Chapter 5.

Stage-Gate®-*TD*

The methodology for handling such technology platform and technology developments is shown in Exhibit 7.7. I call the method *Stage-Gate®-TD*, where "TD" stands for "technology development." The top part of the schematic shows the three stages of the process:

1. **Scoping:** a relatively inexpensive stage involving literature search, secondary research, and detective work. Its purpose is to lay the foundation and to define the scope of the project.
2. **Technical Investigation:** a more extensive stage designed to demonstrate technical feasibility—that you really have something here worth pursuing further.
3. **Detailed Investigation:** the full experimental effort to take the technology to the point where you can start working on specific new product projects or perhaps on a new manufacturing process. During this Detailed Investigation stage, commercial possibilities—for example, some possible new products—are identified and defined, and preliminary market and businesses analyses are conducted on each.

The Applications Path gate is where senior management meets to decide what do with this new technology or capability. Very often, multiple new product projects are defined, which then enter the standard five-stage *Stage-Gate®* framework (across the bottom of Exhibit 7.7) at either Gate 1, 2, or 3 (depending on how far along and defined the project already is).

The TD gates are similar to those in the traditional *Stage-Gate®* framework, except that the gatekeepers usually include a strong contingent of technology people, as well as senior people from key businesses within the corporation—businesses where this new technology will eventually be

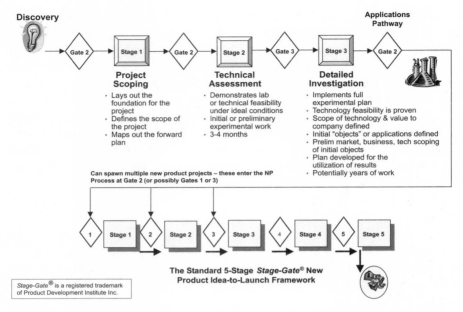

Exhibit 7.7 The *Stage-Gate*®-TD Framework for Technology Developments and Technology Platforms

commercialized. Readiness-check, must-meet, and should-meet questions (in the form of a scorecard) are used to focus the discussions and make more effective Go/Kill decisions (see Exhibit 5.6).

Special considerations for technology development projects: One unique facet of *Stage-Gate®-TD* is the evaluation of the commercial potential for such technology developments.[20] There are very few things one can predict with confidence about these TD projects at the outset, except for one: *Your numbers are certain to be wrong!* If history is any guide, typically one either grossly overestimates or underestimates their commercial potential. But here are best practices that you should build into your *Stage-Gate®-TD* framework to secure more valid projections:

▶ *Target the niche segment:* Once into Stage 3 across the top of Exhibit 7.7, your project team should identify *concrete applications* for the new technology. Recognize, however, that a new technology usually yields products or processes whose performance is inferior in some way to those based on the existing technology. Thus, the mainstream market or application is often reluctant to adopt the new technology.[21] But there is usually a subsegment of users that stands to benefit the most from the new technology's performance characteristics, and can live with its deficiencies. For example, the first digital phones left a lot to be desired: They were bulky, were heavy, had a short battery life, and often lost the signal. But people who really required instant and constant communication adopted the new products, in spite of these drawbacks. Some years later, the mainstream market materialized once the products had improved. The point is: Do not assume a mainstream market or application and certainly do not base your financial projections on the mainstream; rather, search for that segment of users who will strongly benefit from the new technology's performance capabilities, and target them.

▶ *Do fieldwork*: Insist that the entire project team learn firsthand about the various potential applications of the product or new technology and users' potential for adoption. This means multiple site visits, camping out with potential customers or users, and personally experiencing the applications, most likely in Stage 3 across the top of Exhibit 7.7. The better all team members understand potential

Notes for Senior Management

Suggestion: If some of your development projects are technology development (fundamental research, new or disruptive technologies, or technology platform developments), here's my recommendation: Get your *Stage-Gate®* process working for new product projects first (Exhibit 7.3). New products are the easier of the group to design a process for, at least conceptually. But don't try to ram technology developments through this new product process; this will create nothing but frustration, and may even damage the credibility of your well-designed new product process.

Once your new product process is working, then turn to your more visionary projects—science projects and new technology developments—and design a parallel process for them as well. The processes for these TD developments should look a lot like your new product *Stage-Gate®* process, for example, with stages and gates. Even the names of some of the stages and gates may be the same. But the details of the stages and the specific gate criteria you use will be quite unique to these types of projects, as shown in Exhibit 7.7. And more: Use a very different scorecard for rating such projects at gates (Exhibit 5.6). And build in some of the recommended best practices outlined in this chapter to better define the potential and applications for these more venturesome development projects.

applications, market segments, and exactly what features and performance each user seeks, the better the team can converge on the target application and product attributes, and make more reliable estimates of commercial potential.

▶ *Examine parallel applications and existing solutions:* There are very few totally new markets or applications in the world. Usually there is something in existence to benchmark. Even in the case of dramatic breakthroughs, such as the first jet engine or the introduction of xerographic copying, there was an "existing market." Potential users were "solving their problem" in some other way, albeit unsatisfactorily. In offices, people used carbon paper, Gestetner machines, and Kodak's wet photographic process for making copies. The military, the first target users of jet engines, was using piston engines at the time. The trick is to identify the handful of potential customers who stand to benefit from the new solution, to assess how much better the new solution is, and to determine what proportion will convert to the new solution.

▶ *Define at least three resulting objects:* In the case of a new technology, it is often difficult to envision how many and what "objects" (new products, production applications, or commercial applications) the technology might spawn. For example, in the ExxonMobil Metallocene project, when experimental work first began, it wasn't clear whether this would lead to new plastics, or perhaps a new fuel additive. All the researchers had in the early days was "some gummy stuff with interesting properties." However, if the project team has done their homework in Stage 3, they should be able to identify at least *three possible objects*. (If they cannot, then challenge their homework, or whether the technology has any future at all!). Use these three objects to help focus the market and business analysis (that is, do a market and business analysis on each of these three objects in Stage 3 in Exhibit 7.7). Another good rule of thumb is to assume another three objects of equal magnitude, and use these *six objects* as the basis for the financial justification at Gate 3, the Applications Path Gate.

Notes

1. A quotation describing the quality process, which has equal applicability to the new product process. See T. H. Berry, *Managing the Total Quality Transformation*. New York: McGraw-Hill, 1991.

2. This chapter is based on material from many sources. See, for example: R. G. Cooper, "Doing It Right—Winning with New Products," *Ivey Business Journal*, July–August 2000, 54–60; R. G. Cooper, *Winning at New Products: Accelerating the Process from Idea to Launch*, 3rd ed. Reading, MA: Perseus, 2001; R. G. Cooper, "Stage-Gate New Product Development Processes: A Game Plan from Idea to Launch," in *The Portable MBA in Project Management*, edited by E.

Verzuh. Hoboken, NJ: Wiley, 2003, 309–346; and even earlier publications such as R. G. Cooper, "Stage-Gate Systems: A New Tool for Managing New Products," *Business Horizons*, 33, 3, May–June 1990.

3. APQC benchmarking study: see note 29 in Chapter 1.

4. Quotation taken from PDMA best practices study; see A. Griffin, *Drivers of NPD Success: The 1997 PDMA Report*. Chicago: Product Development & Management Association, 1997.

5. PDMA study: see note 4.

6. Parts of this section are taken from an article by the author: R. G. Cooper, "Overhauling the New Product Process," *Industrial Marketing Management*, 25, 6, November 1996, 465–482.

7. The rugby analogy was first introduced in B. Uttal, "Speeding New Ideas to Market," *Fortune*, March 1987, 62–66.

8. Some of these practices are explained in R. G. Cooper, *Winning at New Products: Accelerating the Process from Idea to Launch*, 3rd ed. Reading, MA: Perseus, 2001; R. G. Cooper, Chapter 1, "New Products: What Separates the Winners from the Losers," *The PDMA Handbook of New Product Development*, 2nd ed. New York: Wiley, 2004; and R. G. Cooper, "Third-Generation New Product Processes," *Journal of Product Innovation Management*, 11, 1, 1994, 3–14.

9. See note 2.

10. This early work is reported in R. G. Cooper, "Identifying Industrial New Product Success: Project NewProd," *Industrial Marketing Management*, 8, May 1979, 124–135; also R. G. Cooper, "The New Product Process: An Empirically Derived Classification Scheme," *R&D Management*, 13, January 1983, 2–11.

11. The term "Stage-Gate" first appeared in print in R. G. Cooper, "The New Product Process: A Decision Guide for Managers," *Journal of Marketing Management*, 3, 3, Spring 1988, 238–255. An earlier version had been outlined in previous works; see, for example, R. G. Cooper, *"Winning at New Products*. Reading, MA: Addison Wesley, 1986. *Stage-Gate®* is now a legally registered tradename in a number of countries.

12. *SG- Navigator*™ is a standard best-in-class *Stage-Gate®* framework, available from Stage Gate Inc. at www.stage-gate.com.

13. For more information on the use of lead users in idea generation, see E. A. Von Hippel, S. Thomke, & M. Sonnack, "Creating Breakthroughs at 3M," *Harvard Business Review*, September–October 1999, 47–57.

14. R. Sears & M. Barry, "Product Value Analysis[SM]—Product Interaction Predicts Profits," *Innovation*, Winter 1993, 13–18.

15. For voice of-customer methods and idea generation, see P. Lindstedt & J. Burenius, *The Value Model: How to Master Product Development and Create Unrivalled Customer Value*. Sweden: NIMBA AB, 2003, www.nimba.com.

16. How the gating process links into portfolio management is described in R. G. Cooper, S. J. Edgett, & E. J. Kleinschmidt, "New Problems, New Solutions: Making Portfolio Management More Effective," *Research-Technology Management*, 43, 2, 2000, 18–33.

17. For more information on fast-track versions of *Stage-Gate®*, see R. G. Cooper, *Winning at New Products: Accelerating the Process from Idea to Launch*, 3rd ed. Reading, MA: Perseus, 2001, 147; also note 12.

18. For more information on *Stage-Gate®* for technology and platform developments, see note 17, 166.

19. L. Yapps-Cohen, P. W. Kamienski, & R. L. Espino, "Gate System Focuses Industrial Basic Research," *Research-Technology Management*, July– August 1998, 34–37.

20. Some of these recomended actions for disruptive and radical technology proejcts are from R. G. Cooper, S. J. Edgett, & E. J. Kleinschmidt, *Portfolio Management for New Products*, 2nd ed. Reading, MA: Perseus, 2002.

21. C. M. Christensen, *The Innovator's Dilemma*. New York: HarperCollins, 2000.

8

The People in the Product Innovation War—The Right Climate and Environment, Effective NPD Teams, and the Role of Senior Management

The Troops on the Ground

The innovation war is ultimately won or lost on the battlefield by the ground troops, and how they are led. How you organize your troops, the climate and environment you establish for them, and the role that you, the generals, play decide the final outcome of this vital war. True, you can put in place a superb idea-to-launch process; you can commit the necessary resources and allocate these resources effectively; and you can even boast a brilliant war strategy. But how you manage your people, and the environment you create for them, is one of the strongest *points of performance* in the *Innovation Diamond* (Exhibit 8.1). The three key areas I highlight in this chapter, and which are fundamental to NPD success according to our APQC benchmarking study, are:

1. the nature of project teams and how they are organized[1]
2. the culture and climate within the business in support of product innovation
3. the role of senior management—behaviors, engagement, and commitment

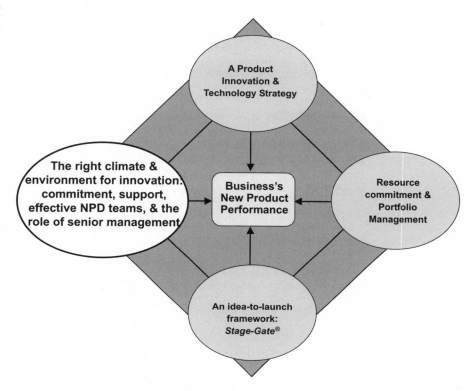

Exhibit 8.1 The Right Climate and Environment for Innovation Is the Final of the *Four Points of Performance* in the *Innovation Diamond*

Effective Cross-Functional Project Teams

The evidence from numerous studies is compelling: How the project team is organized and functions is found to strongly influence project outcomes.[2] Investigations into new product success consistently cite interfaces between R&D and marketing, coordination among key internal groups, multidisciplinary inputs to the new product project, and the role of teams and the team leader.

Successful new product projects feature a balanced process consisting of critical activities that fall into many different functional areas within the business: marketing and marketing research, engineering, R&D, production, supply-chain management, and finance. Maidique and Zirger's study of new product launches in high-technology firms reveals that a critical distinguishing factor between success and failure is the "simultaneous involvement of the create, make, and market functions."[3] Similarly, analyses of

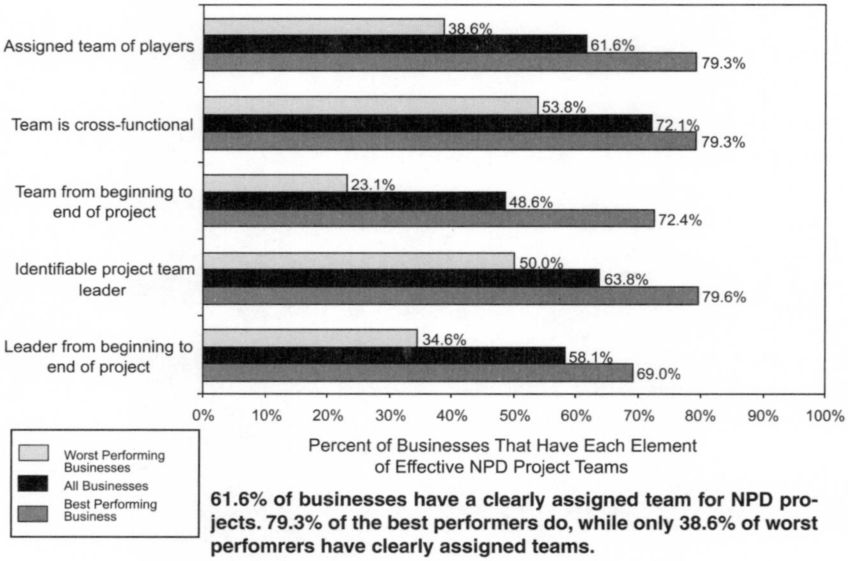

Exhibit 8.2 The Way NPD Project Teams Are Organized Impacts Success

Japanese successes emphasize their attention to manufacturability from the start of development efforts, the location in one place of engineers, designers, and manufacturers, and the conception of management unconstrained by traditional American functionalism.[4]

Our *NewProd*® projects studies show that projects undertaken by empowered, cross-functional teams are much more successful.[5] And our APQC benchmarking study reveals conclusive evidence that team structure and team design are central to new product success. This chapter probes a number of facets of "what makes for a good project team" and what you can do to render your business's team more effective (the benchmarking results on teams are in Exhibits 8.2 and 8.3).

The Way That NPD Project Teams Are Organized

The way NPD project teams are organized is a key success driver; yet in many companies, this team organization is woefully deficient. Look at the benchmarking results in Exhibit 8.2, which shows how much better top-performing businesses organize for product innovation. Here are some things the best do differently from the worst performers, and which you should incorporate into your own business:

Clearly assign a team of players—a cross-functional team—for each significant NPD project. These are people who are part of the project and do work for it—not just a steering group or an advisory committee. I cannot count the number of times I sit in meetings to review individual new product projects, when it comes to the discussion of *who's working on that project*. And often it's not really clear: "It is Mary, or Jack? . . . I think Joe's on it, too!" goes the conversation. Without clearly defined teams, you cannot have clear responsibilities, roles, and accountability!

What is surprising is that this practice is not evident in almost all businesses today. Only 61.5% of businesses have clearly assigned teams for NPD projects, with best-performing businesses outdoing the worst by two to one (79.3% versus 38.5%)—see Exhibit 8.2.

Make it a rule: Every significant project has a defined core team of players—and it's clear who is on the team and who is not. And be sure to distinguish between *core team members* (the folks who are really on the team, and are *responsible for the ultimate outcome*) versus *peripheral players* who show up for the occasional game, do some work, or might attend the odd team meeting. This team definition is particularly important when it comes to team accountability—which people will be held accountable for the end results; and also when it comes to team rewards and recognition—just who receives these? Be single-minded about this: Coming out of every gate, the team should be clearly defined—on paper and signed off on by you, the gatekeepers.

When establishing project teams, make sure they are *cross-functional*, with team members from technical, sales, marketing, operations, and so on. The message here seems to have been heard: The great majority of businesses (72.1%) report that they do indeed utilize cross-functional teams for NPD projects. Best performers use cross-functional teams somewhat more so (79.3%), and worst performers less so (53.8%). Note that the use of cross-functional teams is now such a pervasive approach in NPD that it does not strongly discriminate between best and worst performers—almost everyone uses cross-functional teams! Nonetheless this is so common among best performers that I include cross-functionality as a best practice.

Keep your project teams small and dedicated. Although many people may work on a project during its life, the *core team* should number no more than eight people, according to studies done at AT&T. The ideal number is five to seven, and, where possible, core team members should be *dedicated to the project 100% of their time!* From my observations of hundreds of project teams, I would far rather have a team of two or three full-time people (that is, 100% dedicated to my project) than a team of 10 half-time people.

Why not the team of 10? First, I never get my 50% of their time. Second, they lack ownership: They have other important things going on. And finally, communication is a nightmare. Give me the small, dedicated team any day!

Keep the team on the project from beginning to end—not just on the project for a short while or for a single phase. On occasion, I see management change the entire team as the project approaches the goal line: They send in the "commercialization team" to get the product into the market. While this move might sound great in theory—a specialty team executing the last play—it doesn't work too well in practice. Projects that are handed off from one group to the next often lose momentum. My suggestion: If you need specialty players for the final few plays, then *add commercialization people* (for example, add production people and some salespeople to the team) rather than replacing the entire team and leader. Make it a rule: Keep the key knowledge-holders on the project team until the end of the game!

Almost half of businesses (48.6%) embrace this beginning-to-end team approach, and the practice is particularly evident among best performers (72.4%; see Exhibit 8.2). Note that while it is tempting to change the players on the team as the project moves from stage to stage, the drawback is loss of momentum, passion, knowledge, and accountability. Indeed, it is difficult to fathom how anyone can be held accountable for a project's outcome if the players keep changing with every play!

Put in place a clearly identified team leader as champion of the project, responsible for driving the project. Note that this team leader is a *full member of the team*, analogous to a captain of a football team (and not some executive who manages or cheer-leads from the sidelines). And while everyone on the project team is accountable for the project's end result, there is one person—the team captain or leader—whose head and shoulders are above the rest on that football field! Again, this is a fairly common best practice, with 63.8% of all businesses and 79.5% of top performers defining team leaders for projects clearly. Worst performers are decidedly weaker here, with only about one-third embracing this practice.

Ensure that the project leader is responsible for the project from idea through to launch: She carries the project right through the process, and not just for one or a few stages. In 58.1% of all businesses and 69% of best performers, the leader stays as project leader for the entire project. In this way, accountability is enhanced, key knowledge is not lost, and project momentum is maintained. Worst performers are weaker here, with only 34.6% maintaining the same project leader.

Structure your project teams carefully—pay attention to *organizational design*. What type of organization structure brings many players from different walks of life in the business together in an integrated effort? In short, how do you take a diverse group of players and turn them into a team? It's clear that the traditional functional organizational structure does not suit many of the needs of product innovation. Indeed, functional approaches—where the project is divided into functional segments, and each functional department handles its piece of the project—leads to the poorest new product performance.[6] Tom Peters argues strongly in favor of project teams: "the single most important reason for delays in development activities is the absence of multifunction (and outsider) representation on development projects from the start."[7] He continues: "The answer is to co-mingle members of all key functions, co-opt each function's traditional feudal authority, and use teams."

Move to a team approach that cuts across functional lines. The three approaches that appear to work best are:[8]

- *Balanced matrix:* A project manager or team leader is assigned to oversee the project and shares the responsibility and authority for completing the project with the functional managers. There is joint approval and direction.
- *Project matrix*: A team leader is assigned to oversee the project and has *primary* responsibility and authority for the project. Functional managers assign personnel as needed and provide technical expertise. Functional areas become the "resource providers" here.
- *Project team*: A project manager is put in charge of a project team composed of a core group of personnel from several functional areas. The functional managers have no formal involvement or authority. Here, the team works outside the traditional organizational structure. This approach is best used for very major and complex projects.

All three organizational approaches above work well with a formal idea-to-launch framework in place.

"Ring-fence" your project team resources. Have you ever noticed that when you assign people two types of tasks—*important* tasks and *urgent* tasks—the urgent tasks always seem to dominate? For example, you might have a technical group that is assigned both firefighting tasks (customer issues, or problems on the production floor) as well as new product projects. What dominates? Usually the urgent items requiring a quick fix. That's fine in the very short term; after all, these items are urgent. But the longer-term result is that your new product projects are sidelined and take forever to get done.

The solution: Ring-fence your innovation or NPD resources! Isolate your NPD people, and put a fence around them. Best performers do: They set up dedicated *innovation groups* to undertake NPD (see Exhibit 4.2). So if you have a larger group of people working on product development part-time, consider splitting these people into separate groups, and then *ring-fence your NPD people*. That is, make some of them dedicated resources—full-time to product development—rather than dividing them among many duties. These ring-fenced resources or the "innovation group" includes technical people, but also marketing and production people, whose full-time job is also product development!

With a dedicated group in place, you can now draw on people from this group to staff your important NPD projects. That is, these ring-fenced people now make up the majority of project teams, so that project teams are populated with dedicated, focused people. By contrast, assigning busy people with many jobs to a new product project often means they simply don't get the work done on the project—other tasks get in the way.

> *An example:* Kraft Foods uses a dedicated group called Innovative Applications (IA) that drives much of the new product development. The IA group is a multiple-discipline group designed to help R&D successfully innovate and work with business teams to build and expand growth opportunities and leverage technical knowledge and expertise within R&D. This group consists of 10 or more people who are focused full-time on providing this support to NPD and the organization; they work primarily on the pre-development end of the process.[9]

Make your idea-to-launch framework more cross-functional. One way to promote more effective cross-functional teams is to design and implement an idea-to-launch framework that deliberately cuts across functional boundaries and forces the active participation of people from different functions. Make every step or stage in the process a multifunctional one. Resist the temptation to have a "Manufacturing stage" or "Marketing stage," where a single department or function owns that stage. That is, your new product process must build in different tasks and provide checks and balances that require the input and involvement of these various functions.

> *For example:* A project cannot proceed into a full-scale development effort until a detailed market assessment has been completed and a manufacturing appraisal is complete. Without the active participation of both manufacturing and marketing people, the project does not get released to development—it goes nowhere!

If one looks closely at the *Stage-Gate®* framework in Chapter 7, cross-functionality is embedded within the process from beginning to end. For

Notes for Senior Management

Design your organization for product innovation. Product innovation is not a one-department show! It is very much a multidisciplinary, cross-functional effort. Organizational design—how you organize for new products—is critical. Except for the simplest of products and projects (line extensions and product updates), product innovation must cut across traditional functional boundaries and barriers.

How well does your business fare on the important team factors? Consider the five items in Exhibit 8.2—the ones found to be closely linked to better performance—and rate your own project teams in your business. This rating can be done informally, or perhaps as part of the post-launch review on completed projects that I suggested earlier.

Some suggestions:

- For every significant project, and exiting from every gate, there should be a clearly assigned project team. Members should be drawn from the various required functional areas, and there should be a clearly designated project leader as champion. The project leader can be from any functional area.
- Keep the team small, and with as dedicated (full-time) players as possible.
- Make sure that the project team members and the team leader are on the project from beginning to end. More players can be added as the project nears commercialization, but the key knowledge-holders should remain onboard and be fully accountable.
- Consider how your project teams are organized. Try one of the three recommended models outlined above: the balanced matrix, project matrix, or project team structure.
- Speaking of dedicated resources, if your business is a larger one, consider ring-fencing resources: a 100% dedicated group whose full-time job is product innovation. Make sure this is a cross-functional group, not just technical people.
- Review your idea-to-launch process to make sure that it really does foster a cross-functional approach. If your stages are "owned" by any one function, or if all the gatekeepers at any gate are from one department, then blow the whistle—it's time to rethink your idea-to-launch framework.

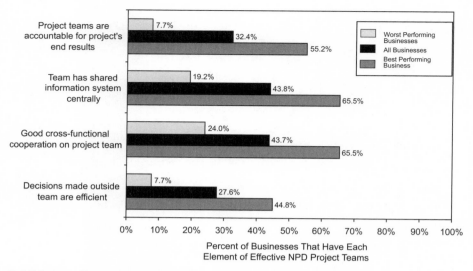

Exhibit 8.3 Characteristics of Effective Cross-Functional Teams

example, the process outlines so many activities from different departments that it's almost impossible to go from idea to launch without engaging a cross-functional team! Similarly, at every gate, the gatekeepers are a cross-functional group of management, so that all functions buy into the project. If one follows this process, your NPD effort cannot help but to become a cross-functional one!

More Characteristics of Effective NPD Teams

That's not all there is to enabling effective NPD teams, however. Our APQC study went on to uncover a number of additional characteristics of teams in top-performing businesses (shown in Exhibit 8.3). In descending order of impact, they are:

Project teams must be accountable for their project's end result—for example, for ensuring that projects meet profit and revenue targets and time targets. Team accountability is a pivotal best practice, and indeed strongly separates best from worst performers by a factor of eight to one! Indeed, only 7.7% of worst businesses hold their teams accountable for results, while 50% confess to absolutely no accountability at all. By contrast, two-thirds of best performers hold NPD teams accountable. Overall, this is a weak area, with only one-third of businesses embracing this best practice!

How does senior management instill a sense of accountability across project team members? In Chapter 7 in the section "Goal 10: Performance Metrics in Place," I outlined a recommended approach:

▶ Require that the project team presents projections of key metrics—first year sales, NPV, launch date—at Gate 3 to senior management as part of their business case.

▶ Then, at each subsequent gate and especially at your post-launch review (Exhibit 7.3), check the team's performance against these metrics.

Most businesses never go back and check project results against initial promises made, so there can be no hope of accountability—what gets measured gets done!

Enable sharing of information among the project team members via a central information system. This practice means having a centralized communication system that permits sharing of project information, and allows several team members to work concurrently on the same document, even across functions, locations, and countries. This is a particularly strong facet of best performers, with almost two-thirds having such a central shared-information system; worst performers are much weaker here, with only 19.2% having such a system. And as project teams become more transnational, the need for an effective IT-based communication system becomes even greater. The *Accolade*™ system, offered by Sopheon Inc., and *SG-Navigator*™ from Stage-Gate Inc. are excellent examples of information and decision support systems for NPD.[10]

Promote good cross-functional cooperation on the team (for example, not too much time and effort wasted on politics, conflicts, and interdepartmental prejudices). Surprisingly this is a moderately weak part of most businesses' new product efforts, with only 43.7% of businesses reporting good cross-functional cooperation within new product project teams. Top performers fare much better (66.5% with excellent cooperation); worst performers are much weaker here (24.0% with good cooperation). Some things that promote good cooperation and conflict minimization:

- Select your project team leaders carefully. "Good people skills" and certain personality traits rather than "technical skills" are much more important criteria to use in selecting leaders. Positive characteristics to look for in a good team leader are credibility, enthusiasm and passion, intrepreneurship, people skills, project management skills, and project knowledge (in that order).
- Provide team training. Such training focuses on how to be a team member, how to communicate as a team, and so on—techniques designed to minimize conflicts and politics. And, speaking of training, do provide training to your team leaders on how to lead a team.

- Team building exercises—a social or outdoor event—at the beginning of a major project helps to foster better cooperation and understanding among team members.
- Provide leadership yourself: At the gate meetings, promote the notion of a unified NPD project team. Make sure your project teams understand that they are to function as a team with a single goal, and together have *total project accountability* (rather than individual team members being functional representatives, each responsible for their own functional part of the project).

To foster cooperation and communication, ideally, team members should be located close to each other. Physical proximity as one of the keys to good teamwork is the conclusion of studies done in a number of firms. 3M reports that physical distances beyond 100 meters thwart team interaction severely. Co-location is one solution: Team members from different functions in the company are relocated in one area or department, even if for only several days a week. A team office is another solution. Another is to rely on frequent but quick team meetings—one per week (and make sure that absentee team members are sent notification of the decisions made).

Improved electronic communications helps to overcome the physical distances that plague some project teams. So make these tools available via IT to your project teams: group software (such as *Lotus Notes*™ or a project Web page); project management software (such as *Microsoft Project*™); teleconferencing and videoconferencing capabilities; and IT that is specially designed for NPD (such as *SG-Navigator*™ or *Accolade*™).[11] Be sure to provide training on these new technologies: In far too many companies we studied, the tools were available but team members failed to exploit them fully due to a lack of knowledge of how to use them!

Decisions outside the team should be handled efficiently. Some businesses have designed procedures to facilitate these outside-the-team decisions. Some examples:

- Build the "capital appropriations request" right into the Gate 3 or 4 meeting, as some businesses do (rather than holding a separate committee meeting some weeks later).
- Most businesses require that all key decision makers attend the gate meeting, or send a substitute with full signing power (so that the project leader does not have to run around "seeking signatures" from executives, one by one).

Overall, outside-the-team decisions is a weak area on average, with only 27.6% of businesses handling such decisions well; by contrast, 44.8% of best performers handle this well.

Notes for Senior Management

If you seek ways to improve the performance and the effectiveness of your NP project teams, consider building in some of the best practices listed above and found to separate best from worst performers:

- Make project teams accountable for the performance results of the project. Establish performance metrics at Gate 3, and then review the project results versus these at the post-launch review.
- Provide good IT support to enhance the sharing of information. This is vital if team members are at different physical locations.
- Foster team cooperation. Do this through careful project leader selection; training for team members and leaders; appropriate work and office facilities and locations (for example, a team office); team building exercises; and IT support.
- Make it easier for the team to handle outside-the-team decisions—some examples were given above.

The Climate and Culture for Innovation and NPD

A second organizational ingredient essential to making this cross-functional team work is *climate and culture.* The climate must encourage and reward creativity and innovation. Exhibit 8.4 shows clearly that climate and culture, and certain practices associated with creating a positive climate, is one of the strongest common denominators of top-performing businesses. Here are some concrete actions for the leadership team:

Provide a supportive climate for entrepreneurship and product innovation. A supportive climate is a major difference between the best and worst performers, with 62.1% of best businesses scoring very strongly here. By contrast, only 7.7% of poor performers have a supportive climate. Indeed, in 34.6% of worst performers, the climate was rated as "very unsupportive." On average, businesses perform moderately weakly here: Only 37.1% of businesses report a climate that supports entrepreneurship and innovation. Overall I rate the creation of such a supportive climate and culture as *one of the top best practices.*

An example: One Danish major pump manufacturer (considered a best-in-class firm) openly promotes NPD at every opportunity. NPD is evident everywhere: in the company's annual report, which devotes more pages to product innovation than to finances; its showcase of new products that occupies its entire headquarters front lobby; and its campaign of posters seen throughout company premises emphasizing

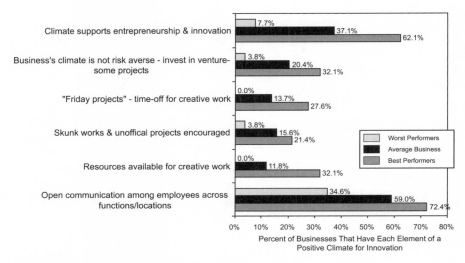

Exhibit 8.4   The Right Climate and Culture for NPD

innovation. Even the company's airport shuttle-bus and commercial trucks highlight the message with three words in huge print on the sides of vehicles: "Be Think Innovate." And the message works: The company boasts a very motivated staff—both junior and senior people—who are strongly committed to product innovation.

Don't be overly risk-averse. Best performers appear to be far less risk-averse—management is not afraid to invest in more venturesome projects. Indeed, about one-third of top performers opt for riskier projects (although risk-averseness is a weakness overall: On average, only 20.4% of businesses take on riskier projects). Almost no worst performers undertake such projects. In fact, 61.5% of worst performers indicate that they undertake only exceptionally low-risk NPD initiatives! Management's fear of venturesome projects sends out a clear signal to employees: Innovation, creativity, and entrepreneurship are not welcome here!

Encourage "Friday projects"—top businesses allow time off or scouting time for innovative projects. You cannot expect your employees to turn a switch on for one hour each week and suddenly become creative! If you want your organization to be creative, then you've got to *provide the time for people to be creative and innovative.* Many top-performing businesses provide resources and time off to creative employees to work on their own projects—that is, projects of the employees' own invention and choosing. In some businesses, the employee does not even require approval from a supervisor to move ahead; only a peer review is needed. According to management at 3M, such "Friday projects" continue to be a major source of creative innovation. Note from Exhibit 8.4 that not one worst performer does this at all! Overall, scouting time provision is a very weak area, with only 13.7% of businesses providing this.

> *Some examples:* 3M provides its technical people with 15% of their time to work on their "unapproved" personal projects. Rohm & Haas allows technical employees to have 10% "scouting time" to do their own projects; and many a successful new product project has been initiated as a "boot-strapped" project using spare time and spare money. Kraft Foods has a similar policy, where early front-end teams have unscheduled time (up to 15% of a person's time) for creative thinking and experiments.

For major projects, set up skunk works. The term "skunk works" comes from the U.S. aircraft industry during the Second World War. At the time, design teams were tasked with numerous aircraft developments at an unprecedented pace. So short was office space that many teams at Lockheed were actually housed outside the engineering offices in tents. This "outside the company" location proved to be an advantage: The teams were left alone and did not have to endure the typical company bureaucracy, hence they moved quickly and successfully. Needless to say, given the confined quarters, the long hours, the hot sun, and a tent environment, the place began to smell pretty badly—hence the term "skunk works." Today, a skunk works refers to a project team, typically dedicated, which works *outside the official bureaucracy of the company*. The team and leader may report directly to a senior executive, but typically not to their individual functional bosses. And in some cases, the team is physically off-premises.

Our APQC study reports that in some best-performing businesses, skunk works projects are encouraged. By contrast, almost no worst performers have such skunk works; indeed, in the great majority of worst performers (79.6%) skunk works are very much discouraged or not allowed.

> *Some examples:* On one visit I made to a team at the Masonite Corporation in Chicago (a manufacturer of wooden panel doors), I was surprised when my airport limo dropped me off at a shopping mall. But the address was right! The innovation team had rented a remote office in a shopping center, moved in second-hand furniture, and set up shop. The team leader reported directly to the executive committee of the business, but the rest of the project team members were free and unfettered to move ahead quickly on several major projects. I recall the incident vividly, because never before or since have I met such an

enthusiastic, bubbling, and passionate team. I guess that's what Lockheed discovered in the 1940s too.

A word of warning: You don't want all your projects run this way. Soon there would be nobody left in the company to mind the store! But for one or two major projects, where speed and success are vital to your organization, this skunk works model could be right.

Provide support for creative employees and their projects. A significant number of best performers (32.1%) provide support and resources for creative employees to pursue their own projects: seed money, equipment, and facilities. But worst performers don't at all. This is a very weak area overall, with only 11.8% of businesses providing such resources. This practice dovetails with the free-time or "Friday projects" policy above.

Foster open communication. Best-performing businesses (72.4%) provide for open communication among employees across functions, departments, and locations. This helps to stimulate creativity, and makes for more effective cross-functional communication on project teams. Worst performers are much weaker here, with only 34.6% providing open communication.

Climate and culture is also about rewards, recognition, and incentives. People behave certain ways because they are motivated to do so. So if your employees appear uncreative and non-entrepreneurial, perhaps you should look at the reward-punishment system in your business. Exhibit 8.5 provides a list of reward and incentive practices that best performers adopt. Each one is feasible, because there are companies that we studied that are doing exactly this:

Reward project champions. The majority of best performers (58.6%) recognize and/or reward their NPD project leaders and entrepreneurs (new product champions or product innovators). But this is a weak area on average, with only 28.8% of businesses providing such rewards, and worst performers not doing this at all.

> *Some examples:* Air Products & Chemicals recognizes that innovation is critical, so much so that the CTO has made it his number one priority. Innovations awards, as well as a Chairman's Award, are offered each year for ideas that have been commercialized. Rewards can be up to $100,000, an indication of the importance the company accords its product innovators.
>
> Other leading companies also place emphasis on recognizing the people who lead projects and are champions for innovation. At Kraft, for example, successfully leading an NPD team is considered a vital and important step in one's upward career path.

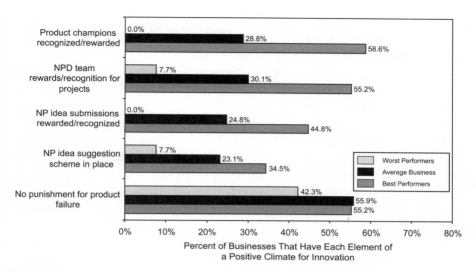

Exhibit 8.5 Rewards Are Part of a Positive Climate and Culture for NPD

Better yet, provide rewards for the entire project team. This is also a weak area on average: In only 30.1% of businesses, when an NPD project team does a good job on their project (gets to market on time, meets sales revenue targets, or has a winner) are they rewarded or recognized. Best performers are much stronger here: 55.2% reward their teams; but note that 34.6% of worst performers provide no reward whatsoever to project teams.

> *Some examples:* 3M provides cash awards to about 10% of its employees annually for doing innovative and creative things. Milliken has a *hall of fame*, whereby individuals and teams are publicly recognized for their contributions to innovative projects.

Recognize and reward new product ideas. The best performers often provide rewards or recognition to employees who submit new product ideas (44.8% of top performers do). Not one worst performer in our APQC study rewards innovation ideas, while on average only 23.1% of businesses provide such rewards—again a fairly weak area.

> *Some examples:* At Kraft Foods, recognition for ideas is important. For example, in the meals division, the division general manager awards employees with *light bulbs* for developing ideas; and there are also awards for "Innovator of the Month" and "Innovator of the Year." Recognition at Kraft is typically not monetary, but involves peer praise

and pride of ownership, which is viewed as more effective than financial rewards. The company works hard at ensuring people know that new product ideas are important and valued.

Bausch & Lomb uses limited monetary rewards as a method to reward new ideas. The employee receives anywhere from $5 to $5,000, depending on how far the idea progresses through their NPD process.

Put a visible new product idea suggestion scheme in place. If ideas are to be rewarded, then it makes sense to have an active and receptive idea capture system in place. This is a fairly common practice in best-performing businesses, with 34.5% of best performers having a strong, visible idea scheme. Only 7.7% of worst performers do, and again this is a weak area across all businesses. Several caveats here:

- First make sure that your product innovation idea scheme is not combined with the "general purpose idea scheme" in your business—the one where employees submit ideas on how to save money. New product ideas are very different types of ideas, and need to be solicited, handled, and screened differently.
- Publicize your idea scheme widely. In many businesses I visit, employees are not even certain whether or not such a scheme exists!
- In order to facilitate the flow of ideas, set up an *idea capture and handling system* as described in Discovery in Chapter 7.

Avoid punishment for failure. Incentives and rewards are only half the climate battle. At the same time, your climate must *avoid punishment for failure*. The only way to ensure no failures is to take no chances at all. So, if failures are punished, expect little in the way of risk taking and entrepreneurial behavior: People hunker down and keep their heads low!

> *An example:* At one Guinness business, the new managing director, facing a very negative climate for innovation, declared that henceforth, there would be no penalty for product failure, assuming the team had done a decent job. He went as far as to promise that *a party would be held* instead, complete with Guinness stout served—a traditional Irish wake for the failed product "to celebrate everything we have learned."
>
> *Another example:* In one major and quite conservative North American bank, the project leader stood before a senior gatekeeping committee comprised of senior VPs and was obviously very nervous. He was about to present a negative report and recommendation "to kill the project now." In spite of a valiant rescue attempt by his team, the project was headed for disaster. To his surprise, the senior executive chairing the meeting broke out in applause; this was quickly followed by

clapping from the rest of the VPs in the room. He explained: "A correct kill must be considered a success. Instead of dropping another $7 million on this project, I'm cutting my losses . . . you just saved me $7 million. Thank you for your frank and honest assessment of the situation." Far from being fired, as the project leader feared, he went on to drive the replacement project to a very successful result, and was subsequently promoted.

Removal of fear of failure is particularly evident in best performers, and indeed in most businesses studied, in order to encourage more innovative and risk-taking behavior (although this should not be confused with lack of accountability): 55.2% of best performers do not punish people for failure in NPD; by contrast, in 34.6% of worst performers, there is exceptionally high fear of failure.

Notes for Senior Management

If the goal is to improve the climate and culture for product innovation in your business, then look at the list of items and the illustrations of best practice above. Some actionable items include:

- Create a positive climate for innovation by supporting and embracing entrepreneurship and innovation openly throughout your business—with your words as well as your actions.
- Don't be afraid to take on venturesome projects if they are well thought-out. And make sure everyone is aware that you allow and encourage these projects.
- Provide scouting time and make resources available to creative, passionate employees to pursue their dream projects; allow skunk works or outside-the-bureaucracy projects.
- Encourage open communication between functions, locations, and countries. No silos allowed!
- Put a new product idea submission scheme in place, and then reward or recognize idea generators.
- Speaking of rewards, don't forget to reward and recognize project team members and leaders for their efforts. Set up a "hall of fame" in the front lobby of your office building, where you showcase your new products, and, most important, the teams that developed them.
- Make it a rule: no punishment for hard work that resulted in a failed project! And remember: A "correct kill" is also a success. That decision just saved you a bag of money and troubles! Make sure your people understand this, so that they're not afraid to take on venturesome higher-risk projects or to present negative results.

Get Your Climate and Culture Right for Innovation

The right climate and culture for product innovation is a pervasive topic, with many elements and facets. And it's sometimes difficult to put one's arms around what is meant by "climate and culture," or worse yet, what to do about it. One thing is clear: You cannot ignore climate and culture if exceptional new product results are the goal. Indeed, some elements of climate and culture outlined above are the strongest discriminators between best and worst performers uncovered in our APQC benchmarking study.

The climate and culture for product innovation is surprisingly and dangerously weak in many businesses, however. Particular weaknesses include anything to do with off-line or creative but unofficial work: free time or scouting time, resources to support creative projects, and skunk works and underground projects. Yet a significant proportion of top-performing businesses embrace and support this type of activity. Another very weak area is idea submission from employees: no idea scheme in place, and no rewards or recognition for ideas. And finally, the third major area of weakness is the unwillingness to invest in more venturesome projects—a general risk-averseness.

Senior Management Practices and Roles

Senior management must lead the way in product innovation, providing the leadership and committing the resources.[12] The topic of senior management commitment and the role of senior management in product innovation contains a number of vital best practices. Note that all but one of the practices and roles of senior management listed in Exhibit 8.6 significantly discriminate between the best- and worst-performing businesses:

Senior management must be strongly committed to new product development. Top management commitment to product innovation exists in the great majority of top-performing businesses, and indeed is one of the strongest common denominators among best performers. Whenever I visit a business for the first time, I always wait to hear about management's commitment to product development; I've learned that this is usually a key indicator of whether or not the business will succeed in the innovation war. At Mega Bloks (introduced in Chapter 1), senior management had been strongly committed to NPD right from the beginning. "It's been the leading engine of our growth for as far back as I can remember," declared a senior executive. The same is true of EXFO Engineering. The CEO, who founded the company, confessed that "I started the company on the basis of a new product that I conceived, and that's still the basis for our growth. I am committed to NPD."

In 79.3% of best performers, the story is the same: strong senior management commitment to NPD. By contrast, this commitment to product innovation exists in only 26.9% of worst performers (see Exhibit 8.6).

Keep score in NPD. And make new product metrics part of senior management's annual and personal objectives. The point about keeping score and measuring NPD performance was highlighted as a best practice in Chapter 6. Recall from Exhibit 6.5 that in 62% of top-performing businesses, senior management measures and reports *overall new product results for the business* (e.g., percentage of sales or profits achieved, success rate, on-time performance, etc.). By contrast, only 30% of poor-performing businesses keep score. Exhibit 6.8 provided insights into popular metrics used to measure the business's overall NPD performance results.

Being the *overall scorekeeper* is a key senior management role. But there's more than just keeping score. The metrics must be tied to senior managers' personal objectives and bonuses. All behavior is caused, and that's true for senior people as well. If your business seeks improved product innovation performance, then *pay people to achieve this!* That is, make NPD performance metrics, such as percentage of sales or profits generated by new products, an explicit part of senior management's personal and annual objectives; and then tie bonuses and variable pay to this metric. This is *the number two discriminator* between best and worst performers among all

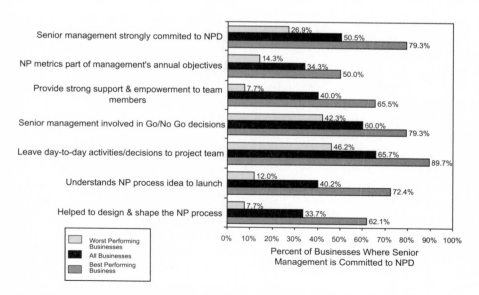

Exhibit 8.6   Senior Management Practices, Roles, and Commitment to NPD

practices listed in Exhibit 8.6, with 50% of top businesses having such metrics tied to personal objectives and rewards, and only 14.3% of worst performers.

> *An example:* One important change the CEO of ITT Industries made was to revamp the measurement system for general managers and managing directors. Traditionally, the key performance metrics for business unit heads had been short-term financial results: profits and costs meeting targets. In order to encourage more innovation and to reward successes, the CEO declared that "percentage of sales from new products" would be tracked by business unit, and senior managers also measured against this metric.

Ironically, in spite of its apparent importance, this area is rated weakly in Exhibit 8.6, with only 34.3% of businesses making new product metrics part of senior management's performance objectives, the weakest of all senior management practices.

Provide strong support and empowerment to the people working on new product projects. And transfer power and authority to the project team and leader. A dedicated project leader with some power and authority is essential for timely, successful projects. Power here means the ability to control what people—the team members—do with their time. And authority means the ability to make certain decisions.

The team leader must *have formal authority and power* (this means shifting authority or power from functional heads). Specifically, the leader and team must have the authority to make project decisions, and not be second-guessed, overruled, or micro-managed by the functional heads or senior management. And the leader (and team) must have some control over how the project team members spend their time (as opposed to the functional bosses of team members controlling their subordinates' time and meting it out to the team leader).

Gates are where the transfer of power and authority from functional managers to the team leader and team takes place. Here, the functional bosses, who are the gatekeepers, approve projects; they *also approve the transfer of their resources* (people and money) to the project leader and team. So another rule is: Coming out of each gate, not only is the project team formally defined, but the *resources assigned to the team should be clear*—people and their time (person-days and percent of their time), as well as dollars.

Team support, empowerment, and authority is a key driver of performance, but also an area of some weakness. In only 40% of businesses overall, and in 65.5% of best performers, top management provides strong support and empowerment to people working on project teams. By contrast, strong senior management support for NPD teams is evident in only 7.7% of worst performers, and 42.3% provide no support whatsoever.

Get engaged in your new product projects and in your idea-to-launch framework. . . but in the right way! For example, in top-performing businesses, the senior people are very much involved in the Go/Kill and spending decisions for new products: They have a central role in the gate review process, with top management in 60% of businesses overall, and in 79.3% of best performers, acting as gatekeepers and making these Go/Kill decisions (see Exhibit 8.6).

Some words of warning: Engagement does not mean micro-managing projects! Rather, in top performers, senior mangers tend to leave the day-to-day activities and decisions in a new product project to the project's leader and team. Most businesses score very strongly here: In 65.7% of businesses overall, and in 89.7% of best performers, senior people do not micro-manage projects.

More words of warning: Engagement does not mean driving your personal "pet project" to market regardless. Recall from Chapter 1: Executive-sponsored pet projects get to market, but have higher than average failure rates once there. The problem is that no one in the company wants to tell you that your personal project is a dog—that "the emperor wears no clothes"!

Make sure that you understand your business's NPD process: For management to play an effective role in NPD, they must understand their business's NPD process, and particularly be aware of their own role and responsibilities in the process. This is not always the case (only true for 40.2% of the businesses), but is clearly a best practice—a major discriminator between best- and worst-performing businesses, with 72.4% of best performers scoring very high here. Indeed, in 48% of worst performers, senior management does not understand the NPD process at all!

Even better, senior management should help to design your business's new product process:

> *An example:* As one senior person in a major flooring manufacturer put it: "Our leadership team [of the business] helped to design our new product process. Our senior VP of marketing actually chaired the task force, and got the rest of us [the executives] involved in designing gate criteria, agreeing on a set of 'rules of engagement' to guide our behaviors, and even outlining how we were going to run gate meetings. So it became very much 'our process' too—we bought in."

Again, this is a weak area (occurs in only 33.7% of businesses), but apparently an important one—the number four discriminator between best and worst performers in Exhibit 8.6. Note that in 62.1% of best performers, senior management was very engaged in the design of their new product process.

Notes for Senior Management

The role of senior management in leading the product innovation effort of the business cannot be understated. This topic area separates best and worst performers in a major way. All practices listed above are important—either they discriminate between our top and poorer businesses, or they are widely practiced among the best—and should be part of your senior management practices, notably:

- Ensuring that you and the rest of the leadership team in your business are committed to product innovation as the ultimate and enduring engine of growth and prosperity for your business.
- Measuring NPD results, and making them an explicit part of senior management's annual objectives and bonuses.
- Making sure that senior management provides the necessary support, empowerment, and authority to project team leaders and members. This transfer of power or authority usually takes place at the gates, where senior management meets the project team, reviews their project, and, if Go, approves the resources. Along with resource approval should go some degree of power and authority transfer as well.
- Involving senior management in projects and in the process in the right way—for example, as gatekeepers making Go/Kill decisions. But avoid the temptation to micro-manage projects or to drive executive "pet projects"!
- Engaging senior management in the design (or periodic overhauling) of your business's NPD process, and making sure that they understand it. Some best practice businesses provide extensive gatekeeper and senior management training on their idea-to-launch framework, and on the roles for senior management and "rules of engagement"—I call this training "gatekeeper boot-camp."

Gatekeeping—A Vital Role for Senior Management

As go the gates, so goes the process! So focus on the gates and get the gates right. If the gates don't work, the idea-to-to-launch process is broken too.

Thus, senior managers in most businesses are very much involved in the crucial Go/Kill decisions for NPD projects (see Exhibit 8.6): Gatekeeping is a key role for senior management, and an important facet of your idea-launch framework.

Effective gatekeeping is an elusive goal for many leadership teams, however; and it does not happen by accident. Too often, senior executives confess that they are less than satisfied with their project gate meetings— that these gate meetings are inefficient, take too long, are poorly run and organized, and often don't even yield a tangible decision! So how can you become more effective in your roles as a gatekeepers and the quality assurors of the new product process?

The critical role of gatekeepers is to *facilitate* the *rapid commercialization* of the *best projects*. It is your job to ensure that projects receive a timely and fair hearing, that objective and consistent decisions are made, that resources are allocated and commitments kept, and that roadblocks are cleared out of the way. Good gatekeepers achieve these goals by:

- *Making timely, firm, and consistent Go/Kill decisions.* Too often I witness gatekeeping teams that cancel gate meetings, or fail to make the decision in a timely fashion. Yet they are the first to complain about long cycle times and projects taking too long to reach the marketplace.
- *Prioritizing projects objectively.* Projects must be prioritized at gate meetings: Is this a strong green light project, or a weak green light, or a yellow light? If all your projects are top priority, then none of them is! And these prioritizations must be made on the basis of objective, visible criteria, and supported by facts, not just opinions of the gatekeepers. There is no room for politicking and opinioneering at gate meetings!
- *Establishing visible deliverables for successive gate meetings.* Deliverables are based on a standard menu for each gate. But each project is unique, and may deviate from the standard deliverables list. The gatekeepers must agree to a list of needed deliverables for the project in question, and ensure that the project leader understands what is required of him or her.
- *Committing and ensuring availability of necessary resources.* Resource commitments must be made at gates. There no sense having a gate meeting, deciding on "Go," but failing to assign the needed resources. Recall that the gatekeepers are the people who "own" the resources required for the next stage, and hence are in a position to make the resource allocation decision right at the gate meeting.
- *Mentoring and enabling project teams.* The traditional notion of a gatekeeper as "judge and critic" is obsolete in progressive businesses.

Rather, the gatekeeper is very much an enabler, helper, and mentor, providing resources and assistance, and facilitating the rapid execution of the project.

▶ *Setting high standards for quality of execution of project tasks.* Gatekeepers are also the quality assurors in the idea-to-launch process, ensuring that projects unfold as they should. Recall from Chapter 7 that gates are the *quality control check-points;* so that means that you, the senior mangers, become in effect the *quality controllers* or *assurors* of the process. In practice, this translates into challenging project teams when deliverables are weak or substandard; and also into providing clear guidelines (when exiting a gate meeting) as to what the expectations are for deliverables for the next gate.

The five key roles of the gatekeepers are outlined in Box 8.1.

Box 8.1   The Five Roles of Gatekeepers

The Bankers: To make Go/Kill and prioritization decisions and to commit and provide the necessary resources for the project.

The Enforcers: To ensure that the new product process works—to instill discipline.

The Quality Assurors: To ensure that projects are unfolding as they should— high-quality work and fact-based deliverables.

The Mentors: To help project teams chart their path forward, to provide advice, and to share their wisdom.

The Godfathers: To help project teams overcome obstacles and move forward—to remove red-tape and other roadblocks to the timely completion of the project.

Making the Gates Work

Most businesses' leadership teams develop and agree to their "rules of the game" and also to the procedures for gate meetings. These might sound like a bit of a nuisance, and not the most exciting task you face. But at best, gate meetings are tricky affairs to make work well, so perhaps your leadership team should take the time to review and develop these rules. After all, any war-game or team sport needs some rules of engagement in order to help to direct the total effort and bring some discipline to the field. So I outline a sample set of "rules of engagement for gatekeepers" that I have collected from a number of companies. Read the list in Box 8.2, and you'll appreciate the wisdom of having such a set of rules of engagement for your own senior management team.

Many businesses also have well-defined gate procedures: These are attempts to deal with deficiencies at gate meetings in the past. These gate procedures typically deal with how the project information will be presented, how the project will be evaluated or scored, and how the decision will be made. Note the importance of these gate decisions, so a little struc-

---

Box 8.2 Use These Gatekeeper "Rules of Engagement"

1. Gatekeepers must hold the meeting and be there. Postponed or cancelled meetings are not an option. If you cannot attend, your vote is "Yes" (or you can send a designate with your proxy vote).

2. Gatekeepers must have received, read, and prepared for the meeting. Contact the gate facilitator or project team if there are show-stoppers or killer variables. No "surprise attacks" at the gate meeting!

3. Gatekeepers cannot request information or answers beyond that specified in the deliverables: no playing "I gotcha." Gates are not a forum to demonstrate your machoism, political clout, or intellectual prowess.

4. Gatekeepers cannot "beat up" the presenter. Give the project team an uninterrupted period to present. The question-and-answer session must be fair, not vicious.

5. Gatekeepers must make their decision based on the criteria for that gate. Gatekeepers must review each criterion and reach a conclusion. Each gatekeeper should use the scorecard to rate the project.

6. Gatekeepers must be disciplined: no hidden agendas; no invisible criteria; decisions based on facts and criteria, not emotion and gut feeling!

7. All projects must be treated fairly and consistently: They must pass through the gate. There is no special treatment for executive-sponsored or "pet projects"; all are subjected to the same criteria and the same rigor.

8. A decision must be made, within that working day! If the deliverables are there, you cannot defer the decision—this is a system built for speed.

9. The project team must be informed of the decision, immediately and face to face.

10. If the decision is Go, the gatekeepers support the agreed-to action plan: commit the resources (people and money); and agree to release times for people on the project team (**Note:** No one gatekeeper can over-ride the Go decision or renege on agreed-to resources).

11. If the decision is Hold, the gatekeepers must try to find resources. The project cannot remain on Hold for more than three months: It's up or out! (This rule puts pressure on gatekeepers to make tougher decisions—some real Kills—or to commit more resources.)

ture that promises to promote effectiveness is a desirable element. I provide a best-practice gate format or procedure in the Appendix.

Notes for Senior Management

At the beginning of this book (back in Chapter 1), I outlined the things that senior management must get right in order to win the innovation war. As we approach the end of the book, and now that you've had a chance to see all the research results and all the details of the *Innovation Diamond* and *its four points of performance*, it's fitting that you reflect back on these key action items for senior management:

1. You must embrace a long-term commitment to product innovation as the engine of growth and prosperity in your business.
2. Then, develop a vision, objectives, and strategy for product innovation in your business, driven by (and linked to) your business's objectives and strategy.
3. Next, install a systematic, high-quality idea-to-launch framework in your business, and practice discipline, following the principles of the process.
4. Be sure to make available the necessary resources. . . you cannot win games without players on the field!
5. Practice effective portfolio management. Make sure that you focus your scarce resources on the right development initiatives. And resist the temptation to try to undertake too many projects for your business's limited resources.
6. And finally, foster innovation in your organization, creating the right climate and culture for product innovation, and supporting and enabling effective cross-functional teams.

Notes

1. APQC benchmarking study: see note 29 in Chapter 1. Some of this chapter is taken from R. G. Cooper, S. J. Edgett, & E. J. Kleinschmidt, "Benchmarking Best NPD Practices—Part I: Culture, Climate, Teams and Senior Management Roles," *Research-Technology Management*, 47, 1, 2003, 31–43.

2. A. L. Page, "PDMA New Product Development Survey: Performance and Best Practices," paper presented at PDMA Conference, Chicago, November 1991; see also A. Griffin, *Drivers of NPD Success: The 1997 PDMA Report*. Chicago: Product Development & Management Association, 1997; A. Griffin & J. Hauser, "Integrating R&D, and Marketing: A Review and Analysis of the Literature," *Journal of Product Innovation Management*, 13, 1996, 191–215; and E. Olson, O.

Walker, R. Ruekert, & J. Bonner, "Patterns of Cooperation during New Product Development among Marketing, Operations and R&D: Implications for Project Performance," *Journal of Product Innovation Management*, 18, 4, 2001, 258–271.

3. M. A. Maidique & B. J. Zirger, "A Study of Success and Failure in Product Innovation: The Case of the U.S. Electronics Industry," *IEEE Transactions in Engineering Management* EM-31, November 1984, 192–203; also B. J. Zirger & M. A. Maidique, "A Model of New Product Development: An Empirical Test," *Management Science*, 36, 7, 1990, 867–883.

4. See Maidique and Zirger: note 3.

5. *NewProd®* projects studies: see note 30 in Chapter 1.

6. E. W. Larson & D. H. Gobeli, "Organizing for Product Development Projects," *Journal of Product Innovation Management*, 5, 1988, 180–190.

7. T. J. Peters, *Thriving on Chaos*. New York: Harper & Row, 1988.

8. E. W. Larson & D. H. Gobeli, "Organizing for Product Development Projects," *Journal of Product Innovation Management* 5, 1988, 180–190.

9. The Kraft Foods case study is reported in APQC benchmarking study. See note 1.

10. *Accolade™* by Sopheon; one of my colleagues, Dr. Scott Edgett, was on Sopheon's external design advisory team as the software was developed. See www.sopheon.com and www.prod-dev.com. See also note 11.

11. *SG-Navigator™* is an electronic IT version of *Stage-Gate®*, available from Stage-Gate Inc. (www.stage-gate.com). See also: *Accolade™* by Sopheon in note 10.

12. See R. G. Cooper & E. J. Kleinschmidt, "Benchmarking the Firm's Critical Success Factors in New Product Development," *Journal of Product Innovation Management*, 12, 5, November 1995, 374–391.

9

Taking Action—
Executive Summary

If you're going through hell, keep going. . .
—Winston Churchill

Whatever you can do, or dream you can, begin it.
Boldness has genius, power and magic in it.
—Goethe

Twenty-Five Ways to Win the Product Innovation War

"Give me the three main bullet points—what I have to know in order to win the new products game!" exclaimed an impatient managing director of a major European food business. The setting was an in-company conference, and I had just begun my presentation, when he blurted out his request. My reply was: "It isn't that simple . . . as in any war or game, a number of factors lead to victory." Now that you've read this book, you have seen many concepts and prescriptions on how to win at new products in the last eight chapters. It's a daunting list, but no one said that leading at product innovation was going to be easy or could be boiled down to a handful of quick fixes!

In spite of the complex nature of winning at product innovation, and in spite of my reply to this managing director, in this final chapter I do try to integrate and simplify—to reduce some of the complexity, and to distill the essence of the book into a 25 key messages and major calls to action: a fast summary of the book.

So here are the 25 messages:

It's War and Winning Is Everything

1. New product development is a war, where victory ultimately decides the fate of your business. Do you know you are at war?

Do you and the other members of your leadership team recognize that you are indeed at war, and that this war merits your undivided time and attention? And are you leading your business the way generals would run their warfare operations? Specifically . . .

- Have you mapped out a strategy for this war—a product innovation strategy?
- Have you defined the battlefields or strategic arenas where you wish to fight or attack?
- Have you thought about tactics—about the details of how you'll drive products to market quickly and effectively?
- Are you dealing with the people issues—creating the right spirit, climate, and culture, and organizing your troops effectively in order to win this war?

What Distinguishes the Best Performers

2. Businesses that boast the *four points of performance* in the *Innovation Diamond* fare much better in this product innovation war (Exhibit 2.8). Take steps to incorporate this *Innovation Diamond* into your business.

Recall, the *four points of performance* are:

- *Strategic:* Top performers put a product innovation and technology strategy in place, driven by the leadership team and the strategic vision of the business. This product innovation strategy guides the business's NPD direction and helps to steer resource allocation and project selection.
- *Resource investment and focusing on the right projects—portfolio management:* Top performers commit sufficient resources to undertake their new product projects effectively; and they boast a portfolio management system that helps the leadership team effectively allocate these resources to the right areas and to the right projects.
- *An idea-to-launch framework for doing NPD projects right:* A best-in-class new product process or *Stage-Gate®* game plan—a framework that drives new product projects from the idea phase through to

launch and beyond—exists in top-performing businesses. This idea-to-launch framework emphasizes quality-of-execution, upfront homework, voice-of-customer input, and tough Go/Kill decision-points.

▶ *The right climate and environment for innovation:* Senior managers in top performing businesses create a positive climate and culture for innovation and entrepreneurship; they foster effective cross-functional NPD teams; and they are properly engaged in the NPD decision-making process.

3. **Keep score! The place to begin is with *an audit* of your new product performance.**

I began this book by urging you to keep score—to start tracking your new product performance. And keeping score is a theme throughout the book. Begin by comparing your performance results with those for average and best performers in the charts in Chapter 2:

▶ percentage of revenues and profits coming from new products—Exhibit 2.1
▶ new product success, fail, and kill rates—Exhibit 2.2
▶ time-to-market and on-schedule, on-budget performance—Exhibits 2.3 and 2.4
▶ percentage of projects that meet objectives—Exhibit 2.5
▶ a variety of other performance metrics—Exhibit 2.6

4. **If you're not happy with the results of this performance audit, track down the causes. Do an audit of your current development practices.**

How well is your business performing in terms of the *four points performance* in the *Innovation Diamond*? And how do you rate on the many best practices identified in the bar charts throughout the book?

Undertake internal benchmarking by lowering the microscope on your current new product practices. Rate your practices in terms of the *four points of performance* above. For a more detailed audit, use the items in the many bar charts:

▶ best practices in developing a product innovation strategy—Exhibit 3.2
▶ how best-practice businesses focus and allocate resources to project teams—Exhibits 4.2 and 4.3

- portfolio management best practices—Exhibit 4.4
- quality of execution of key activities (idea-to-launch)—Exhibit 6.1
- best practices embedded in the idea-to-launch framework—Exhibits 6.2 to 6.5
- the way that project teams should be organized—Exhibits 8.2 and 8.3
- creating the right climate and culture—Exhibits 8.4 and 8.5
- the role of senior management—Exhibit 8.6

Recall that there are standard audit tools available, such as *SG-Benchmarker*™, to help you with this audit.

A Product Innovation Strategy for Your Business: What Markets, Products, and Technologies?

5. **Doing business without strategy is like sailing a ship without a rudder. New product strategy pays off.**

Those businesses that lack goals for their total new product effort, where arenas or areas of strategic thrust have not been defined, where the strategy and projects are short-term in nature, and where the strategy is not well-communicated to all, are at a decided performance disadvantage. If your organization does not have an explicit, written new product strategy, complete with measurable goals and specification of arenas as a guide to your business's new product efforts, now is the time to begin developing one.

6. **Strategy development is the job of the leadership team of the business. This is how senior people become engaged in project selection and portfolio management processes—by charting your business's innovation strategy.**

Here's how to proceed (from Chapter 3):

- Spell out your *new product goals*: for example, what percentage of sales or profit or growth new products will contribute. Use gap analysis.
- Undertake a *strategic assessment*. Assess your markets and industry looking for opportunities; watch for disruptive or step-change technologies; and identify your strengths and core competencies, and what you could exploit to advantage.
- Map your battlefields: That is, *identify arenas of strategic focus*. Draw an arena grid for your business: Use two dimensions (products and markets, as in Exhibit 3.8) or three dimensions (customer groups, applications, and technologies, as in Exhibit 3.10). Locate your home base,

and move out on each of the three axes, identifying other customer groups, applications, and technologies.

▶ Now that you've identified a list of possible arenas, try to rate each on the two key dimensions of *arena attractiveness* and *business strength*. Draw an arena assessment map to see in which sectors your arenas lie (as in Exhibit 3.11).

▶ Prioritize your arenas or battlefields, looking for those in the desirable best bets sector, but perhaps seeking a balance by including some from the good bets and the high-risk bets sectors.

▶ Define your attack strategy and entry strategy. Decide how you'll win on each battlefield: the strategy may be to be the industry innovator, the first to the market with new products; or to be a "fast follower," rapidly copying and improving upon competitive entries. And decide how you will enter each arena: internal product development, licensing, joint venturing, or acquisitions of other firms.

Product Innovation Strategy to Portfolio Management— Resource Commitment and Deployment

7. Determine the right level of NPD investment for your business— don't get caught in a crippling "resource crunch."

Have you committed sufficient resources to achieve your business's NPD goals? Or are you heavily under-resourced, and face tough decisions regarding resource commitment for the future? (As a quick check, compare your R&D spending with industry averages in Exhibit 1.5.) And are you caught in the resource crunch in NPD, with all the problems that brings: long times to market, lack-luster launches, and no blockbuster new products?

Use the four fundamental approaches to help you, the leadership team of the business, decide how many resources to commit to product development or how much to invest in R&D in your business. These four approaches are:

- investment level based on the strategic role of your business
- strategy, goals, and task approach
- competitive parity
- investment level based on demand created by your NPD opportunities

8. Translate your product innovation strategy into spending decisions—implement an effective portfolio management system.

A vital and related question is this: Are you allocating your scarce and valuable NPD resources in the right way—to the right markets, product types, and projects?

Strive to achieve at least some of the five goals of an effective portfolio management system (although very few businesses do get all five):

- Seek *strategic alignment*, so that your portfolio of projects truly reflects your business's strategy (all projects are "on strategy" and support your strategy; the breakdown of spending mirrors your strategic priorities).
- *Maximize the value* of your portfolio. That is, pick projects so that the sum total of the values of these projects in your portfolio is the maximum possible for a given spending level. (Hint: Start by finding out what your portfolio is worth today by putting a valuation on all projects in your portfolio; add them up.)
- Seek the *right balance* of projects in terms of long-term projects versus short-term ones; or high-risk versus lower-risk projects; and across various markets, technologies, product categories, and project types.
- Ensure *portfolio sufficiency* versus your overall product innovation goals. Make sure that when you add up what your portfolio of projects will yield, this meets or exceeds your stated goal.
- Balance the *number of projects with resources available.* Don't overload your pipeline; rather, achieve a balance between resources required for the "Go" projects and resources available.

9. **Start with strategic portfolio management: Establish** *strategic buckets* **to decide where you want to spend your NPD resources or money.**

Strategy becomes real when you start spending money. Thus, deciding your ideal *spending breakdown* or *deployment of development resources* helps to translate strategy into reality (middle left part of Exhibit 4.5).

Strategic buckets are a powerful tool here: Strategic buckets is a simple concept, but has profound implications. Instead of just letting the portfolio be decided by the projects you select, reverse the order, letting strategy decide what the mix and balance in the portfolio should be.

Here is the approach:

- Select appropriate dimensions: Project types, business areas (markets, sectors, product lines), and geography are commonly employed dimensions.
- Determine the size of the buckets (how much to spend in each)—use a modified Delphi management approach (Exhibit 4.7). Look at best practice companies as a guide to splits by project types (Exhibit 4.9).
- Reconcile the numbers of projects underway in each bucket with the strategic buckets spending limits. That is, do you have too many projects in any area or bucket? Or perhaps not enough?

◗ Use these buckets to allocate funds and resources to different types and categories of projects. And recognize that projects in different buckets can use different criteria for rating and ranking them.

The result: Over time and with some discipline, your spending or deployment should begin to mirror your strategic priorities.

10. **Develop a strategic product roadmap. Map out the major development initiatives that you will need in order to win on your key battlefields or strategic arenas.**

The product roadmap ensures that your list of major projects contributes to (or is essential for) the realization of the business's strategy and goals. A strategic product roadmap is an effective way to map out this series of key assaults in an attack plan. Note that this roadmap should be strategic, with place-marks for major projects, some of which are yet to be defined. And it must be a timeline for the longer term (not just a list of products and projects for this year)

In developing your roadmap, be sure to rely on:

◗ strategic assessment—identifying those products and projects that are necessary for you to enter and be successful in your chosen arenas (from item 6 above).
◗ a portfolio review of your existing product offerings—forecasts of the life cycles of current products, and the identification of gaps in the current product line.
◗ competitive analysis—your products and product lines relative to your competitors' current and probable future offerings.
◗ technology trend assessment—technology forecasts and the identification of what new technologies, and hence new platform developments, will be required.
◗ market trends assessment—pinpointing specific initiatives that you must undertake to stay ahead of these trends.

Portfolio Management for New Products—Picking Winners and Investing in the Right Projects

11. **Now move to tactical portfolio management—focusing resources on the right development projects.**

Establish a hierarchical approach to portfolio management, as in Exhibit 5.1. Recognize that there are strategic decisions (directional and high-level) and tactical decisions (project selection and prioritization). The strategic portfolio decisions were dealt with above in items 9 and 10 above. But recognize that project decisions—Go/Kill, prioritization, and resource allocation—must still be made.

Two decision processes complement each other here:

▶ your idea-to-launch *gating process*, which focuses on individual projects
▶ your *portfolio review* approach, which looks at the entire set of projects

12. Make use of project selection tools to help you make more professional decisions in your gate meetings and portfolio reviews.

Doing projects right is tough, but picking the right projects is even tougher. The evidence strongly suggests that most leadership teams stumble here. So introduce a little professionalism into your Go/Kill and prioritization decision process. Here's how:

a. Use one of the financial models—NPV or ECV—to help make gate Go/Kill decisions; but also use the *productivity index* calculated from the NPV or ECV for ranking projects at portfolio reviews.
b. Incorporate these financial metrics into your balanced scorecard (item 13 below).
c. Use a bubble diagram to display the risk profile of your portfolio, either the popular risk-reward diagram in Exhibit 5.7 or the newness diagram in Exhibit 5.9.
d. Show the balance in your portfolio by using two or three pie charts. Break down your resources by project types, geographies, and business areas. And compare these pie chart splits—the "what is"—with your strategic buckets—the "what should be."
e. And make sure someone has done the sufficiency calculation as well as the resource capacity analysis and presents these results at your portfolio review for debate and discussion.

13. For best results, rely on a balanced scorecard approach to project selection.

The selection of the right development projects is not as easy as cranking the financial numbers and making Go/Kill decisions from this spreadsheet analysis. For one thing, the numbers are usually wrong. In fact, those businesses that dwell mostly on the numbers—using financial criteria to rate, rank, and select projects—end up with the worst portfolios!

Instead, develop and use a *balanced scorecard approach*, where a number of factors known to drive success are included in the scorecard. Use this scorecard at the gate meetings, with the leadership team physically scoring projects. Tally and display the scorecard results on a big screen; debate the results; and then make the Go/Kill decision.

If you are doing quite different types of projects in different buckets, use *different scorecards* for these different project types (for example, the scorecard in Exhibit 5.5 for normal new products and in Exhibit 5.6 for radical innovations and technology developments).

Building Best Practices into Your Idea-to-Launch Framework

14. **Put in place a best-in-class idea-to-launch framework to drive new products to market . . . quickly and efficiently.**

Virtually every top-performing company in the product innovation war has a first-rate idea-to-launch process in place, such as *Stage-Gate®*. If you do not have such a process, or if your current method is cumbersome, bureaucratic, and doesn't yield the results you want, get rid of it or overhaul it! If your current idea-to-launch process is more than two years old, it's probably time for a good overhaul anyway.

Once you do design and implement your idea-to-launch framework, make sure that both senior management and project teams understand, embrace, and stick to this process. Here, the devil is in the details—how the process is implemented and used. Learn to live your idea-to-launch framework!

15. **When you implement your idea-to-launch framework (or overhaul your old one), be sure to build six vital best practices, especially into the stages or plays of the game:**

▶ Emphasize quality of execution of key tasks from idea to launch: no short-cutting and no corner-cutting. Eighteen key activities were listed in Exhibit 6.1 that are pivotal to NPD success.

▶ Seek competitive advantage through superior new products: differentiated products that offer the customer or user unique benefits and provide the user better value for money.

▶ Ensure that the voice-of-customer is built in throughout the entire NPD idea-to-launch framework. This means the whole project team interfacing directly with customers or users, listening to their problems, and understanding unmet needs and desires.

▶ Demand sharp, early product definition—the target market, product concept and positioning, the value proposition, and the features and specs—before any project enters the Development stage. And make sure this definition is fact-based and signed off by the entire project team.

- Insist on solid upfront homework by the project team before the project is released to the Development stage. And make sure your NPD framework incorporates a good dose of upfront or front-end homework, both technical and marketing.

16. Build tough gates or Go/Kill decision-points into your idea-to-launch framework.

Focus, focus, focus! Learn to drown some puppies—that is, make sure that some projects really do get killed! Strive for a funneling approach, where projects are successively culled out at each gate until only the best survive and enter Development. These Go/Kill gates must have visible criteria, defined deliverables, and designated gatekeepers. Use the project selection tools outlined in Chapter 5 and items 12 and 13 above—such as the productivity index and the balanced scorecard method—to make for more effective Go/Kill gate meetings.

17. Put multiple performance metrics in place. What gets measured gets done.

These metrics should measure performance in three areas:

- how successful or profitable your projects are (as part of a post-launch review)
- how well your NPD process is working
- how well your business is doing at product innovation

You need at least several metrics per area, as no one metric does the whole job. Further, overemphasis on a single metric may actually encourage or reward the wrong type of management behavior (for example, the "percentage of sales" metric).

A World-Class *Stage-Gate*® Idea-to-Launch Framework for Your Business

18. Integrate these best practices above into a best-in-class new idea-to-launch framework. It should be robust and comprehensive, yet be simple, easy to follow, and easy to use. And there should be an intuitively logical structure to the framework.

As you walked through the typical *Stage-Gate*® framework in Chapter 7, you should have noted the simple elegance and logic of the model. There are just five stages and five gates for the full model, each simply defined and identified. And the flow logic is clear.

- Gates are like the huddles in a North American football game. They each have a common format:
  - inputs or deliverables—what the project leader must deliver to each gate, specifically the information that management needs to make a timely Go/Kill decision
  - criteria—upon which the Go/Kill and prioritization decision will be made (ideally, visible criteria and in scorecard format)
  - outputs—the decision (Go/Kill/Hold/Recycle); and if Go, the next steps and resources approved
- The stages are like the plays in that football game. They are defined by their purpose and also by the activities executed within them. Stages build in a number of best practices, and include both mandatory and highly recommended activities. Activities are undertaken within stages by the cross-functional team in parallel or rugby-style in order to accelerate projects to market.

19. Your idea-to-launch process must be flexible and scalable.

Your *Stage-Gate®* framework should suit the risk and size of different types of projects. If not, your people are probably trying to ram both large and small, simple and complex projects through the same model, and are ending up frustrated and with much make-work on their hands.

Define different types of projects according to size, complexity, and risk level. Then map out different processes or frameworks to suit each: a three-stage *Stage-Gate® Express* version for extensions, modifications, and improvements; and even a two-stage framework for simple sales and customer requests.

20. Handle your visionary or discovery projects—technology developments and technology platforms—in a special way.

Technology developments, more radical innovations, and technology platform projects should be part of any progressive business's portfolio of development projects. Consider setting up a separate strategic bucket to ensure that resources are set aside for such projects (as in Exhibit 4.6)—otherwise they'll be crowded out by more pressing short-term projects.

Then develop and use a special *Stage-Gate®* process for these projects. Just because discovery projects are special and less well-defined does not mean they should be totally free-form: A little discipline helps here too. This idea-to-application process for TD-developments should look a lot like your new product *Stage-Gate®* process, complete with stages and gates. Even the names of some of the stages and gates may be the same. But the details of the stages and the specific gate criteria you use should be quite unique to these types of projects, as shown in Exhibit 7.7. For example, use a more visionary scorecard at gates as in Exhibit 5.6 to ensure that these technology development and discovery projects get a fair hearing, and aren't killed or sidelined for the wrong reasons.

The People in the Product Innovation War—
The Right Climate and Environment, Effective
NPD Teams, and the Role of Senior Management

21. **Winning the product innovation war is very much a team effort. Spare no effort to ensure the effectiveness of your cross-functional teams.**

A clearly assigned project team, with members from the various functional areas, must be designated for every significant development project. There should also be a clearly identified project leader as champion (who can be from any functional area). Try to keep the team small, with dedicated (full-time) players. And avoid hand-offs, ensuring that the team members and leader remain on the project from beginning to end.

Adopt one of the three recommended organizational structures for teams outlined in Chapter 8: the balanced matrix, project matrix, or project team structure. If your business is a larger one, ring-fence your NPD resources: a 100% dedicated group, whose full-time job is product innovation (a cross-functional group, not just technical people).

Finally, make project teams accountable for the performance-results of the project. Establish performance metrics at Gate 3, and then review the project results versus these at the post-launch review.

22. **Your troops must be motivated to win the innovation war, so create the right climate and culture for product innovation.**

Support innovation openly throughout your business with your words as well as your actions. And take on venturesome projects if they are well thought-out. Communicate this to all. Provide scouting time and make resources available to creative, passionate employees to pursue their own projects; and allow skunk works or outside-the-bureaucracy projects.

Install a new product idea submission scheme, and then reward or recognize idea generators. Also, reward and recognize project team members and leaders for their efforts. Try setting up a "hall of fame" in the front lobby of your office building, where you showcase your new products and the teams that developed them. And remember: no punishment for hard work that resulted in a failed project; and a "correct kill" is also a success.

23. **Follow the example of leadership teams in winning businesses—your leadership team should take the following key actions:**

▶ Measure your business's NPD results, and make these results an explicit part of senior management's annual objectives.

▶ Provide the necessary support, empowerment, and authority to project team leaders and members (this transfer of power takes place at the gates).

▶ Senior management must be active in projects in the right way—for example, as gatekeepers making Go/Kill decisions. But avoid the temptation to drive executive pet projects or to micro-manage projects from on high!

▶ Understand what it takes to be an effective gatekeeper. If in doubt, enroll in "gatekeeper boot-camp."

▶ Develop and live by a set of gatekeeper rules of engagement.

24. **Senior management must lead in this innovation war. To summarize, there are six major actions which you, the leadership team, must undertake in order to win the new products war:**

a. You must embrace a long-term commitment to product innovation as the engine of growth and prosperity in your business.

b. Then, develop a vision, objectives, and strategy for product innovation in your business, driven by (and linked to) your business's objectives and strategy.

c. Next, install a systematic, high quality idea-to-launch framework in your business (such as *Stage-Gate®*), and practice discipline, following the principles of the process.

d. Make available the necessary resources . . . you cannot win games without players on the field!

e. Put an effective portfolio management system in place. Focus your scarce resources on the right development initiatives, and resist the temptation to try to undertake too many projects for your business's limited resources.

f. Finally, foster innovation in your organization, creating the right climate and culture for product innovation, and supporting and enabling effective cross-functional teams.

25. Make a commitment to move forward in order to win this product innovation war.

Cut and paste Churchill's famous quotation which began this chapter on your office wall: "If you're going through hell, keep going." Now reread items 1–24 above and highlight the actions and items most relevant for you and your leadership team. Then move forward . . .

Appendix

Effectively Run Gate Meetings— A Good Procedure

1. The dates for leadership-team gate meetings are pre-established for the year (dates are often tied into another meeting, such as the Executive Committee Meeting). The date for a specific project's gate is decided at its previous gate meeting.

2. Deliverables materials are electronically delivered to gatekeepers one week prior:
   - Use a standard format for most deliverables (for example, use templates). This makes it easier for both project teams and gatekeepers.
   - The project team must submit by this one-week deadline; otherwise the project is removed from the gate agenda.

3. Major questions and show-stoppers:
   - If gatekeepers spot major issues or potential showstoppers, or have key questions, they should contact the gate facilitator or project team in advance. No surprises at the gate meeting!

4. Hold the gate meeting!
   - Cancellations or postponements are unacceptable unless deliverables are not ready.
   - Hold the meeting even if a Kill decision is anticipated . . .
     – to achieve closure
     – to agree on lessons
     – to celebrate a correct Kill
   - Video and teleconferencing are okay.

5. The entire project team is present.

6. A head gatekeeper is nominated or designated (optional). She or he follows up with the project team regarding any loose ends after the gate meeting.

7. Meeting procedure:
   ● The project team has 15 minutes to present . . . uninterrupted.
   ● A Q&A session ensues (facilitated).
   ● The facilitator takes the gatekeepers through the list of criteria.
     – Readiness-check and must-meet criteria are displayed on video projector and discussed. A consensus "No" kills or recycles the project.
     – Should-meet criteria are rated independently on scorecards by the gatekeepers.
   ● The scores from scorecards are tallied and displayed on video projector.
   ● Debate and discussion by gatekeepers follows (facilitated).
   ● Consensus is reached (decide in advance how consensus will be reached).

8. The decision is made:
   ● Go/Kill/Hold/Recycle.
   ● The prioritization level is established for the project:
     – The project is compared to active and on-hold projects (use the various portfolio charts in Chapter 5).
     – The effect on the portfolio (other projects) is discussed.
   ● The Action Plan and required next-gate deliverables are agreed to.
   ● Resource commitments are made (people, times and person-days, dollars).
   ● Date for next gate is set.

9. The project team is informed in person, immediately and face to face.

Index

A. D. Little, 14
Abell, D. F., 72
Accolade(TM), 247, 248
Air Products & Chemicals, 100, 111, 166, 189, 194, 252
American Productivity and Quality Center (APQC), 20, 30n. 21, 33–34, 46, 56, 57, 92–93, 102, 109, 122, 166, 179, 184, 192, 200, 201, 240, 246, 251, 253
Apple Computer, 1
At Risk simulation model, 143
attack strategies, 60, 80, 88; customer-friendly strategy, 82; differentiator strategy, 81; low-budget conservative strategy, 82–83; low-cost provider strategy, 81; niche player strategy, 82; strategies based on innovativeness, 80–81 (*see also* defender businesses; fast-follower businesses; innovator businesses; reactor businesses)

Bacon, Francis, 91
balanced scorecard, 143–144, 155, 161, 273–274. *See also* scoring models
base business, 84
basic research projects. *See* technology development (TD) projects
Bausch & Lomb, 112, 166, 186, 254
benchmarking: benchmarking studies, 20, 21, 23, 30–31n. 29, 92–93; internal benchmarking, 268–269

Berry, C. A., 83–84
Berry, Thomas H., 200
best performers, 9, 32; dedication of resources to product innovation, 94–96; identifying, 46; and portfolio management, 109–113; and resource allocation, 94–96. *See also* performance metrics; specific case histories
best practices, 20, 167. *See also* gates; marketing best practices; performance metrics; product definition; quality of execution; superior new products; upfront homework; voice-of-customer
Bio-Pro, 177
Black and Decker, 81
Boeing, 12
Booz-Allen & Hamilton, 17, 55–56
Boston Consulting Group (BCG) portfolio model, 99–100, 147
Bourgeois, Dan, 5, 7
Bradley, Omar, 1
Bstieler, Ludwig, 19n
bubble diagrams, 147, 153, 154, 155, 156, 159, 273; bubble diagrams that capture newness-to-the-firm, 149–150; bubble diagrams with axes derived from scoring models, 149; risk-reward bubble diagrams, 147–149
business and product innovation strategy, 53